Microsoft® Solutions Framework Essentials

Building Successful Technology Solutions

Michael S. V. Turner

PUBLISHED BY
Microsoft Press
A Division of Microsoft Corporation
One Microsoft Way
Redmond, Washington 98052-6399

Copyright © 2006 by Michael Turner

Library of Congress ISBN-13: 978-0-7356-2353-8
ISBN-10: 0-7356-2353-8
Library of Congress Control Number 2006928844

Printed and bound in the United States of America.

1 2 3 4 5 6 7 8 9   QWT   1 0 9 8 7 6

Distributed in Canada by H.B. Fenn and Company Ltd.

A CIP catalogue record for this book is available from the British Library.

Microsoft Press books are available through booksellers and distributors worldwide. For further information about international editions, contact your local Microsoft Corporation office or contact Microsoft Press International directly at fax (425) 936-7329. Visit our Web site at www.microsoft.com/mspress. Send comments to mspinput@microsoft.com.

Acquisitions Editor: Ben Ryan
Project Editor: Lynn Finnel
Copy Editor: Christine Palaia
Indexer: Lee and Tony Ross of Pamona Corporation

Body Part No. X12-70908

To my wife, Lauren, who enabled me to take this journey.

To my children, Isabelle, Benjamin, and Noah, who inspire me.

Contents at a Glance

Table of Contents

Acknowledgments

Although this is the fourth iteration of Microsoft Solutions Framework, prior MSF material was mostly limited to Microsoft white papers, training materials, and MSF practitioners' knowledge. To continue with a cohesive lineage, this book draws upon those sources as a basis and a foundation. As such, key contributors to MSF v3 are acknowledged in the Appendix.

This book would not have been possible if not for the collaboration and healthy debate with the architects of Visual Studio Team System (VSTS): Sam Guckenheimer, Grandville "Randy" Miller, and David J. Anderson. A special thanks to Randy for numerous hours of collaborative introspection and reflection on how to distill MSF into the best it can be.

A huge thank you to the MSF Champs who added endless value to forming and shaping this book. In particular, I would like to thank Rossen Blagoev, Andrew Delin, Nathan Dolly, Francis Gan, Robert Fontaine, Alan Hakimi, Tim Litton, David Lymburner, Carroll Moon, David Preedy, Dave Svab, and Peter Williams.

Last and certainly not least, I would like to thank my editor, Lynn Finnel, and copy editor, Christina Palaia. They worked their magic to polish this diamond in the rough.

—Mike Turner

Introduction

Successfully delivering solutions, any solutions, involves an ever-changing blend of skill, wisdom, luck, and often technology. Too many times, teams focus just on technology. This book is an attempt to quantify, simplify, and enable those other components—yes, even luck. The book is a result of my belief that a team can increase their odds of success on all fronts through thoughtful and reflective application of Microsoft Solutions Framework (MSF).

This book describes and explains the Microsoft Solutions Framework (MSF)—a collection of key concepts, foundational principles, and proven practices from Microsoft and from dedicated and passionate practitioners around the world. They are an amazing bunch, continually looking to improve and streamline how teams deliver solutions. It is an honor to write this book on their behalf.

Who Should Read This Book

This book was written for any team or organization, technical or nontechnical, that is looking for some commonsense guidance on how to deliver solutions successfully. This book is not for a particular role on a team; it is meant to stimulate thinking of all team members. Hopefully, the team will come away with a common taxonomy and common understanding of the foundational elements needed to have a successful team, project, and solution.

How to Apply the Information in This Book

If a team or organization lacks the fundamentals of solution delivery, it would be detrimental for a team to try to implement all aspects discussed herein. It is better to pick out a few implementable aspects and achieve a few successes. Then reread this book and, from your new vantage point, pick out a few more implementable aspects, whether you choose to improve existing ones or adopt new ones.

If a team is having issues in a few aspects of their solution delivery approach, read the whole book to get an overall understanding of the concepts. Then revisit those trouble areas with an eye toward process improvement ideas.

What Essentials Have Changed with MSF v4?

Although the fundamentals have mostly remained the same, Microsoft is refreshing MSF to clarify and adapt terms and concepts to be more understandable to a broader, global audience. Key changes, additions, clarifications, and enhancements to MSF v3 are highlighted in the following section. Please note that these concepts are discussed in detail in subsequent chapters.

Changed

Key changes to MSF v3 that are implemented in MSF v4 have been in the following areas:

- Foundational principles
- Key concepts
- Team Model
- Process Model

A few miscellaneous changes are also highlighted.

Foundational Principles

The following summary maps the principles currently found in MSF v4 to those currently in *MSF for Agile Software Development* and *MSF for CMMI Process Improvement* as well as in MSF v3. In some instances, a couple principles have been merged or recast as a key concept (now called *mindsets*).

MSF v4 Principle	Agile and CMMI (v1)	MSF v3
Foster open communications	Same	Same
Work toward a shared vision	Same	Same
Stay agile, expect and adapt to change	Stay agile, adapt to change	Stay agile, expect change
Invest in quality	Quality is everyone's business, every day (This applies to an individual's behavior and is therefore a mindset—merged into pride in workmanship mindset.)	Same
Partner with customers	Same	New
Deliver *incremental* value	Flow of value: incremental delivery of value Make deployment a habit: implies team readiness Frequent delivery	Always create shippable solutions: implies solution readiness
Make mindset		Focus on business value: make sure what is being delivered has value (This applies to an individual's behavior and is therefore a mindset.)

MSF v4 Principle	Agile and CMMI (v1)	MSF v3
Empower team members	New	Same
Establish clear accountability and shared responsibility	New	Same
Learn from all experiences	New	Same

Key Concepts

Key concepts have been renamed as *mindsets*, but they are still key concepts. To help clarify the difference between a principle and a key concept, and especially because these concepts apply to individual behavior, calling them mindsets seems to represent better that understanding. As with the prior table, the following summary maps the mindsets in MSF v4 to those currently found in *MSF for Agile Software Development* and *MSF for CMMI Process Improvement* as well as in MSF v3.

MSF v4 Mindset	Agile and CMMI (v1)	MSF v3
Foster a team of peers	Same	Extended to include trust. Trust is essential for many of the aspects of MSF to work properly.
Focus on business value	Quality is defined by customer: "Everyone on the team should be...focused on delivering something that the consumers need, want, and will derive value from."	Transferred from principles and merged with: Customer-focused
Keep a solution perspective	New	Solution mindset
Take pride in workmanship	Pride of workmanship Quality is everyone's business, every day (transferred from principles)	Quality mindset Zero-defect mindset
Learn continuously	Willingness to learn	Willingness to learn
(Merged into deliver incremental value principle)	Frequent delivery	
(Moved to proven practices)	Get specific early	
Internalize qualities of service	Qualities of service	Design principles, but there needs to be more awareness so it needs to be internalized—too often considered after design is done

MSF v4 Mindset	Agile and CMMI (v1)	MSF v3
Practice good citizenship	Same	New
Deliver on your commitments	New	Fixed ship date: Stimulate creativity by removing the option of moving the ship date

Team Model

A very welcome change is that *role clusters* remain. To help emphasize that the Team Model has always been about advocating for different aspects of delivering a solution and for their respective stakeholders, role clusters were renamed to *advocacy groups*.

As we reexamined the model, it made sense to make the most significant change to MSF Team Model, namely, adding an Architecture Advocacy Group. This group should seem familiar because most of the relevant aspects of this group were extracted from the Program Management Advocacy Group and the Development Advocacy Group.

The Release Management Role Cluster was renamed to Release/Operations Advocacy Group. This change was made to emphasize the critical need for the solution delivery team to be closely coupled with the Solution Operations team. Because not all solutions are deployed to an operations environment, the term *release* was retained in the name.

As part of reexamining the Team Model, we clarified and expanded the functional areas within each advocacy group. Added to this, we clarified, distilled, and expanded some of the key responsibilities and activities of each of the functional areas.

Process Model

The MSF v3 Process Model underwent the most change. Although the underlying concepts have remained the same, it made sense to separate the process and activities of building a solution (i.e., enactment) from the process and activities of running a project (i.e., governance). As such, Process Model was renamed *Governance Model*.

Other changes were made to help emphasize the agile, overlapping, and iterative nature of MSF v3. Namely, the five phases are now call tracks (e.g., Plan Track)—as in tracks of activity. To emphasize that MSF v3 has always had a broader applicability to more than just the software development domain, the *Developing Phase* was renamed *Build Track*. Although the term *milestone* is commonly used in project management circles, to emphasize the agile nature of MSF v3, the term *checkpoints* is used instead. The Governance Model still has major and interim checkpoints.

The Process Model was changed somewhat to better emphasize the iterative name of MSF v3. For instance, some clarity was added about decomposing the major tracks of activity into *work streams* and further still into *swim lanes*.

Miscellaneous Changes

A few miscellaneous but important changes are as follows. The term *defects* has been replaced with *issues*—a term more fitting our litigious society. To emphasize the applicability of MSF v3 beyond software development, the term *bug* has also been replaced by *issue*. Accordingly, the two bug-related interim checkpoints have been renamed. The *Zero Bug Bounce* checkpoint has been renamed *Issue Log Cleared*. The *Bug Convergence* checkpoint has been renamed *Issue Convergence*. In the Build Track (formerly called the Developing Phase), the *Proof of Concept Completed* interim checkpoint was renamed *Prototyping Completed* to better reflect that not all projects include a proof of concept; however, most do include prototyping efforts.

New

A few key elements have been added to MSF v4 that often build off of or clarify a topic lightly covered in MSF v3, namely, the following:

- Scheduling process
- Risk mitigation trigger
- Empowerment readiness
- Requirement prioritization
- Governance track

Scheduling Process

Although not new for the project management community, an approach to scheduling that reflects the MSF principles and mindsets has been added into MSF v4. The real value of this section is the numerous lessons learned that accompany the explanation of this process.

Risk Mitigation Trigger

Although not a common practice in the project management community, it is a practical addition to MSF v4. It enables more options for a cost-conscious approach to risk mitigation.

Empowerment Readiness

MSF continues to be a strong proponent of empowering team members. However, not all team members are ready or able to be empowered. Empowerment readiness is a means added into MSF v4 to assess the degree to which each team member is ready to be empowered to perform a given task.

Requirement Prioritization

New with MSF v4 are a few sections discussing requirements prioritization. Examples of a simple means to prioritize as well as a more comprehensive means are provided.

Governance Track

As identified in the changes to the Process Model section, MSF v4 has a new track of activity, namely, the Governance Track. This track of activity spans the enactment tracks (e.g., Envision Track) to provide guidance on running the project.

Significant Clarifications and/or Enhancements

Many aspects of MSF v3 have been clarified and/or extended. A few key aspects of note include these:

- Readiness Management Discipline and Process
- Risk Management Discipline and Process
- More projects plans for Master Project Plan
- Supporting environments: more than just development and test environments
- Stakeholder analysis
- Defining high-level requirements
- Decomposing and refining requirements
- Added qualities of service (QoS) requirements
- Acceptance criteria: user, operations, and customer
- Clarified differences between conceptual, logical, and physical designs efforts
- Types of testing: regression, functional, usability, system

Help Evolve MSF

This book is a snapshot of a changing and evolving body of knowledge and practices. You are welcome to contribute to this body of knowledge. Go to *http://www.microsoft.com/msf* for general MSF information and tools. Additional MSF communities, resources, and services are available at *http://www.NorthStarAnalytics.com/msf*.

Training

Microsoft and its certified training partners offer an array of MSF classes, including a course based on MSF Essentials. Please visit the following Web site for more information:

http://www.microsoft.com/learning/training/

Support for This Book

Every effort has been made to ensure the accuracy of this book. As corrections or changes are collected, they will be added to a Microsoft Knowledge Base article.

Microsoft Press provides support for books at the following Web site:

http://www.microsoft.com/learning/support/books/

Questions and Comments

If you have comments, questions, or ideas regarding this book, or questions that are not answered by visiting the sites above, please send them to Microsoft Press by sending an e-mail message to

mspinput@microsoft.com

or by sending postal mail to

Microsoft Press
Attn: Microsoft Solutions Framework Essentials *Editor*
One Microsoft Way
Redmond, WA 98052-6399

Part I
Solution Delivery Fundamentals

Chapter 1

What Is MSF and Is It Right for You?

There are many great approaches to solutions development. So, why would *Microsoft Solutions Framework (MSF)* be right for you, your project, and/or your organization? To help answer that question, you must first understand what you are actually looking for. Are you looking for a few "nuggets" to improve your current development approach, or are you looking for a new soup-to-nuts approach? Or maybe, are you just curious about how Microsoft approaches solutions development? This book answers these questions by sharing with you an industry-proven approach to delivering solutions. It provides years of Microsoft solutions delivery experience and lessons learned distilled into a flexible and scalable framework. The framework can be adapted to meet the needs of any project (regardless of size or complexity) to plan, build, and deploy business-driven technology solutions.

This book explains the foundational principles and proven practices of the Microsoft Solutions Framework. MSF provides an adaptable framework for successfully delivering solutions faster, requiring fewer people, and involving less risk while yielding higher quality results. MSF helps teams directly address most common causes of technology project failure to improve success rates, solution quality, and business impact. Created to deal with the dynamic nature of technology projects and environments, MSF fosters the ability to adapt to continual change within the course of a project.

MSF has a long history of helping teams and organizations become more successful in delivering business-driven solutions. MSF is a deliberate and disciplined approach based on a defined set of principles, models, disciplines, guidelines, mindsets, and proven practices. It contains a set of natural checks and balances that work to maximize quality and agility without adding undue governance. MSF is applicable to any effort that involves thinking about what needs to be accomplished; planning how to accomplish it; doing it; making sure it meets expectations; and wrapping up the effort, including learning from the effort. MSF has been successfully used on projects from the very simple to the very complex, from small teams to an enterprise.

The History and Origins of Microsoft Solutions Framework

MSF is in its fourth iteration. This version update, like previous version updates, comes in response to changing environments and an increased and broader understanding of how teams deliver solutions. The original version of MSF was first introduced in 1994 as a loose collection of best practices from Microsoft's product development efforts and Microsoft Consulting engagements. As shown in Figure 1-1, MSF has been evolving ever since based on deliberate learning from successful, real-world best practices of Microsoft product groups, Microsoft Consulting, Microsoft's internal Operations and Technology Group (OTG), Microsoft partners, and customers. Elements of MSF are based on well-known industry best practices and incorporate Microsoft's more than 30 years of experience in the high-tech industry. These elements are designed to work together to help practitioners and managers address many significant challenges encountered throughout a technology life cycle.

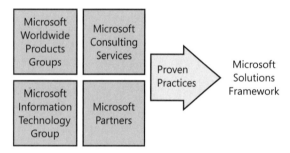

Figure 1-1   Origins of MSF

MSF uses this pool of real-world best practices, which have been proved both internally and externally. It simplifies, consolidates, and verifies them for easier understanding and adoption. Now a robust and mature framework, MSF is managed and developed by a dedicated product team within Microsoft, with guidance and review from an international advisory council of subject matter experts. MSF also continues to draw upon current Microsoft experience. Other teams within various Microsoft lines of business regularly create, find, and share best practices and tools internally. Learning from these internal project efforts is consolidated and distributed outside of Microsoft through MSF.

Why a "Framework"?

No single method or process optimally applies to all projects. Yet, the need for guidance exists. To compound this challenge, few technology efforts are either "pure" software development or infrastructure efforts. Accordingly, MSF was assembled to be an adaptable and scalable framework. It was thought that a framework would better enable an organization to adapt this information easily into a methodology that fits its needs—not change an organization to fit a methodology. The trade-off of this decision is that the resultant guidance is sometimes less prescriptive than what people generally expect. Microsoft recognizes this, too, and built a new suite of products to enable a project team to pick as much MSF prescriptive guidance as they need.

New with version 4, Microsoft provides prescriptive instances of MSF through its Microsoft Visual Studio Team System (VSTS) product line. As shown in Figure 1-2, Microsoft currently offers two application development approaches (e.g., *MSF for Agile Software Development* and *MSF for CMMI Process Improvement*). Other instances in the application development family and in other domains such as *infrastructure deployment* are planned. Note that an organization is also able to define its own MSF-based instances.

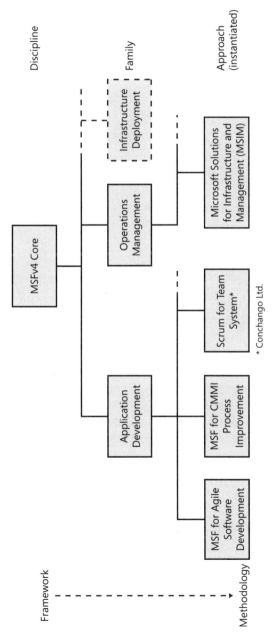

Figure 1-2   MSF family tree

Figure 1-3 offers an alternate view of the MSF family. As shown, MSF v4 Core encompasses and extends MSFv3. Each domain (e.g., application development and infrastructure deployment) incorporates parts of MSF that are applicable to that domain. Each instance of MSF might also incorporate domain-specific guidance that exists outside of MSF.

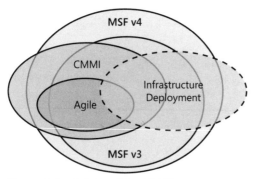

Figure 1-3   Relationship of MSF content

How Is MSF Different?

At some level of abstraction, key elements of most frameworks and methodologies are fundamentally the same. Often, what makes them different is the order, emphasis, and combination of those key elements.

MSF does not claim to have a silver bullet that other frameworks lack. To the contrary, many aspects of other methodologies are compatible with an MSF approach. Each aspect of MSF is structured to be adapted to meet the needs of a given situation. Even though MSF can be adapted to be very similar to other methodologies, MSF provides a richness that goes beyond the others and fills the gaps of most methodologies. This ability to adapt MSF often presents itself as a quandary when compared to specific prescriptive methodologies. So, when you consider MSF, remember it is a framework that is intentionally presented as guidance with recommendations—not a cookbook, prescriptive methodology.

Key Elements of MSF v4.0

The key elements of MSF are briefly discussed here; the context for their relationship to each other is discussed in detail in subsequent chapters. These elements could be used individually or adopted as an integrated whole. Collectively, they create a solid yet flexible approach to the successful execution of technology projects.

- **Foundational principles**   Core principles upon which the framework is based. They express values and standards that are common to all framework elements. They should be adopted by the team and applied in how team members operate among themselves as well as how they work within their organization and with stakeholders.

- **Mindsets**   Beliefs that team members should internalize to guide their personal behavior.

- **Models**   Schematic descriptions or "mental maps" of how to structure project teams and processes (Team Model and Governance Model—two of the major defining elements/components of the framework).

- **Disciplines**   Areas of practice using a specific set of methods, terms, and approaches (Project Management, Risk Management, and Readiness Management—the other major defining elements/components of the framework).

- **Proven practices**   Techniques, methods, or processes that have been demonstrated to work under a variety of real-world conditions.

- **Recommendations**   Optional but suggested practices and guidelines in the application of the models and disciplines.

Summary

MSF is a practical, flexible and proven approach to delivering solutions. It has been successfully applied to a range of project types with varying complexities and within an assortment of environments. Refined and evolved over a dozen years, MSF provides guidance in not only how to define, design, build, stabilize and deploy a solution, but also how to organize, ready and govern the team to handle the dynamic nature of solutions delivery.

MSF is structured as an adaptable and scalable framework upon which specialized and prescriptive methodologies can be built. It includes a set of natural checks and balances that work to maximize quality and agility without adding undue governance. That way, MSF can be a basis for both an agile as well as a formal approach to solutions delivery. By providing a solid and comprehensive foundation, organizations can create their own methodology that is tailored to their needs or select from a range of pre-packaged MSF-based approaches such as *MSF for Agile Software Development*.

Chapter 2
Understanding Solution Delivery Environments

Seemingly, half of the effort of delivering a solution is understanding and operating within a delivery environment. In consideration of this, MSF provides guidance not only on how to work within teams, but also on how to work within a delivery environment, including understanding business drivers, people capabilities, and project constraints.

Once a team understands their environment, they need to figure out how to be successful. This chapter lays out elements of understanding and operating within delivery environment(s). It discusses assessing an environment, optimizing typical constraints derived from environmental challenges, overcoming common environmental challenges, and converting challenges into opportunities.

Assessing Environmental Challenges

When you try to understand an environment, you must consider many types of influences, drivers, and constraints. Typically, an environment is a complex ecosystem that requires understanding and the balancing of many internal and external challenges such as these:

- Business environment
    - Economic
    - Legal
    - Regulatory
- Corporate culture: internal challenges
- Internal governance: process and procedure challenges
- People challenges
- Technology challenges

Organizations that overcome these challenges derive better results for their business through higher solution and service quality, improved customer satisfaction, and working environments that attract the best people in the industry. These factors translate into a positive impact on bottom lines and improvements in an organization's strategic effectiveness.

Business Environment

Projects must operate in an ever-changing business environment that has a complex relationship between legal, regulatory, and economic influences. Rates of change in both business and technology are accelerating, including shorter product cycles, increasingly diverse and complex solutions and services, and evolving business models. Most managers know all too well that increasingly they are expected to do more with less. They are also faced with rapidly changing external requirements (e.g., regulations and legislation such as Sarbanes-Oxley [SOX]).

Often, project teams are caught between opposing external forces. For example, consumers' demands for features are growing while their demands for reliable, simplified and secure operations are growing, too. Organizations are now faced with rising competitive pressures just to keep up. Add to all of that pressures of internationalization and globalization. In short, demands and pressures just from a business environment require that a project team have nimble and agile solution delivery processes.

Corporate Culture

An important component to understanding a delivery environment is assessing where both a project team and the organization lie in the solutions delivery landscape. This landscape is a multivariable cultural assessment of an organization. Corporate cultures and behaviors range from being slow to adopt new technology to the other end of the spectrum where a project team or organization leads a market through innovation and adopting new technology and new thinking—a mature, learning organization. Figure 2-1 categorizes these cultures and behaviors into eight regions on a continuum.

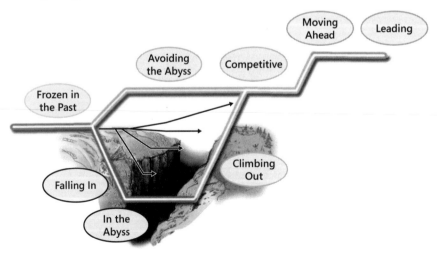

Figure 2-1   Continuum of corporate cultures and behaviors

Frozen in the Past

The path that leads up and over the abyss in Figure 2-1 indicates a safe and well-tread path. Organizations that follow this path are slow to change and adopt new technology and new thinking; usually they wait for innovation to be proved out in industry. They are tactically focused and cost driven. This position is not necessarily bad because it helps organizations avoid pitfalls experienced by less careful organizations. However, these organizations often have a burdensome bureaucracy.

The Abyss

When an organization tries to use new technology or new thinking but is not quite ready to adopt it, it often heads down the path leading into the abyss—a path where instead of advancing the project or organization, the organization ends up hurting itself. This organization is starting a death spiral into the abyss. The abyss is a place where teams spend more time, energy, and money on tools and fixing processes rather than on solutions delivery. Organizations sliding into the abyss realize rising costs, rising complexity, and ineffective delivery. Although few organizations avoid the abyss, how deep they fall into the abyss usually depends on how soon they make their culture work for them rather than the other way around. Nevertheless, what do organizations do to avoid or climb out of the abyss? They figure out how to deliver solutions effectively within their culture (sometimes in spite of it) while meeting ongoing business needs.

Potential

Organizations with positive momentum coming out of the abyss are following the path that leads upward to where the organization makes progress incrementally in maturing its solutions delivery. It finds ways to simplify and reduce complexity, adopts a strategic focus (i.e., becomes proactive instead of reactive), focuses on value as opposed to cost, and learns how to become nimble and able to change quickly. Through hard-won maturity, these organizations become competitive.

Leader

As an organization continues to be competitive and continues to mature, it moves ahead of the competition by following the path that leads onward and upward. With continued success, such an organization is rewarded with a leading position in a market.

Internal Governance: Process and Procedure Challenges

Business sponsors are often frustrated by the amount of time and resources it takes to deliver solutions. Although technology challenges are increasing, experience has shown that most of the internal challenges are related to people, processes, tools, and procedures. If an organization is fortunate, it has processes, procedures, and tools that match how it wants to run itself. More typically, organizations use entrenched legacy processes, procedures, and tools that can be characterized in the following ways:

- Are inflexible to change
- Provide low return on investment of time and effort
- Hinder teams' progress rather than enabling it
- Underserve project team needs
- Are ill-suited to the task at hand

People Challenges

Unlike other challenges, people challenges are more oriented around softer skills—which tend to be less tangible and harder to manage. People challenges often include dealing with team morale, internal politics, and the like. Additional common people challenges include these:

- Skills
- Team chemistry
- Organizational structure

Skills

One of the hardest challenges is to assess team member skills properly, and then blend them so that a team is technically complementary and has redundancy in critical skills. As discussed later, MSF attempts to address this challenge through its *Readiness Management Discipline.*

Team Chemistry

A challenge often overlooked is team chemistry. Not only does a team need to make sure they are technically and functionally complementary, they also need to make sure they have complementary personalities and traits—part of the set of natural built-in checks and balances. For example, if a team has a hard-charging person that is very good at working through problems, that person often needs to be paired with a more detail-oriented person who can ensure quality and completeness. Without this balance, a team is at risk.

Organizational Structure

As discussed later, most organizations have an organizational structure (e.g., hierarchical) that rarely enables high-performance teams. Organizations often underestimate how hard it is to run a business one way and run a project another. For instance, if team members are accustomed to working in a hierarchical organization, it is difficult for them to change suddenly to a more empowering organizational structure. But beware of the old adage: "Be careful what you wish for...." People want to be empowered, but when it becomes a reality, they often feel "lost" and feel as if they are "aimlessly wandering" around a project until they internalize empowerment and start leading themselves.

Another side effect of becoming an empowered team is that executives, who are accustomed to a hierarchical model of doing business, sometimes realize they have an inadequate understanding of what it takes to deliver solutions in an empowered structure.

Technology Challenges

As technology evolves, so do technology challenges. Technology challenges manifest themselves in many ways that arise from all aspects of delivering a solution, including needing more skilled resources and more dynamic tools that must work across more diverse environments. Added to this is the pressure to increase qualities of service (e.g., availability, scalability, and maintainability). These challenges present potential for an organization to spiral into a technology black hole. Without careful governance, costs and schedules can quickly get out of control. To mitigate these occurrences, organizations should have a solution road map as well as an understanding of how to take advantage of new technology to provide increasing return on investment.

Optimizing Constraints

Environmental challenges can be overwhelming. When presented collectively, these challenges can paralyze a team—as proved by the large number of projects that fail (e.g., the Standish Group reported that in the year 2003, only 34 percent of 30,000 application development projects succeeded, while 15 percent failed and 51 percent were challenged).[1] A team should distill these challenges into constraints that can be addressed by the solution delivery process as well as project governance. Although MSF does not provide a prescriptive means of identifying constraints, a few good published methods do (e.g., Theory of Constraints).[2,3] Constraints need to be thoughtfully balanced throughout a project so that as impacting events occur, a team understands how to navigate calmly and rationally through each event. In addition, constraints are used to define and prioritize project trade-offs. Because multiple projects potentially are needed to realize a solution, solution constraints also need to be defined, prioritized, and decomposed into subordinate project constraints. Successful teams quickly and continually optimize project constraints. Listed here are a few common constraint categories:

■ Costs

■ Process

---

1   The Standish Group International, "10th Annual (2003) CHAOS Report," *CHAOS Chronicles* 3 (2003): 406.

2   E. M. Goldratt, *What Is This Thing Called the Theory of Constraints?* (Croton-on-Hudson, NY: North River Press, 1990).

3   H. W. Dettmer, *Goldratt's Theory of Constraints: A Systems Approach to Continuous Improvement* (Milwaukee, WI: ASQC Quality Press, 1997).

- Tools
- Schedule
- Quality
- Scope
- Legacy solutions
- Risk
- Technology

Costs

Typically, the biggest cost to a project is labor. As such, it is very important to determine: a cost-effective blend of required skills and capabilities to deliver a solution; how to organize a team to achieve optimal skill balance and team chemistry; and which processes and procedures are optimal to maximize team throughput and minimize unnecessary rework.

Process

A team should use just enough process to be repeatable and effective. Too much burdens a team. Too little makes for an inefficient team. Many times a team does not realize it has too little process until something extraordinary occurs. It is easy to have "good" process in "good" times. The true test of a process is whether it helps teams navigate out of troubled waters.

Tools

Everyone gets caught up in the allure of time-saving tools. Remember that one of the tenants of MSF (and life) is "keep it simple." Only use a tool if team members have positive and productive experiences with it. Otherwise, the tool(s) might be doing more harm than good to a project.

Schedule

Many "trade-off triangles" are commonly used (e.g., *good*, *fast*, or *cheap*). Regardless of which is used, time is always a factor. Time to delivery is most often driven by external considerations.

Quality

A tough challenge is to figure out the right level of quality for a solution as a whole and for each of its subcomponents. Too little quality might enable a team to churn solutions out faster but will cost an organization in many well-quantified ways, such as increased customer support and decreased customer satisfaction. Compromising quality classically defers costs rather than removes them. On the other hand, too much quality has well-quantified downfalls, too, such as increased project costs and being slower to market.

Scope

Typically, you should consider two areas when assessing project scope, including requirements and features. First, how much and how well should a team document? It takes time to capture as well as to maintain the scope. So what is the right level? A team should document just enough to communicate adequately and clearly. This might mean that different subteams have different levels of documentation. Please note that team members are likely to come and go. Therefore, the lowest level at which to communicate might be at the level of a future team member. Few teams have time or resources to go back and add more detail.

The second area to consider is that solutions with broader scope typically take longer to deliver. Because requirements usually have a short half-life (i.e., documented requirements quickly tend to get out of sync with sponsor needs and expectations), keep the number of requirements per release as low as possible.

Legacy Solutions

Is it better to integrate with legacy solutions or replace them? The answer to this question often involves many business and technical factors and perspectives.

Risk

As discussed in detail in Chapter 5, "Managing Project Risks," risk is the quantified potential of unplanned activities and events that could adversely affect a project. Although managing risk is a regular part of running a project, and so is not a constraint to optimize, two common influences on how a project team manages risk are constraints to optimize: namely, (1) tolerance to risk, and (2) how much effort should be spent proactively addressing risk.

Each organization and each project have an explicit or implicit tolerance to risk. It is much harder for a project team to balance their constraints when their tolerance is implicit. One means of quantifying an organization's tolerance to risk is to understand where it is on Moore's Technology Adoption Life Cycle,[4] described and depicted as follows (see Figure 2-2).

- **Innovators**   "Willing to take a risk on a good idea"; risk explorers who use new or prerelease technology, often to gain a strategic advantage

- **Early Adopters**   "Waits to hear a few good anecdotes"; risk visionaries who see potential inherent in new technology but who are more practical in trying to use it for a competitive advantage

- **Early Majority**   "Needs solid anecdotal evidence"; risk-cautious people who perceive new technology as an enabler but who are unwilling to assume too much risk

---

4 G. A. Moore, *Crossing the Chasm* (New York: HarperBusiness, 1991), 15.

- **Late Majority**   "Wants to see three good case studies at similar organizations"; risk-adverse people who are willing to consider new technology (at least new to them, but not new to the market) but who are not willing to adopt it until proven examples and case studies of others achieving return on investment (ROI) exist

- **Laggards**   "Wants solid proof that something works"; risk avoiders who are risk intolerant and often are "forced" to adopt technology because of external reasons (e.g., Sarbanes-Oxley compliance)

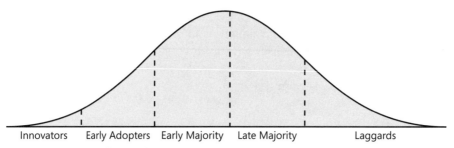

Innovators   Early Adopters   Early Majority   Late Majority   Laggards

Figure 2-2   Quantifying risk using Moore's Technology Adoption Life Cycle

The second influence on how risk is managed on a project relates to how proactively a team addresses risk. If a team proactively addresses risk, they often avoid risks and lessen the impact of those that are realized. However, tangible work needs to be included into project plans to proactively avoid what might or might not be realized. How a team addresses risk is therefore a constraint that is project specific and one that needs to be reasoned out. For example, consider a risk of work stoppage caused by a blizzard. A team can mitigate this risk by enabling remote access so team members are able to work from home. A project being run in colder climates might consider adopting this mitigation, whereas a project being run from warmer climates might consider it too administratively expensive. It all comes down to a balance of how tolerant a project team is to unplanned activities or events versus how much time and effort it takes the team to manage risks.

Technology

Should a team proceed with proven technology, or should they try to take advantage of "new and improved" technology to gain some advantage (e.g., better tools for faster development)? Answering this question typically relates to how much risk a project can handle and how much support is available for a project team and for an operations team once a solution is deployed (e.g., obsolete technology typically has support but at a premium cost). Typically, a project uses a mix of technologies on the maturity continuum to maximize benefits while managing risks. The following terms and definitions are taken from Wikipedia, and considered a common means of classifying technology maturity:

- **Bleeding edge**   Any technology that shows high potential but hasn't demonstrated its value or settled down into any kind of consensus. Early adopters may win big or may be stuck with a white elephant.

- **Leading edge** A technology that has proven itself in the marketplace but is still new enough that it may be difficult to find knowledgeable personnel to implement or support it.

- **State of the art** When everyone agrees that a particular technology is the right solution.

- **Dated** Still useful, still sometimes implemented, but a replacement leading edge technology is readily available.

- **Obsolete** Has been superseded by state-of-the-art technology, rarely implemented anymore.[5]

Overcoming Environmental Challenges

It might seem daunting to overcome environmental challenges especially because most seem beyond the control of a team. But without careful and proactive planning, challenges become obstacles. To prevent this from happening, an organization needs to assess quickly whether workarounds are available or whether they need to work through a challenge. The goal is to minimize the impact of any challenges that should present themselves—which usually happens at the worst time possible. Here are a few ideas that can help a team start addressing and hopefully mitigating these challenges:

- Understand business directions, goals, and opportunities.

- Ensure project goals support business goals.

- Communicate with the business in an ongoing dialogue.

- Be as proactive as can be afforded.

- Align responsibilities and tasks based on team member strengths and weaknesses, increasing the odds of team members being able to work efficiently and effectively.

- Take a long-term view to solving challenges.

How much preventable planning is enough? How much is too much? At one extreme, a team that does little planning will need to address challenges reactively. At the other extreme, an organization can do so much proactive planning that it hinders its ability to execute. Ideally, an organization proactively puts measures in place to avoid or mitigate challenges while not adversely affecting its ability to deliver. A question for each organization to determine is: What is appropriate for a team given its circumstance(s)? Organizations often start out being more reactive and become more proactive as they see return on investment for their efforts.

---

5 Wikipedia (http://en.wikipedia.org/wiki/Technology_lifecycle).

Effects of Project Team Morale on the Solution Delivery Life Cycle

A team's ability to overcome challenges is heavily influenced by their morale as it evolves throughout the life cycle. It is natural that project team morale rises and falls as the team experiences various accomplishments and setbacks inherent in a solution delivery life cycle. Figure 2-3 exemplifies typical trends in team morale that I have observed over many years of managing projects. A team usually starts with high hopes and matching high morale. As a solution starts to be defined, team morale often starts to wane (i.e., project realities start to overcome kick-off glee). Most technology practitioners do not care much for the design portion of a project, but once construction starts, team morale usually starts increasing. As construction draws to a close, feature and function trade-offs start to sour the "fun" of building a solution, and team morale starts to oscillate between a set of highs and lows. This continues through solution stabilization such that team morale rises as a solution build is completed only to fall as test results show there are more issues to resolve. However, as a team gets closer to finishing solution stabilization, overall morale trends higher. When a solution is ready for deployment, morale is high once again from the team's renewed sense of pride. This morale high is tempered a bit as initial deployments usually encounter a few issues but returns to a high at the completion of deployment.

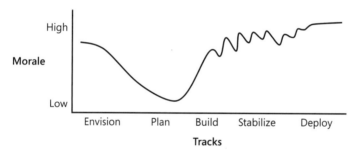

Figure 2-3   Observed evolution of team morale throughout the solution delivery life cycle

Identifying Opportunities Within a Challenging Business Environment

In the middle of difficulty lies opportunity.

—*Albert Einstein*

It seems increasingly hard to deliver solutions successfully in an ever-changing and more demanding business environment. This is good news for those organizations that have the ability and maturity to adapt. This is potentially fatal for those organizations that struggle not only to keep up with technology but also are not able to navigate adequately through challenging business environments. These challenges often are characterized by increasing customer demands, escalating business expectations, increasing business impact of technology-based solutions, increasing technology specialization leading to scarce resources, and increasing customer and organizational globalization. Cumulatively, this results in an overall increase in complexity, which makes it harder and harder for teams to deliver solutions without a means to handle challenges in an expeditious manner.

Changing organizational behavior to address challenges effectively and achieve outstanding results is possible but requires dedication, commitment, vision, trust, and leadership. To accomplish this, links need to be forged between the delivery team and the business—links of understanding, accountability, collaboration, and communication. The delivery team must take a leadership role to remove barriers to their own success. MSF was designed and built to provide a framework for this transition.

Increased challenges are often accompanied by increased opportunities. The question then remains: Are you, your project team, and your organization poised to take advantage of them?

Summary

How successful would a doctor be if he or she were not able to diagnose correctly? Surprisingly, many solution teams do not adequately assess their delivery environment yet expect every project to be successful. Correctly assessing the many facets of a delivery environment is essential to forming accurate project constraints. As discussed throughout this book, project constraints are key to delivering a solution. It is therefore critical to be able to quickly identify these constraints and quickly adapt as these constraints evolve over the delivery life cycle. Although collective team mastery of this ability is challenging, it can yield a bounty of opportunities.

Chapter 3
Foundational Principles, Mindsets, and Proven Practices

Microsoft and Microsoft Solutions Framework (MSF) practitioners have distilled their experience and lessons learned into a set of foundational principles, mindsets, and proven practices. As you will see, these concepts hold true across the various MSF models, processes, and disciplines. This chapter introduces each of these commonsense concepts, but not until you read subsequent chapters will you truly get a sense of how pervasive, interrelated, and powerful they are; and yet how challenging they are to implement correctly.

Foundational Principles

MSF foundational principles are guiding concepts for how a project team should work together to deliver a solution. These principles should be internalized by each team member and applied in how members operate together as a team. These principles also apply to how a team should work with their organization and with stakeholders. At the core of MSF are nine foundational principles:

- Foster open communications
- Work toward a shared vision
- Empower team members
- Establish clear accountability and shared responsibility
- Deliver incremental value
- Stay agile, expect and adapt to change
- Invest in quality
- Learn from all experiences
- Partner with customers

The following sections provide practical insight on some seemingly commonsense principles. Together, these principles express the MSF philosophy, forming the basis of a coherent approach to organizing people and processes for projects undertaken to deliver solutions. They underlie both the structure and application of MSF. Although each principle has been shown to have merit on its own, many are interdependent in the sense that the application of one supports the successful application of another. When applied in tandem, they create a strong foundation that enables MSF to work well in a wide range of projects that vary in size, complexity, and type.

Foster Open Communications

It seems obvious that any project team ought to share information. What is not so obvious is that for a team to be effective and efficient, an appropriate level of information needs to be shared among team members and across the enterprise. A team needs to understand the nature of what needs to be done and how team members and external folks communicate. The hard part is determining an appropriate level for each relationship and what information needs to be shared. For example, should you share the same level of information with an executive as you would share with a team member? Not likely. Nor would that executive likely have the time or patience to appreciate you going to that level. Too many times people confuse flooding someone with data as being the same as sharing information.

Where "open" communications comes into play is twofold. First, it involves sharing the plain truth, and not some slanted spin on information because a sender is fearful that a receiver cannot handle the truth, does not want to hear the truth, or will take punitive action. If an organization establishes an open communications environment, everyone will be better able to adjust plans accordingly.

The second aspect of open communications is that all project information has to be readily available and, more important, actively shared. For instance, open communications is not just making completed deliverables available for others to read in some dark corner of a collaboration site. Open communications is making sure a team knows enough about what each member is working on and knows when they can expect a deliverable or a draft of the deliverable for their review and comment (well before it is due). This could be a challenge because some people do not like to share work before it is done. Worse yet, some still perceive information and knowledge as power and share as little as possible. This "need to know" model of restrictive communications is very counterproductive, especially as the size and complexity of a project team grow.

Open communications is a lofty goal and often culturally very hard to foster. Keep in mind that if not handled correctly, open communications could be very detrimental to a project. It is like drinking from an informational fire hose with the obvious risk that someone drowns in all that information and is less efficient and effective.

Accordingly, open communications does not mean flooding team members with e-mail messages and writing treatise-sized documents. Conversely, open and inclusive communications means sharing just enough information with the current team, and subsequent team(s), to increase their understanding and reduce wasted efforts. An obvious challenge is continually determining what amount of information to share with the various team members and stakeholders.

Open Communications in MSF

As challenging as it might be for logistical, practical, and cultural reasons, MSF encourages being as open and inclusive as possible with communications, both within a team and with key stakeholders. When used throughout an entire project life cycle, open communications fosters active customer, user, and operations involvement. Communication becomes a medium through which a shared vision and performance goals are established, measured, and achieved.

When personalizing and adapting MSF to fit a team's needs, it is necessary to understand what needs to be communicated, when, and at what level of detail. To help facilitate this, the MSF Team Model is structured to support open communications. The MSF Risk Model is structured to openly handle project risks. The MSF Governance Model fosters open communications through incorporation of key checkpoints.

Work Toward a Shared Vision

Every day so many decisions are made at all levels of a project that, unless everyone shares a common vision, quick resolution of decisions could be burdensome and overwhelming. Having a shared vision empowers team members and enables agility so that team members are able to make informed decisions quickly in the context of achieving a vision. A shared vision also helps team members fill requirements gaps as they are discovered. Sometimes when a team is stuck in the present, a vision can provide motivation and hope for the future.

But what is a vision? In business terms, it is a concise description of the overall mission. It provides clear and quantifiable goals without biasing or constraining how they will be accomplished. Typically, this vision goes beyond the current project to paint a long-term and unbounded understanding of what the team is trying to accomplish. A vision is usually held at a solution level where it might take a few projects to deliver on that vision. Conversely, the realization of a vision through a solution definition might need to be decomposed into many projects.

Why is a shared vision so important? When all participants understand a shared vision and are working toward it, they align their own decisions and priorities with a broader team purpose represented by that vision. Without a shared vision, team members and stakeholders might have conflicting views of a project's direction, goals, and purpose and be unable to act as a cohesive group. An unaligned effort is wasteful and potentially debilitating to a team.

Teams often fail to understand that even if they think they successfully delivered a requested solution, without a shared vision, stakeholders might not agree with their assessment. Without a unifying shared vision, it is extremely challenging to measure tactical execution because it depends on which variation of a strategic vision a team is being measured against.

Shared Vision in MSF

Clarifying and getting commitment to a shared vision are so important that it is the primary objective at the beginning of any MSF project. Working toward a shared vision requires the application of many of the other principles that are essential to team success. Principles of empowerment, accountability, communication, and delivering business value each play a part in successful pursuit of a shared vision, which can be difficult and courageous work—work that often needs leadership and personal fortitude.

A shared vision comes into play with the MSF Governance Model. The iterative nature of the MSF Governance Model means that many parts of a solution could be in various stages of completion. To support this approach, a shared vision is required to guide concurrent delivery of these parts toward one coherent and integrated solution. Without a shared vision, the likely impact is that the later stages of delivery will need more, unplanned effort to pull together and integrate the disjointed parts.

The MSF Team Model has all roles (described in Chapter 4, "Building an MSF Team") represented from the beginning of a project. With each role represented, the process of creating shared vision helps to clarify goals and bring conflicts and mistaken assumptions to light so they can be resolved. Once agreed upon, a vision motivates a team and helps to ensure that all efforts are aligned with project goals. It also provides a way to measure success.

Empower Team Members

> *On the best teams, different individuals provide occasional leadership, taking charge in areas where they have particular strengths. No one is the permanent leader, because that person would then cease to be a peer and the team interaction would begin to break down. The structure of a team is a network, not a hierarchy.*
>
> —*Tom DeMarco and Timothy Lister,* Peopleware: Productive Projects and Teams

How often are you on a project where everything is clearly mapped out and not likely to change? Odds are...not often. Empowering teams is one of many ways not only to survive in this type of ever-changing environment, but also to enable team members to creatively find ways to be successful. Lack of empowerment not only diminishes creativity but also reduces morale and thwarts the ability to create high-performance teams.

Like many of these principles, "empower team members" is a catchy phrase that companies like to espouse but often have limited success in truly achieving. Having an environment that supports empowering team members is summed up in a couple of questions: Does an organization truly trust a project team to make the right decisions for a project? Do team members trust each other? Often team members understand their own area and are able to make good decisions for their area but feel limited in their ability to make good decisions that have effects beyond their area (i.e., think global, act local). If team members feel empowered, responsible for the whole solution, and have a shared vision, there is a greater chance they will make good project-level decisions. And as discussed in the section titled "Work Toward a Shared Vision" earlier in this chapter, to be agile, team members must be empowered to make decisions given the vast number of decisions that must be made every day.

Empowering team members means there is a level of trust that all team members will deliver on their commitments. Likewise, stakeholders are able to empower and trust the team. Building a culture that supports and nourishes empowered teams is challenging and requires steadfast support by an organization. It also includes creating an environment so that team members feel safe taking reasonable risks (referred to as *personal safety*).

If done successfully, empowerment engenders more confidence in a team and its abilities. For example, with open communications about roles and responsibilities, project management should be more at ease with greater degrees of empowerment. If they clearly know what is expected of them, most people are able to rise to most challenges and deliver quality solutions. With trust and empowerment comes a benefit of being able to rechannel efforts into delivering a better quality solution as opposed to monitoring and policing team members. That is not to say there should be no monitoring, just that heavy-handed, burdensome, and bureaucratic activities should wane as empowerment is successfully instituted.

Empowering team members must be done in a thoughtful way to help bring along those that are not ready for empowerment. A body of research can be used in assessing how ready team members are for empowerment (i.e., *situational leadership*).[1] Although positioned as advice to leaders, this research involves how to better understand team members and subsequently how team leads might appropriately interact with other members on various tasks. As such, in assessing how ready team members are for empowerment (i.e., *empowerment readiness*), it is helpful to consider how much tasking and encouragement each team member requires.

Understanding Empowerment Readiness by Using the Situational Leadership Model

Hersey and Blanchard developed a *Situational Leadership Model*. This model purports that successful leadership is more than just having certain behavioral traits; it is how those traits are applied in different situations. Based on the notion of "it depends," it is a leader's responsibility to diagnose and identify appropriate leadership styles given a team's and/or team member's readiness to perform.

As provided in Table 3-1, this research describes team members within four developmental levels. These levels are expressed in terms of their competence to perform a given task

---

1 Paul Hersey, Kenneth Blanchard, and Dewey Johnson, *Management of Organizational Behavior*, 7th ed. (Upper Saddle River, NJ: Prentice Hall, 1996).

and their commitment to performing the task (commonly paraphrased as *skill vs. will*). Because a developmental level is assessed per task or task type, a team member might have different developmental levels for different types of tasks. As reflected in the table, these levels reasonably describe empowerment readiness, starting with little to no empowerment and gradually cultivating each team member to become fully empowered—one who needs nominal tasking or encouraging and is confident and self-driven.

Table 3-1   Developmental Levels Within the Situational Leadership Model

Develop-mental Level	Competence Level	Commitment Level	Description
D1	Low competence	Low commitment	Budding experience and confidence. Needs extensive support and assistance in understanding and performing the task. As such, motivation is low. Empowerment readiness is very low.
D2	Some competence	Low commitment	Growing experience and confidence. Still needs support and encouragement. Might be skilled and confident in other areas, but this is a new task type. Empowerment readiness is low.
D3	High competence	Variable commitment	Experienced and moderately motivated, often because of wavering self-confidence in ability to complete the task without support. Empowerment readiness is moderate.
D4	High competence	High commitment	Experienced, confident, and motivated. Able to complete tasks quickly with little guidance or support. Empowerment readiness is high.

Given these categories, this research espouses that leaders must use one of four matching leadership styles, described here, depending on team member and collective team readiness. The styles differ in the amount of direction and support offered.

- **Directing (S1)**   Leader defines roles and segments work into small, manageable tasks that are closely supervised. Although he or she lacks competence in a specific area, the team member(s) usually is motivated and eager for direction on how to get started. Usually, one-way communications are used. Typically for new or inexperienced team members.

- **Coaching (S2)**   Leader encourages team member(s) to start to make lower-level task decisions to cultivate confidence and motivation. Leader still defines roles and tasks but starts to engage team member(s) in definition and decision making. Starts to build relationship and basis for two-way communications. Typically for experienced team members that need some assistance.

- **Supporting (S3)**   Leader focuses on reinforcing confidence and motivation while the team member(s) competence enables him or her to be empowered to make low-level decisions. Starts to build a trust relationship through increased empowerment. Leader starts to take a more hands-off approach as the focus shifts to coaching and becomes less lower-task focused. Typically for motivated team members with increasing confidence and when tasking is counterproductive.

■ **Delegating (S4)**   With the relationship established and empowerment earned, leader provides high-level guidance and direction, and is involved in decision making and problem solving as needed. Typically for peak performers where it is best to be hands-off.

The research suggests that team leads adapt and personalize their leadership style to align with each team member's developmental level when interacting with that person regarding a specific task or task type. Figure 3-1 illustrates the situational nature of a team lead's interactions and relationships with team members—and a team as a whole.

Figure 3-1   Understanding empowerment readiness using the Situational Leadership Model

Raelin[2] also addresses overall team development and the application of Situational Leadership. He suggests that leaders also consider stages of team development, such as Tuckman's[3] model of a group's natural cycle: *forming, storming, norming,* and *performing.* Specifically, a *directing* leadership style is appropriate to help establish a team during a *forming* stage; a *coaching* leadership style is appropriate to cultivate a team during a *storming* stage; a *supporting* leadership style is appropriate to encourage a team during a *norming* stage; and a *delegating* leadership style is appropriate to monitor a team during a *performing* stage.

---

2 Joseph Raelin, *Creating Leaderful Organizations: How to Bring Out Leadership in Everyone* (San Francisco: Berrett-Koehler Publishers, 2003).

3 Bruce Tuckman (1965). "Developmental Sequence in Small Groups," *Psychological Bulletin* 63 (1965): 384–399.

Empowering Team Members in MSF

Empowerment has a profound impact on MSF. The MSF Team Model is based on the concept of empowered equals (i.e., team of peers). People and organizations outside of a team also need to empower and trust team members to make good decisions in light of a shared vision. This helps to eliminate the two extremes commonly found on teams: (1) relying on the "boss" to make hierarchical-based decisions, and (2) decision by committee, which often leads to analysis paralysis. MSF advocates empowering team members to help with their productivity and ability to remain agile while expecting change.

Establish Clear Accountability and Shared Responsibility

Empowered team members often feel more accountable for their decisions and willing to be jointly responsible for a project. More team member accountability leads to higher quality. For example, if a team member represents that he or she has completed a task but it is found not to be at the right level of quality, that team member is responsible for completing tasks to stated quality levels. To not make this punitive, every team member shares responsibility for the overall solution and its deliverables. This fosters stronger members of a team to be motivated to help bring along others. For example, if one part of a solution lacks sufficient quality or is delayed in delivery, the whole project team assumes responsibility; should one team member fail to deliver, the team fails to deliver (it's an "all for one and one for all" mentality).

Accountability and Responsibility in MSF

Much of what is espoused here is based on team members being sufficiently self-motivated to be accountable and responsible. When first adopting MSF, this is not often the case, and as such, more governance is needed. Keep in mind that this is exactly opposite the spirit of MSF. However, as a team successfully adopts MSF, individual accountability coupled with empowerment is a good goal to work toward.

Because MSF structures a team to be an interdependent network rather than a hierarchy, team members are jointly responsible for overall management of a project. This is not to imply that shared responsibility for managing a project negates the need for a project manager role. What it does mean, as discussed later, is that everyone is empowered to manage proactively all aspects of their portion of a solution, and to share in assuming a project is successful. A project manager role has specific responsibilities in contributing to that success but is not the "boss."

Deliver Incremental Value

> *Agile managers understand that demanding certainty in the face of uncertainty is dysfunctional. They set goals and constraints that provide boundaries within which creativity and innovation can flourish.*
>
> –Jim Highsmith, What Is Agile Software Development?

There are two facets to delivering incremental value. The first involves making sure what is delivered has optimal value to stakeholders. The second facet involves determining optimal increments in which to deliver value (i.e., frequency of delivery).

Classically, solutions are defined from requirements, decomposed into a collection of work packages, which in turn are assembled into schedules to accomplish that work based on the capability of a team and project constraints. Although there is nothing wrong with that approach, it sometimes appears that a disconnect exists between requirement gatherers and a delivery team when it comes to understanding what value is contained within work packages. Because delivery of value is determined by stakeholders, requirement gatherers are better positioned to understand intrinsic value. All groups (requirement gathers, delivery team, and stakeholders) need to work together to make sure each work package contains the maximum possible amount of high-value components of a solution.

To mitigate the disconnect about what is high value (given it often changes over time), a variation of this approach is to make sure that work packages are small enough such that a clear, quantifiable understanding of the value contained within each work package exists. This short-cycle, iterative approach provides more frequent opportunities to validate with stakeholders that what is being delivered has value. This enables a team to focus on incrementally and continuously delivering high value to the customer(s), not burning down resources and the schedule by delivering mixed-value work packages. Also, smaller work packages usually translate into smaller batches of risks and issues to monitor and resolve. Hence, often it is easier to deliver incrementally. Therefore, completing small, cohesive work packages provides a progressive flow of quantifiable value to the customer(s) at regular intervals, as opposed to less frequent delivery of larger work packages that contain mixed levels of value (often referred to as *earned value*: "The value of completed work expressed in terms of the approved budget assigned to that work for a schedule activity or work breakdown structure component"[4]).

The second facet of delivering incremental value centers around determining how frequently a team should deliver. The answer is project specific and lies in the balance between the cost to prepare and deliver a solution versus benefits gained with frequent delivery. The cost to prepare and deliver a shippable solution is measurable. It is the amount of tangible disruption of a project team. For example, a team might need to address issues as part of a solution stabilization and deployment effort, whereas these issues might have been worked out as part of the regular course of development in a longer iteration (i.e., net-net: issues were resolved at a much higher cost to a project because they needed to be resolved sooner as part of stabilization instead of being addressed in development).

A key benefit gained with frequent delivery is that nothing is more motivating than seeing a solution come together and start to take shape. It gives everyone a better understanding of realized value contained within a solution. Team members who did not quite grasp a shared

---

4 Project Management Institute, *A Guide to the Project Management Body of Knowledge (PMBOK Guide),* 3rd ed. (Newtown Square, PA: Project Management Institute, 2004), glossary.

vision then start to see a tangible solution. Skeptical sponsors are able to "touch" a solution, are reassured that a return on their investment is starting to be realized, and are able to provide more concrete feedback as to how a solution satisfies their needs and expectations. In addition, architects who formed a vision start to share with others tangible evidence of that vision. It also benefits those roles that depend on early and frequent delivery to accomplish and progress or advance their work. It provides them with a snapshot of a solution that is not too out of phase with the solution being developed. For instance, deployment and operations teams need something as soon as possible to start refining their plans and activities. If a solution is not available until the end of a build track, odds are that deployment issues will appear.

A side benefit is that by making deployment a habit and by practicing and testing deployment procedures, even with early solution prototypes, the costs to prepare and deliver a solution are reduced because the whole team learns how to make deployments run smoothly and predictably. Additional benefits of institutionalizing frequent delivery as soon in a life cycle as possible include the following:

- Enables team members to hone their contributions and skills
- Helps drive out issues earlier, hence improving quality sooner
- Builds trust among team members and externally with sponsors and stakeholders
- Enables agility so as to accommodate continuous change in customer needs and requirements
- Provides a reliable indicator that a project is on track and that a team is functioning well together
- Enables quality verification and validation, continuous improvement, increased productivity, and overall better economic performance
- Improves readiness, including solution deployment readiness and team deployment readiness
- Conditions a team into the habit of making regular deliveries
- Helps to continuously engage team members (i.e., not let them "go dark")

Delivering Incremental Value in MSF

If it makes sense to deliver incremental value, why do teams sometimes deliver large blocks of questionable value? Why do they sometimes leave integration of solution components—often the ones necessary to realize value—until the end? MSF avoids this by guiding teams to make frequent deliveries of incremental value, even though a solution might not be functionally complete.

MSF uses its two models to drive incremental delivery of value: Governance Model and Team Model. The MSF Governance Model is structured to support frequent and iterative development and deployment. The MSF Team Model is structured to make sure that all aspects of what is being delivering are of high value. Combined, these models enable a team to deliver value quickly and incrementally for stakeholder review.

To help understand and quantify value, a team needs to be customer focused. Being "customer focused" is another one of those catchy phrases that people and organizations banter around. But what does it really mean on a day-to-day basis to be customer focused? From a mechanical perspective, being customer focused is being able to trace each activity, deliverable, and feature back to a customer or user requirement. However, within MSF being customer focused is much more. The MSF Governance Model combined with the MSF Team Model enables a feedback loop to convey cost implications of delivering value. Because MSF is flexible and adaptable, should the costs of delivering incremental value start to outweigh the benefits, the process easily can be adjusted to rebalance the return on investment.

Stay Agile, Expect and Adapt to Change

Change happens...surprises should not.

Because change happens often, and usually at the worst possible moment, having an agile way to handle change means that the common disruptions caused by change are often minimized. Staying agile means an organization is ready for change and is able to smoothly adapt and adjust. As discussed later, one of the best ways to handle change is to have a good understanding of project constraint prioritizations and have a process that quickly considers and assesses what to do regarding the change. For example, if a change surfaces, its impact is assessed and rational steps are taken to adjust project activities accordingly.

Although change happens, an effective change control process throttles the amount of change to enable a team to optimize their productivity and creativity. Relating magnitude of change with team agility (i.e., their capacity to handle change) provides an understanding of how productive and creative a team likely will be. For example, as depicted in Figure 3-2, a team with low agility likely will have rapidly decreasing productivity as the volume of change increases (1). Conversely, a team with high agility likely will not incur a significant decrease in productivity as the volume of change increases (2). Figure 3-3 relates the amount of change to team member creativity. A team likely will realize an increase in creativity as change increases, but there is a turning point at which a team becomes overloaded with change (3) and additional change starts to deteriorate team dynamics, causing a reduction of creativity (4).

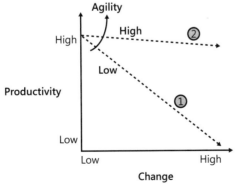

Figure 3-2 Relating team productivity to magnitude of change and team agility

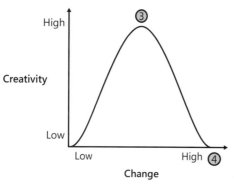

Figure 3-3   Relating team creativity to magnitude of change

Agility in MSF

Although MSF has little to no influence over whether change happens, MSF does provide an orderly, measured, and agile means to handle change when it does occur. Through open communications and empowerment, MSF enables teams to be agile and to act on change.

MSF has designed both its Team and Governance Models to anticipate and manage change. The MSF Team Model fosters agility for teams to address new challenges by involving all team roles in key decisions, thus ensuring that issues are explored and reviewed from all critical perspectives. In addition to changes coming from external origins, project teams should expect changes from stakeholders and even from within a team itself. For instance, teams must recognize that project requirements can be difficult to articulate at the outset and often will undergo significant modifications as possibilities become clearer to participants.

The MSF Governance Model, through its iterative approach to building project deliverables, provides a clear picture of deliverable status at each progressive stage. It enables stakeholders and team members to identify and respond to change effectively. This minimizes negative effects and disruptions caused by change while optimizing any benefits.

Invest in Quality

> *Quality improvement is a never-ending journey. There is no such thing as a top-quality product or service. All quality is relative. Each day, each product or service is getting relatively better or relatively worse, but it never stands still.*

> —*Tom Peters*, Thriving on Chaos

Clarity Point   *Quality* is an overloaded term with many implicit and explicit meanings; quality within an MSF context is consistent with these definitions:

■   "Meeting or exceeding customer expectations at a cost that represents value to them" (Harrington and Harrington)[5]

---

5 H. J. Harrington and J. S. Harrington, *Total Improvement Management: The Next Generation in Performance Improvement* (New York: McGraw-Hill, 1994), 23.

- "Conformance to requirements" (Crosby)[6]
- "Fitness for use" (Juran)[7]
- "The total composite product and service characteristics of marketing, engineering, manufacturing, and maintenance through which the product and service in use will meet the expectations of the customer" (Feigenbaum)[8]

  I selected these definitions because they are in harmony with different aspects of how quality is ingrained in MSF. Harrington and Harrington's definition resonates with a balanced approach to delivering value. Crosby's definition aligns with the MSF mindset of delivering on your commitments. Juran's definition emphasizes user experience. Feigenbaum's definition parallels the drivers for the MSF Governance Model.

How tolerant are end users of quirky behavior or, worse yet, partial working solutions? Will they be patient with unexpected behavior? If a solution involves finances, is it acceptable to "misplace" or "find" a few dollars? Many organizations espouse *quality*, often a loosely defined term, but lack the understanding of how to quantify quality. Solutions that involve infrastructure operations are usually more mature in this area. Typically, they have established agreements such as Service Level Agreements (SLAs) that specify quality in measurable terms. For instance, a vendor providing a messaging service can be nonoperational for only up to 15 minutes a month. Often, this is phrased as: "How many 9s are needed?" A service that is available for three 9s, for instance, would be operational 99.9 percent of the time.

Quality, or lack thereof, is defined in many ways. Quality can be seen simply as a direct reflection of the stability of a solution, something achieved through consistent process, or can be viewed as a complex trade-off of delivery, cost, and functionality. Quality must be quantified, defined, and planned. It does not happen accidentally. It requires investment of time and resources. It involves a mix of prevention and verification. Efforts need to be explicitly applied to ensure that quality is embedded in all solutions and services that an organization delivers. Organizations sometimes make a mistake of demanding the "highest-quality solutions" from their delivery teams. This request is dangerous because, unless explicitly defined, a team might understand this to mean five 9s or better (i.e., five 9s equates to about five minutes per year of downtime—typically very costly to achieve). An organization should avoid unnecessarily driving up the cost of delivering a solution as a result of excessive quality. Each organization should understand what the right level of quality is for all aspects of a solution—from software components to user manuals.

Most important, thinking about what the right levels of quality are encourages teams and individuals to develop a mindset centered on quality improvement. Quality improvement is everyone's business, every day. The idea of quality improvement complements the basic human desires of taking pride in your work, learning, continuous improvement, and empowerment. An investment in quality therefore becomes an investment in people, as well as in processes and tools. Successful quality management programs recognize this and incorporate

---

6 P. B. Crosby, *Quality Is Free: The Art of Making Quality Certain* (New York: McGraw-Hill, 1979).

7 Joseph M. Juran, *Juran on Leadership for Quality: An Executive Handbook* (New York: Free Press, 1989).

8 Armand V. Feigenbaum, *Total Quality Control*, 3rd ed. revised (New York: McGraw-Hill International, 1991).

quality into the culture of an organization. They all emphasize the need to invest continually in quality because quality expectations typically increase over time. Standing still is not a viable option.

Entire industries have evolved out of the pursuit of quality, as witnessed by the multitude of books, classes, theories, and approaches to managing quality (i.e., quality control) as well as monitoring quality (i.e., quality assurance). Promoting quality involves a continual investment in processes, tools, and training. Efforts to improve quality include a defined process for building quality into solutions and services through deliberate evaluation and assessment of outcomes (i.e., measurement). Enabling these processes with measurement tools strengthens them by developing structure and consistency. However, an organization and/or a team can overrely on measurements rather than retain a holistic quality perspective. Measurements should be one of many indicators of quality. If an organization or a team relies too much on metrics, team members might start to focus myopically on metrics and potentially skew them. The result is that these skewed metrics give others a false sense of solution quality.

> **Lesson Learned**   Many organizations do not know how to quantify quality for various solution elements. As such, they do not sufficiently know how to plan quality into a project and how to assess quality effectively at various checkpoints. This classically presents a challenge in that if a project team needs to deliver in an environment that does not assess quality, they rarely achieve the prescribed quality level required for each checkpoint. Instead, a team likely will declare satisfaction of a checkpoint based on a point in time not related to achieving a quality threshold.

Investing in Quality in MSF

Facilitating quality underlies every aspect of MSF. MSF tries to bolster an increase in quality through a set of natural checks and balances in its Team, Governance, and Risk Models. Team members who are held accountable for their activities and deliverables are naturally motivated to behave in ways that produce higher-quality solutions. MSF promotes the ability to capture lessons learned, which by its very nature provides a validation of activities and deliverables that helps drive an increase in quality awareness.

Each team member is accountable to the team and to respective stakeholders for achieving quality goals. In this sense, each team member is accountable for a share of the quality of the eventual solution. At the same time, overall responsibility is shared across the team of peers because any team member has the potential to cause project failure.

The MSF Team Model holds everyone on the team responsible for quality while committing one group to managing the processes of testing. A test group drives a team to make the necessary investments throughout a project's duration. This ensures that quality levels meet all stakeholders' expectations. In the MSF Governance Model, as project deliverables are progressively produced and reviewed, testing verifies and validates quality—starting at the beginning of a project life cycle and continuing through each track of activity. This model defines key checkpoints while suggesting interim checkpoints that, led by a test team, measure a solution against quality criteria established by stakeholders and the team. Conducting reviews at these checkpoints ensures a continuing focus on quality and provides opportunities to make midcourse corrections as necessary.

An essential ingredient for instilling quality into solutions and services is development of a learning environment. MSF emphasizes the importance of learning through the Readiness Management Discipline, which identifies the skills needed for a project and supports their acquisition by team members. Obtaining appropriate skills for a team represents an investment; time taken out of otherwise productive work hours plus funds for classroom training, courseware, mentors, or even consulting can add up to a significant monetary commitment. The Readiness Management Discipline promotes up-front investment in staffing teams with the right skills, based on the belief that an investment in skills translates into an investment in quality.

Learn from All Experiences

> *Those who do not remember the past are condemned to repeat it.*
>
> —*George Santayana,* The Life of Reason

If all levels of an organization do not learn from what previously worked and did not work, how will anyone improve next time? It must be understood and appreciated that learning happens at all levels: at a project level (e.g., refining a project-wide process), at an individual level (e.g., how to better interact with other team members), and at an organizational level (e.g., adjusting which quality metrics are collected for each project).

Capturing and sharing both technical and nontechnical experiences are fundamental to ongoing improvement and continuing success. Here are a few reasons why:

- Enables team members to benefit from success and failure experiences of others
- Helps team members to repeat successes and avoid mistakes
- Institutionalizes learning through techniques such as reviews and retrospectives

When you look at the marginal increases in the success rate of technology projects while acknowledging that the major causes of failure have not changed much over time (see Table 3-2), it would appear that as an industry those in business have not learned from their failed projects. Taking time to learn while on tight deadlines with limited resources is difficult to do, and tougher to justify both to teams and stakeholders. However, failure to learn from experience is a guarantee that failures will be repeated and a team once again will suffer through associated project consequences.

Table 3-2   Top 10 Causes of Project Failure

Rank	Cause	Frequency (%)
1	Incomplete requirements	13.1
2	Lack of user involvement	12.4
3	Lack of resources	10.6
4	Unrealistic expectations	9.9
5	Lack of executive support	9.3
6	Changing requirements and specifications	8.7
7	Lack of planning	8.1
8	Didn't need it any longer	7.5
9	Lack of IT management	6.2
10	Technology illiteracy	4.3

Source: Standish Group International, *Extreme Chaos* (West Yarmouth, MA: Standish Group International, 2000)

Learning from All Experiences in MSF

MSF assumes that focusing on continuous improvement through learning leads to greater success (referred to as *kaizen*, the Japanese word meaning "philosophy of ongoing improvement").[9] MSF builds in natural checkpoints and reviews that help a team reflect and assess successful and not-so-successful aspects of a project. Knowledge derived from one project that then becomes available for others to draw upon decreases uncertainty surrounding decision making based on inadequate information. Planned checkpoints throughout the MSF Governance Model help teams to make midcourse corrections and avoid repeating mistakes. Additionally, capturing and sharing this learning create best practices from processes that went well.

MSF emphasizes the importance of organizational- or enterprise-level learning from project outcomes by recommending externally facilitated project checkpoints and post-project reviews. This information records not only the success of a project, but also characteristics of the team and the process that contributed to its success. Sharing lessons learned from multiple projects facilitates an environment of open communications, and as such interactions between team members take on a forward, problem-solving outlook rather than one that is intrinsically backward and blaming.

Partner with Customers

How often is a project successful by simply throwing the result over the "proverbial" wall and hoping that a team met customer expectations? Success is a joint effort. That is not to say that customers do a team's work. However, it is to say that customers should work closely and incrementally with a delivery team to ensure a solution meets their expectations. Partnering

---

9 *MSN Encarta Dictionary,* http://encarta.msn.com/encnet/refpages/search.aspx?q=kaizen.

with customers is mutually beneficial because it helps drive down uncertainty, shortens the time to resolve requirement questions, and increases a team's understanding of the solution value propositions through regular contact.

Partnering with Customers in MSF

The MSF Team Model represents an advocacy model that attempts to involve all stakeholders, including customers and users. The model differentiates between customers and users, and dedicates a separate set of advocates on a team for both. As discussed in much more detail later, *customers* are the people sponsoring and/or paying for a project. *Users* are the people who intend to use a solution.

Mindsets

Foundational principles guide how a team should be oriented to maximize success, but what about orienting team members as individuals to maximize success? This orientation is called a *mindset*. A mindset orients each team member as to how he or she should approach solution delivery. Ideally, team members internalize these mindsets to drive their personal behavior. The following are a few mindsets that each team member should internalize:

- Foster a team of peers
- Focus on business value
- Keep a solution perspective
- Take pride in workmanship
- Learn continuously
- Internalize qualities of service
- Practice good citizenship
- Deliver on your commitments

Foster a Team of Peers

If your organization is able to embody the MSF foundational principles, especially empowerment and accountability, does it really make sense to run a project with a hierarchical project structure? If everyone understands the mission and its goals (i.e., shared vision) and understands his or her role and responsibilities in delivering a solution, doesn't it make more sense to treat everyone as a peer? This is not proposing anarchy or managing by committee, but rather that everyone shares responsibility for the successful delivery of a solution. Every role is singularly accountable for its respective aspect(s) of a project while being jointly responsible for a project as a whole. As you will see, there is still a Program Manager role, but that role is focused on delivering a project within project constraints, not on managing team members.

The mindset of a team of peers conveys to a team that each role has a "spotlight" on it at various times throughout a life cycle, that each role is an integral part of a team reaching its quality goals and delivering a solution that best meets all stakeholder needs. When everyone is empowered as equals, MSF avoids disadvantages imposed by a top-down, hierarchical structure of traditional project teams.

In MSF, everyone shares responsibility for the successes or failures of a project; MSF discourages singling out individuals for praise or blame because that undermines the foundation of empowering a team. The lowest level of recognition should be at a team level. Yes, it is nice to recognize star performers, but it should be done in the context of recognizing a team. Although unspoken, a project team usually knows who contributes most. Individual recognition is often better served in private venues such as yearly increases and/or bonuses.

Although each role has equal value on a team, the team of peers exists between roles and should not be confused with consensus-driven decision making. Each subteam (e.g., the test team) requires a form of internal organizational hierarchy for distributing work and managing resources. Team leads for each group are responsible for managing, guiding, and coordinating the team, enabling team members to focus on meeting individual goals.

Essential ingredients in fostering a team of peers are trust and respect. Trust and respect bind a team of peers. For example, team members need to trust that their fellow team members perform to expected levels. An organization must trust a project team to deliver a solution regardless of their selected approach so long as it is within project constraints. Team leads need to trust their team members.

Usually, there are 101 ways to complete every assigned task. As long as team members adhere to project norms and deliver as expected, they should have creative license to perform and accomplish the task. This ties directly into the principle of empowering team members. Without trust and respect, a team of peers starts to falter, which leads to micromanagement and seriously degraded ability to be agile.

Focus on Business Value

It is really quite simple: success is measured in terms of delivering business value. This means not only delivering something that customers need, but also includes delivering something customers want, which has value to them. To deliver value, everyone on a team needs to understand what customers deem valuable. Failing to provide customers with business value puts a project at risk: at risk of getting off course; at risk of spending lots of misdirected time, effort, and money; and even at risk of being cancelled.

Team members usually understand that they need to focus on business value. It is just that they often get distracted. Too many times solutions are delivered with cool features that provide different or little business value. Too many times a team polishes a solution where each successive layer of polish further diminishes business value. Too many times a team mistakenly focuses on those parts of a solution that are business value gap fillers (i.e., those parts of a solution that integrate high business value pieces). Too many times requirements are not stack-ranked based on business value. In short, business leaders fund solution delivery efforts to provide them with increased value or some business advantage. To be successful, as part of a shared vision, a team must understand linkages between their efforts and the business drivers, and must continue to deliver increasing business value.

For a team to better understand how to deliver business value, they need to keep customers in mind for all of those little decisions that every team member makes every day. This means that when team members try to make those decisions, they ask themselves: What way would best serve the customer? Where are their pain points? Keeping customers in mind at a grassroots level naturally percolates up to when those bigger decisions must be made. Most of the time this type of thinking is commonly called *customer empathy*.

Keep a Solution Perspective

Because of the size and complexity of most projects, when a solution is decomposed into actionable pieces, team members sometimes become myopic in their understanding of the ultimate solution. That is why so much emphasis is placed on the principle of having a shared vision. As team members deliver their portions, they need to be mindful of the overall mission, goals, and vision for a solution. Many times a subteam veers away from the vision while optimizing their area and believing they are acting for the common good—only to find that they need to rework major aspects to bring it back in line with a solution; they get caught up in details and lose sight of a solution.

Having a solution perspective is not about how a role contributes to delivering a solution, but is about how a role delivers a solution that fits into a broader solution. In turn, that solution fits into an even broader solution, and so forth. A solutions mindset attempts to foster the ability of team members to holistically consider their respective efforts to develop a stand-alone solution and how they are accountable for its successful integration into a broader solution. A solutions mindset enables team members to carve out a portion of a broader solution and call it their own. This typically drives up a sense of ownership and pride of craftsmanship.

Adopting a solution perspective is also a team normalizer that supports being a team of peers. This approach means that everyone's job is to define, design, build, test, and deploy their solution as opposed to team members aligning themselves with their craft (e.g., I am a developer and therefore my job is to write code).

Having a solution perspective also encourages team members to focus on what is needed to deliver solutions and not to be caught up in lower-level details of how to deliver a solution. They should consider themselves as empowered business owners whose business is dependent on delivering their solution. This level of thinking should help team members resolve many day-to-day issues and decisions.

One way Microsoft fosters a solution perspective is by encouraging team members to adopt their solution and give it a life and personality of its own. Teams do this by creating a unifying solution identity, be it a logo, a cool-sounding code name, a mascot, or some other means where team members identify themselves as a part of a great whole versus a collection of loosely associated individuals (e.g., *project rolling thunder* with logo of a lightning bolt coming from an ominous storm cloud). This approach clearly identifies a project, clearly identifies a team, raises a sense of accountability, and serves as a mechanism for increasing team morale. Printing the team project code name on T-shirts, coffee mugs, and other group gift items is another way to create and reinforce team identity and spirit. This is particularly useful on projects that include virtual teams that are composed of elements from several different groups within an organization.

Take Pride in Workmanship

Unlike the principle of investing in quality, which conveys that a team and organization should take purposeful steps to facilitate quality, this mindset espouses that quality is not something to be delegated. Instead, quality is everyone's responsibility throughout the solution delivery life cycle. This mindset not only includes enabling increased quality within a team member's own deliverables but also includes driving up the quality of process enactment and project governance. Being ever vigilant, any team member can facilitate continuous improvement.

In a successful team, every member feels responsible for the overall solution quality; and every team member takes pride in what he or she produces. However, a team needs to invest wisely—too much can cost a team. At the beginning of a project, a team must determine which level of quality is needed for the various aspects of the project.

Pride in workmanship involves passion and commitment. Taking pride in their work leads team members to perform their work at the highest quality possible, given their constraints, so that if they have to deliver tomorrow, they are able to deliver something of value. It is the idea of having a nearly shippable solution every day. It means that a solution meets or exceeds the quality standard(s) set by a project sponsor and accepted by the team at the beginning of a project.

An analogy that describes this concept is the automobile assembly line. Traditionally, workers put cars together from individual parts and were only responsible for the quality of their own task. When a car rolled off the line, an inspector checked it to see whether its quality was high enough to sell. But the end of a process is an expensive time at which to find problems because corrections are very costly to make at that point. Also, because quality was not very predictable, the amount of time required at the end of the line to determine whether the product was sellable was not predictable either.

More recently in car manufacturing, quality has become "job one." As work is being done (such as when a door is attached or a radio is installed), an inspector checks the work in progress to make sure that it meets the quality standards defined for that particular task. As long as this level of quality continues throughout the assembly process, much less time and fewer resources are required at the end to ensure that a car is of acceptable quality. This makes the process much more predictable because an inspector needs to check only the integration of the parts and not the individual work.

Learn Continuously

Given that most every project, team, and environment have uniqueness, each project presents opportunities to learn, experiment, and refine skills, processes, and procedures. To take advantage of these opportunities, continuous learning and adapting must exist at all levels of an organization—not just be limited to team members.

Unlike a classic master–apprentice relationship, learning while on a dynamic team can come from any area and from anyone. Because innovation can occur with any team member, teams should be open and allow themselves to learn from each other. Encouraging team members to be innovative and to take acceptable risks likely results in success. When a team is given a chance to repeat those successes, it drives process improvement. Having a team learn from less-than-successful efforts is also valuable. Most people say that you learn much more from unsuccessful activities than you do when things go smoothly.

Continuous learning takes commitment from all levels of an organization. Time taken to extract lessons learned might divert time from other parts of a project, but this is a commitment to ongoing self-improvement through the gathering and sharing of knowledge.

Internalize Qualities of Service

As discussed in more detail in Chapter 8, "MSF Plan Track: Planning a Solution," *qualities of service* (QoS) define expected operational characteristics of a solution, such as the level of expected solution availability. It is essential for stakeholders and team members, not just architects, to understand QoS and how satisfying them affects deliverables. Otherwise, stakeholders and team members likely will make implicit assumptions about how a solution will behave. Because these assumptions rarely align, each team member needs to make explicit design decisions from the beginning to ensure QoS are satisfied. That way, implicit assumptions are converted into explicit QoS requirements. And QoS are explicitly designed into a solution from the beginning and are not treated as an afterthought.

> **Lesson Learned** It is very challenging to define QoS unless the customer(s) and the team can articulate the key attributes of a solution. In addition, it really helps if both parties understand the benefits as well as cost and schedule implications of setting QoS levels.
>
> Being explicit about QoS assumptions is very important, especially when the solution being delivered replaces an existing solution. Stakeholders trust that a new solution will provide new and improved features and capabilities, and they are intolerant if a new solution does not at least match existing QoS of the legacy solution.

Practice Good Citizenship

Good citizenship means being trustworthy, honorable, responsible, and respectful in all aspects of how you interact with your fellow team members, with an organization, and with stakeholders and how you participate in a project and help deliver a solution. This includes being an entrusted steward of corporate, project, and computing resources. This includes openly and willingly sharing resources, information, and knowledge. Citizens act on and are mindful of the greater good.

Being a good citizen also means proactive reuse of resources and generating resources that can be reused. In the not-so-distant past, many teams built everything from scratch because it was not practical to reuse or extend existing components, scripts, and collateral. Even if it was practical, many teams resisted (often called the *not invented here* syndrome). With the advent of *service-oriented architectures* (SOAs), the mindset of reuse is more practical. Team members should first think to reuse and extend current assets and standards, not to reinvent unnecessarily.

Deliver on Your Commitments

Despite many embedded checks and balances, MSF runs on trust and empowerment. Trust and empowerment are earned, in part, by team members delivering on their commitments. MSF establishes an environment in which team members and stakeholders are able to trust that their fellow team members will deliver on their commitments. Because a project is a collection of interdependent activities, when one team member does not meet his or her commitments, it imbalances and jeopardizes the whole ecosystem.

To help meet commitments, each team member continually needs to make measured progress and not get bogged down by little obstacles and issues. It often helps if team members assume a frame of mind where missing a commitment (e.g., a deliverable date) is not an option. This should help drive creative decision making and serve as motivation to drive forward.

Proven Practices

Proven practices, sometimes called *best practices*, are relative. They are good for the situation(s) in which they apply and might or might not be good for other situations. In other words, a proven practice in one situation might not be a proven practice in another. Given that, some practices seem to apply to a wide array of projects and project types. Although descriptions of some of these are dispersed throughout subsequent chapters, here are a few general ones to consider:

- Use small, multidisciplinary teams
- Enable teams to work together at a single site
- Define and design a solution with all roles represented (discussed in depth in Chapter 4)
- Motivated teams are more effective
- Get specific early

Use Small, Multidisciplinary Teams

Small, multidisciplinary teams (i.e., typically no bigger than 10 members) have inherent advantages, including the ability to respond more quickly than larger teams can. Therefore, one recourse for large project teams is to create a team of teams (e.g., a lead team or an integration team)—with smaller groups working in parallel. Team members with expertise or who focus in specific areas are empowered with control to act when necessary. Within a team or even within a subteam, multiple disciplines need a specific set of skills. People from various backgrounds, training, and specialization who make up teams or roles all add to the overall solution quality. That results from the unique perspective each brings to his or her role and, ultimately, to an entire solution.

Enable Teams to Work Together at a Single Site

Teams work best in a low communications overhead environment where ideas are free flowing and decision making is real-time. Experience has shown that this is best fostered by teams working together at a single physical site. Because organizations increasingly have global delivery teams, it has become more challenging to be physically colocated. Therefore, virtual colocation is an increasing reality.

Physical colocation, such as working in the same section of a building, sharing offices, or setting aside space specifically for teams to gather, has in the past proved to be the most effective method to promote open communications. This process is an essential ingredient to the MSF team formula for success. Team members must be cognizant of team dynamics in this shared space and be ready to adjust things because colocation does not equal collaboration—it just reduces collaboration barriers. However, there are some colocation risks to be aware of such as disruptive cross-team chatter. For example, if a team is colocated in a team room, goals of free-flowing ideas and real-time decision making are likely achieved, but sometimes a team can be derailed in conversations that consume the whole team unnecessarily. The obvious intent is to keep these eventualities to a minimum.

Although working together at the same physical location is the preferred choice, the nature of business might necessitate *virtual teaming*. Virtual teaming involves team members communicating and collaborating with each other primarily by electronic means—including team members who telecommute. Communication occurs across organizational boundaries, space, and time. Virtually working together could be as simple as everyone being readily available through an instant messaging service. It could also be as elaborate as continual, multiparty video teleconferencing.

Note that without physical organizational boundaries to encapsulate roles in a coordinated unit, virtual teaming requires even stronger communication, trust agreements and relationships, explicit action plans, and automation tools that support tracking of projects and tasks so that action items do not get lost.

A vital component of a virtual team is the ability for each role to depend on and trust in other roles to fulfill their responsibilities. This develops through a blend of culture, good management, and, when possible, time spent working together at the same site. Industry research often finds that little attention is given to communication skills or team fit when members are chosen for virtual teams. This oversight is a key factor in the failure of many of these teams. When setting up a virtual team, look for members with the following characteristics:

- Able to work independently

- Demonstrates leadership skills

- Possesses specific skills required for delivery of a solution

- Able to share knowledge with an organization

- Can help develop effective methods of working

> **Lesson Learned**   If working virtually is necessary, teams should first physically work together to establish working relationships and team dynamics. Having teams work together at a single site also helps to enforce their sense of team identity and unity. Once team members know and understand each other, working virtually becomes more successful.

Motivated Teams Are More Effective

The beatings will continue until morale improves.

—Anonymous

Motivation is a key factor in team member productivity. Some organizations, be it willingly or unwillingly, create an environment that saps away motivation. For example, some organizations use the threat of punishment to motivate teams. These organizations are losing out on being able to take advantage of benefits of highly motivated teams. Any entity, an organization, team, or individual, with low motivation realizes a cascading negative effect. For instance, low motivation usually lowers individual performance, leading to lower quality and lower quantity of output. In an attempt to avoid scrutiny, these entities often resort to the illusion of progress by undercommunicating reductions of goals, scope, and tasks. Usually, an impact of this behavior is discovered too late in the process to recover without significant effort and added costs.

Conversely, there are many positive benefits of a motivated team. Motivating a team involves planning and nurturing—rarely does it happen spontaneously. To achieve this, identify what is likely to motivate each team and attempt to create an environment whereby each team can foster creativity and innovation. With these two base elements of motivation in place, team morale builds. This in turn stimulates team motivation. People who work at Microsoft recognize this as one of the company's defining characteristics. Other techniques that might be used to build motivation are the following:

- Clarify team vision.

- Build team identity using project code names and team paraphernalia, including mascots, T-shirts, and gadgets.

- Spend time getting to know colleagues by way of social or team events.

- Schedule team-building sessions in which team members are able to experiment with different ways of collaborating and interacting; normally outside a work setting.

- Ensure that an individual's personal goals are considered, such as providing opportunities for personal or technical competency development or managing the impact on work–life balance.

- Maximize empowerment felt by individuals and listen to their views.

- Celebrate success.

Get Specific Early

When a team first defines a solution delivery effort, many aspects of a solution are abstract and conceptual. Abstract thinking about a solution is necessary to help paint a broad-brush, conceptual picture of a solution and to establish a shared vision. However, abstractions and conceptual solutions by their very nature intentionally lack definition and detail to foster diversity of thought. This can lead to inconsistent understandings and different interpretations of a solution. Although useful initially, designing in the abstract for too long adds risk to a project and undermines team effectiveness.

A team should attempt to evolve the abstract and conceptual into tangible concepts as quickly as possible. Otherwise, they risk losing time procrastinating about the big picture instead of tackling solvable problems. A team should quickly drive to defining specific examples rather than prolonged analysis of the problem space. By getting to specific examples early in the design process, and developing concrete examples (as exemplified in Figure 3-4), a team better aligns its thinking and reaches consensus on how to implement a shared vision. Using specific examples helps a team not only to reach a shared vision more quickly, but it also helps more quickly drive to consensus on how to approach solution delivery. In addition, it helps to draw out stakeholders' needs and expectations. As such, this approach, supported by clarity about what and how to deliver, reduces project risk.

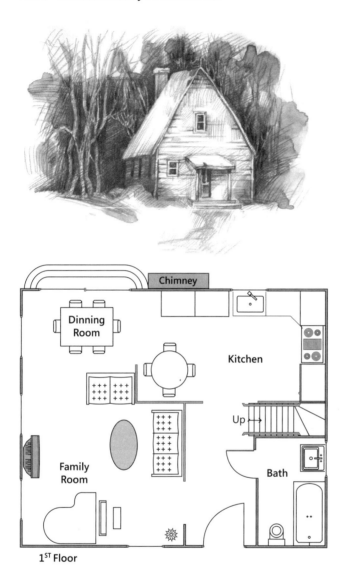

Figure 3-4   Example of moving from abstract to specific

Summary

The foundational principles, mindsets, and proven practices discussed in this chapter are the heart of MSF. They are threaded through every model, process, and discipline. The foundational principles guide how a team should work together and with the organization and stakeholders to deliver a solution. The mindsets orient team member behavior. The proven practices discussed in this chapter, with more to come in subsequent chapters, are time-tested lessons learned with broad appeal. Although these commonsense concepts are easy to grasp, they can be quite challenging to implement well.

Chapter 4
Building an MSF Team

What is the best division of labor when a team is trying to deliver solutions? How does a team make sure it represents the interest of all stakeholders sufficiently? How should a team be structured to facilitate being a high-performing team? How should a team be organized to work naturally toward quality goals? As you well know, many factors influence how to structure a team. Over the years, Microsoft has experimented with various teaming models. What has worked best has been distilled into the following concepts surrounding teaming. The next few sections map how these concepts relate to the Microsoft Solutions Framework (MSF) foundational principles, mindsets, and proven practices.

This chapter describes a scalable and extensible teaming strategy developed, refined, and validated over many years. It represents not only a means to organize a team to represent stakeholder interests but embeds a set of natural checks and balances to help increase quality and minimize bureaucracy. It embodies the MSF foundational principles and incorporates core disciplines and key concepts.

> **Lesson Learned**   Of all the recommendations made within MSF, this one is the most valuable. It is also one of the most difficult to implement. It often involves changing peoples' jobs and what they do on a daily basis. As such, it typically causes great resistance from some people.

MSF Team Model: Team of Advocates

The MSF Team Model describes an approach to structure organizations, teams, individuals, and activities to maximize quality, productivity, and chances for success. It defines interdependent, multidisciplinary roles and their responsibilities, goals, and activities in context of the foundational principles and mindsets (e.g., team of peers).

The MSF Team Model is based on the premise that each team member presents a unique perspective on a project. Yet, for project success, customers and other stakeholders need an authoritative single source of information on project status, actions, and current issues.

To resolve this dilemma, the MSF Team Model combines clear accountability to various stakeholders with shared responsibility among the entire team for overall project success.

The MSF Team Model is perhaps the most distinctive aspect of MSF. At the heart of the Team Model is the fact that projects must embrace the disparate and often juxtaposed perspectives of various stakeholders, including operations, the business, and users. The MSF Team Model fosters this melding of diverse ideas, thus recognizing that projects and their team structure need to be flexible enough to foster those ideas all while supporting the various teams in how they prefer to organize themselves to help foster innovation that comes from those ideas.

Team of Advocates

Building on the team of peers mindset, the MSF Team Model is based on advocacy. A project team and their respective advocacies are segmented into seven groupings (called *advocacy groups*). Each advocacy group, identified in Table 4-1 and depicted in Figure 4-1, champions a few complementary, and sometimes competing,[1] aspects of working together to deliver a solution. Each advocacy group gives its respective external groups a voice on the team and is key to setting and managing the expectations of the external groups, which the team will deliver against (i.e., two-way advocacy). The core of this model is the concept that every team member is an advocate for achieving and championing his or her respective quality goals; advocating for his or her respective stakeholders (i.e., constituents); and advocating for his or her corporate functional area (e.g., the marketing department).

Table 4-1   MSF Advocacy Groups and Their Respective Advocacies

MSF Advocacy Group	Advocates for
Product Management	*Solution definition*: Solution description optimally satisfies stakeholder needs and expectations.
Program Management	*Solution delivery*: Project governance optimally satisfies sponsor(s) needs and expectations.
Architecture	*Solution design*: Solution design optimally satisfies all needs and expectations.
Development	*Solution construction*: Solution optimally satisfies design.
	Solution verification: Solution works as specified.
Test	*Solution validation*: Solution works as expected.
User Experience	*Solution usability*: Solution is fit for use and provides an effective, productive, and efficient user experience.
	User readiness: Users are sufficiently prepared to use the solution.
Release/Operations	*Solution deployment*: Solution is smoothly deployed and optimally integrated into its target environment(s).

---

1 Some of the natural checks and balances structured within MSF are by their very nature competing. For example, a program management team wants to deliver on time, which sometimes means cutting features. Whereas a product management team wants to add as much value to a solution as possible, which sometimes means adding features. More often than not, these are competing goals.

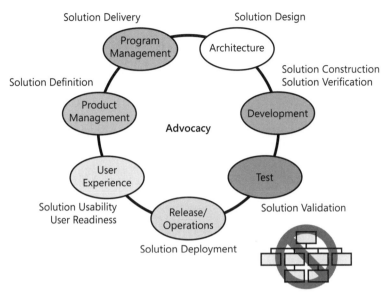

Figure 4-1   MSF Team Model

Although Figure 4-1 presents a logical depiction of the team model and is not an "org chart," there remains a formidable challenge of creating an adaptable, scalable, and flexible team structure that enables the team to advocate for their respective advocacies, namely, the following:

- Quality goals
- Constituents
- Functional areas

The following sections discuss these aspects and how roles relate to advocacy groups, and then provide an in-depth discussion of each advocacy group.

Quality Goals: Team of Quality Champions

MSF is based on a belief that key quality goals must be achieved for a project to be considered successful. Reaching these goals typically requires the application of different sets of related skills and knowledge areas. Failure of one group to achieve its goals jeopardizes a project. Therefore, each group is considered equally important in this team of peers.

These goals drive a team and define a team model. What is important in the adoption of the MSF Team Model is that all quality goals have an advocate on the team. Although it is true that the entire team is responsible for a project's success, the team model associates each quality goal with an advocacy group to ensure accountability and focus. That way, the various project stakeholders know who on the team is accountable for each goal.

Table 4-2 states key quality goals and maps them to their respective advocacy group. Following the table, each goal is discussed.

Table 4-2   **Key Quality Goals and MSF Team Model Advocacy Groups**

Key Quality Goals	MSF Advocacy Group
Satisfied stakeholders	Product Management
Define solution within project constraints	
Coordinate identification and optimization of project constraints	Program Management
Deliver solution within project constraints	
Design solution within project constraints	Architecture
Build solution to specifications	Development
Confirm all aspects of a solution meet or exceed their respective, defined quality levels	Test
Maximize solution usability	User Experience
Enhance user readiness and effectiveness	
Smooth deployment and transition to operations	Release/Operations

Satisfied Stakeholders   To be successful projects must meet stakeholder needs. A solution must match or exceed stakeholder expectations. It is possible to meet budget and time goals but still be unsuccessful if stakeholder needs have not been met. It is also possible to meet stakeholder needs but be unsuccessful if there is an expectation mismatch.

Coordinate Identification and Optimization of Project Constraints   As discussed in Chapter 2, "Understanding Solution Delivery Environments," solution delivery is subject to many constraints (e.g., budget, schedule, and resources). These constraints need to be quantified and their impact determined and balanced so a delivery team knows how best to work within the constraints. Because constraints can come from many aspects of solution delivery, each advocacy group is responsible for identifying and quantifying its own constraints. Optimizing and balancing these constraints for a given project is the responsibility of the Program Management Advocacy Group.

Define Solution Within Project Constraints   As discussed in Chapter 7, "MSF Envision Track: Defining a Solution," a *solution definition* describes how users and administrators use and interact with a solution as well as how a solution behaves and interacts with its host environment(s). The advocates for a solution definition need to collaborate with their constituencies to work through the challenges of defining a solution within project constraints. Because it is not always possible to define a solution within all constraints, trade-offs need to be made.

Deliver Solution Within Project Constraints   These advocates work with their consistencies to deliver a solution that optimally complies with project constraints. As discussed later, MSF provides a means to consider, balance, and optimally satisfy these constraints.

Design Solution Within Project Constraints   A successful design ensures that all aspects of a solution design meet or exceed project constraints, including training plans, pilot plans, deployment plans, and so forth. As discussed in Chapter 8, "MSF Plan Track: Planning a Solution," designing a solution involves a gradual evolution from high-level, conceptual designs to low-level, implementation designs.

Build Solution to Specification   Solution specifications describe in detail deliverables to be provided by a team to customers. It is important for a team to deliver in accordance with the specifications as accurately as possible because the specifications represent an agreement between a team and customers as to what will be built.

Confirm All Aspects of a Solution Meet or Exceed Their Respective, Defined Quality Levels   All solutions have issues. However, as discussed in Chapter 10, "MSF Stabilize Track: Stabilizing a Solution," to achieve defined quality levels, all issues deemed as release-blocking need to be addressed. As discussed later, this can involve everything from fixing an issue to documenting a workaround to closing the issue as "by design."

Maximize Solution Usability   The purpose of a solution is to make it easier for users to perform their work. Otherwise, why would users use a solution? It would likely be easier to perform the work manually. Delivering a solution that is rich in features and content but that is not usable by its designated users is considered a failure.

Maximize User Readiness and Effectiveness   A well-crafted solution and a poorly crafted solution are equally inadequate if intended users do not have sufficient skills and understanding of how to use and interact with either solution. To be successful, solution delivery needs to address user readiness (sometimes referred to as *user enablement*), be it through training, support, or instructional manuals.

Smooth Deployment and Transition to Operations   Often, the work necessary for a smooth deployment and transition to operations is underestimated. A smooth transition consists of not only making sure component parts of a solution are ready but also making sure Operations is ready to receive a solution and is prepared for the ongoing support and sustainability of a solution (i.e., *operational readiness*). How does a project team make sure the Operations team is ready? The answer to this question is very situational. This might include ensuring that training, infrastructure, and support are in place prior to deployment. Oftentimes, it is best to have some of an Operations team on a delivery team so they can bring their knowledge and experiences back to Operations.

Another challenge related to a smooth deployment is the association of the ease of deployment with solution quality. Although seemingly illogical, it makes sense because the first exposure to a solution is with solution installation. If solution installation is faulty, unfriendly, or complicated, it often leads users to assume that the installed solution is similarly flawed, even if that is not true.

Constituents: Team of Ambassadors

The MSF Team Model embodies a team of peers brought together to represent the entire set of constituencies: internal or external organizational entities (groups or individuals) involved with sponsorship, promotion, production, use, administration, and maintenance of a solution. Each advocacy group is accountable for representing specific needs of its constituencies. No advocacy group's interests are more important than another's. With each group contributing its unique perspective of its representative constituency, together these views provide the necessary checks and balances to ensure that a team produces the right solution.

The MSF Team Model advocates basing team decisions on sound understanding of customers' business and on active stakeholder participation throughout a project. To facilitate deep levels of participation, it is recommended that customer and user advocacy roles within the Team Model are staffed by members of the business and user communities.

> **Clarity Point**   *Constituents* are people or groups of people. The inanimate things that advocacy groups advocate for are called *advocacies*. For example, the User Experience Advocacy Group advocates for solution usability. Said the other way, solution usability is an advocacy of the User Experience Advocacy Group.

Functional Areas: Team of Representatives

A *functional area* is defined as a specialization within a general grouping of activities within an advocacy group. For instance, within the User Experience Advocacy Group, discussed in detail later, there are six functional areas (e.g., User Interface Design); each is responsible for a distinct aspect of user experience.

The MSF Team Model emphasizes the importance of aligning advocacy groups by business needs. Keep in mind that "business needs" are not just customer needs, they also include internal needs coming from the various corporate functional areas (e.g., the training department)— often the internal teams providing staff to be on a project. Team members, therefore, are representatives of their internal team and are advocates for the team's needs.

Foundational Principles Applied to Teaming

The following are the MSF foundational principles applied to the MSF Team Model.

Foster Open Communications

As team size grows, so does the importance of good communications. Open communications is fostered by how a team is structured and what guidance is provided on which cross-team interactions are required.

A team needs to be structured so that clear roles and responsibilities exist. Part of those responsibilities is to establish communications channels among roles. Open communications encourages healthy debate and discussions regarding different aspects of solution delivery.

One tricky aspect of fostering open communications is balancing a team structure that encourages sharing across the advocacy groups but not to a point that grouping team members together reduces productivity. Conversely, separating them too much creates isolated, nonintegrated groups (i.e., team fragmentation).

> **Lesson Learned**   To try to achieve open communications, some teams invite the whole team to status meetings such that everyone can hear each other's status firsthand. This is often counterproductive and does not achieve the intended goal. Most subteam members have too-detailed status for it to be of interest to others. Plus, it usually takes a very long time to go around the room soliciting status from everyone. When the project has subteams, a more effective strategy might be to have each subteam conduct their status meeting followed by a team-lead status meeting, or vice versa. This way, only the cross-team-relevant status is raised at the project team lead meeting.
>
> When there is a need for very close coordination, try a daily, first-thing-in-the-morning "stand-up" meeting (i.e., the meeting is so short that people do not have time to sit down). This is a quick sync-up of only the pressing issues for that day. If there is nothing to share, the meeting is over in minutes. The meeting should be time-boxed to no more than a half hour.

Work Toward a Shared Vision

Establishing a shared vision is facilitated by appropriately organizing a team into feature and function teams (discussed in the sections titled "Feature Teams" and "Function Teams" later in this chapter). When it is important to have a cross-role understanding of a solution, feature teams work best. When it is important for cross-solution consistency, function teams work best.

Empower Team Members

The MSF team of peers mindset is an empowering concept. Each team contributes to the management and success of delivering a solution. There is preferably no "boss" telling team members what to do. Ideally, it is up to a team to reach consensus on what is best and how to implement. As such, each advocacy group is responsible for self-organizing to be able to best deliver on their commitments.

Establish Clear Accountability, Shared Responsibility

Everyone is responsible for a solution and is held accountable for performing his or her assigned role. The team of peers mindset does not cloud accountability; there is always a single person that is accountable for each aspect, task, and deliverable. Sharing responsibility across a team of peers means that everyone succeeds or fails together—unlike other models where the overall manager is responsible.

Deliver Incremental Value

Although all advocacy groups strive to add business value to a solution, two advocacy groups are dedicated to it (i.e., Product Management to connect with customers, and User Experience to connect with users). Both groups work with the others on the team to make sure what is being built incrementally has high customer value.

Stay Agile, Expect and Adapt to Change

One aspect of staying agile is the ability to reorganize a team structure to fit best how a team thinks it will work best. For instance, let team members organize themselves—including if it means rearranging tables in their team room. Many times organizations are not flexible enough and force a team to fit into an existing structure that rarely is optimal for the team.

Being agile also means that team members should be comfortable with being added to a team and rolled off as needed to respond to changing requirements and changing needs for skills necessary to deliver a solution. Too many times, team members get comfortable on a team and feel slighted if they are rolled off. If an organization's culture supports this dynamic staffing concept, it likely will be an invigorating culture that enables employees to seek tasks that they want and are skilled at providing.

Invest in Quality

Breaking up a team into seven advocacy groups, even if it is just locally, requires a concerted effort to communicate openly and collaborate effectively. However, structuring a team this way helps increase quality through a set of natural checks and balances where each role is validated by another. It enables each group to focus on its mission and create natural tension with competing goals. For instance, Product Management often tries to get as many features into a release, whereas Program Management wants to deliver within constraints and therefore tends to minimize the number of features.

Learn from All Experiences

Setting up a balanced team is not easy. Often, there are too many outside influences and challenges for a team to assemble their "dream team." As such, an organization must amass a body of experience and knowledge in teaming strategies that work. This includes how to divide into subteams, team chemistry, distributed teaming, and collaboration tools that support colocated teams as well as globally dispersed ones.

Partner with Customers

The MSF team roles are set up to maximize coordination with customers—each advocacy group has a distinct set of constituencies. To advocate successfully, each advocacy group must establish a good working relationship with its constituencies. Through these relationships, a team can better represent customer expectations, requirements, issues, and concerns.

MSF Team Model Fundamentals

Before discussing MSF Team Model advocacy group particulars, a few underlying topics need to be discussed, namely, how roles relate to advocacy groups and functional areas; how the MSF Team Model fits within an organization; and how project management discipline is needed across a team.

Relating Roles to Advocacy Groups and Functional Areas

It is important to understand the differences between an advocacy group, a role on a project team, and a functional area and how team members fit into the whole picture. As stated previously, an *advocacy group* is a clustering of like responsibilities, goals, and activities for the express purpose of advocating specific quality goals, constituencies, and internal corporate functional areas, as exemplified in Figure 4-2. Each advocacy group (e.g., Development) can subdivide its work into a more refined collection of responsibilities, goals, and activities that is assigned to specific functional areas (e.g., Database Development). The specifics of which functional areas are relevant vary from project to project.

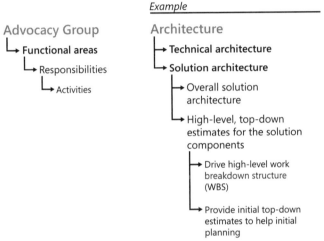

Figure 4-2 Example of an advocacy group decomposed into functional areas and responsibilities

A *role* is a logical means to refer to the lowest subdivision of labor and responsibility across all advocacy groups (i.e., it is the lowest level on a team structure within each advocacy group). Roles can be at different levels across a team (i.e., it is very likely that all roles will not be at the same level of specialty). For example, if an advocacy group does not use functional areas, the "role" maps to the whole advocacy group (e.g., "tester" would generically refer to the Test Advocacy Group). If an advocacy group uses functional areas (e.g., the Test Advocacy Group decides to split their work into functional testing and systems testing), a role maps to each functional area (e.g., functional tester and systems tester). If an advocacy group feels it is necessary to decompose their functional area into subspecialties, a role maps to the subspecialty level.

On small teams (e.g., system performance tester), a role is typically at an advocacy group level because there might not be enough people to specialize. On moderate-sized teams, roles are most often assigned at a functional area level. On large teams, a solution is complex enough that functional areas often need to be subdivided into specialty areas. As such, roles on large teams are defined to match that level. Note that one role is not the same as one person—multiple people might perform the same role (e.g., many team members might fill the role of "tester"). Alternatively, to scale down a team, a team member might take on more than one role.

Note that roles do not equate, imply, or suggest any kind of corporate organization chart or set of job titles because these vary widely by organization and team. Most often, project roles are staffed by people distributed among different corporate entities and sometimes within the business user community, as well as by external consultants and partners. To help clarify this for stakeholders and team members, it is best to document each team member's corporate position and title (e.g., Director of Finance) and his or her role on a project (e.g., Business Analyst role within the Product Management Advocacy Group). It is key to have a clear determination of the individuals on a team that are fulfilling a specific role and its associated functions, responsibilities, and contributions. Otherwise, by default, people assume a team member's corporate role matches that person's project role, which is often an incorrect assumption.

Define and Design a Solution with All Roles Represented

Although not everyone on a team might have helped define or design a solution, each advocacy group should have a representative involved. This is essential because each one represents a different aspect of solution delivery. Each has a unique perspective of a solution and its relationship to his or her individual objectives, as well as a team's objectives. Representatives from every advocacy group collaborating on the definition and design of a solution leads to a richer solution. This might be foreign to some organizations that typically rely heavily on their technology folks (e.g., architects) to come up with a design. However, solution designs that consider operations, user readiness, testability, and so forth tend to be more successful over the life of a solution.

To put this in perspective, it is unfortunate but true that sometimes a well-designed solution has deployment issues (e.g., problems with legacy system integration). Typically, this is because a team put most of their efforts into feature design and not enough into deployment design. Although this might have looked like the right decision during planning, that decision can delay the whole rollout because it necessitates reworking a solution for it to be deployed successfully. Another example of this is designing a solution to facilitate testing. In this case, solution deployment could be delayed because testing was not performed as expeditiously as expected.

The MSF Team Model Is *Not* an Organization Chart

One question that often arises when applying the MSF Team Model is: "Who is in charge?" An organization chart describes who is in charge and who reports to whom. In contrast, the MSF Team Model describes key roles and responsibilities for a project team, but does not define a management structure of a team from a personnel administration perspective. In many cases, a project team includes members from several different organizations, some of whom might report administratively to different managers.

Certain situations might arise, however, in which a team does not come to consensus on an issue. After spending due diligence in trying to come to agreement, the role of Program

Management must step up and temporarily take the primary lead to break a gridlock and move a project forward. It is during these instances that team members understand the leadership that has typically been shared among the roles must be temporarily shifted to an authoritative style to break the deadlock. This understanding creates a stronger level of acceptance and buy-in from the team on the need for an authoritative decision. As soon as the issue has been resolved and a team is able to get back into consensus, there is an immediate shift back into shared leadership responsibilities. A team of peers can be flexible and adaptable enough to handle these challenges successfully yet remain a nonhierarchical approach to project teaming.

Use Small Teams, Working in Parallel with Frequent Synchronization Points

Many books discuss ideal team size. There is no universally correct answer. Conversely, each solution delivery approach or method has its own ideal. For instance, some agile approaches effectively use pair programming (i.e., team size equals two) whereas others suggest breaking a project team into groups of between 5 and 10 people. Irrespective of how a team is organized, a goal is to have efficient teams that work in parallel and that can easily integrate and synchronize their efforts. Influences on making this team-size decision include how easily project work lends itself to decomposition and the skills of a project team (i.e., more senior folks are better able to work independently).

Project Management Discipline

Why is it that when most people see or hear something like "project management discipline" they either recoil or snicker about the lack of discipline on their team? So with this type of visceral reaction, why would MSF advocate that everyone needs to exhibit good project management discipline? Because a key to building trust that leads to empowerment is when everyone develops mutual confidence in each other's ability to manage themselves and their portion of solution delivery adequately. This is not to say everyone needs to be a project manager; it is to say that to varying degrees all team members need to exhibit good project management discipline. It is also a key to scaling up a project team. Without adequate project management rigor, scaling up a project team quickly erodes into dysfunction.

According to the Project Management Institute, "Project management is the application of knowledge, skills, tools and techniques to project activities to meet project requirements.[2] It is about using a body of knowledge and best practices to better enable a team to reliably deliver, adequately plan for risk, and reasonably manage its sphere of influence as opposed to being "the boss." It is about looking beyond the obvious, and planning for the unknown and the uncertain. It is confidently assessing and estimating what needs to be accomplished given project constraints and risks.

---

2 Project Management Institute, *Project Management Body of Knowledge (PMBOK) Guide,* 3rd ed. (Newtown Square, PA: Project Management Institute, 2004), sec. 1.3.

Part of developing good discipline is when team members assemble their own body of knowledge for the various types of projects and roles they might encounter. Whether managing a large program or a small solution component, a team needs context from which to understand how its current situation compares to other efforts. Figure 4-3 is an example of one such context. In this example, perceived project management complexity is mapped to perceived technical complexity for each project. As an organization starts to form a landscape of project types, each team builds off this experience to mature various successful approaches and behaviors to increase their ability to deliver reliably and repeatedly on commitments. In other words, a team is maturing their project management discipline.

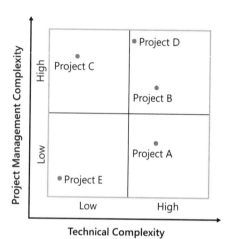

Figure 4-3   Example of assessed project complexity

Part of increasing each team member's project management discipline is broadening their project management awareness and maturing their delivery of activities. If done right, project management should be perceived as value-added activities that "protect" a team and enables them to focus on doing their work. The following project management planning activities should be considered for every effort and implemented as appropriate:

- **Communications Plan**   How, when, and what information to share with various stakeholders and with the team

- **Roles and Responsibilities**   Who does what, how they fit into a team structure, and what their responsibilities are

- **Integrated Master Schedule**   A consolidated set of activities (e.g., work breakdown structure (WBS)) with assigned resources (e.g., Resource Assignment Matrix)

- **Staffing Plan**   How to assess required skills and abilities to identify and recruit personnel needed to deliver a solution

- **Readiness Plan**   How to bring team member knowledge, skills, and abilities to levels required to perform the assigned roles

- **Risk and Issue Management Plan**   How to handle risks and issues as they arise

- **Configuration Management Plan**   How to handle changes to a solution as it is incrementally built and deployed

- **Change Management Plan**   How to handle changes to the negotiated agreement on project scope, cost, and assigned resources

- **Quality Management Plan**   How to measure and assess achievement of quality goals

- **Test Plan**   How to approach making sure a solution not only adheres to the requirements but also that the requirements are what are needed and expected

- **Pilot Plan**   How to validate a solution through limited-release usage

- **Training Plan**   How to bring user readiness up to necessary levels

- **Deployment Management Plan**   How to deploy a solution to its destination(s)

- **Change Enablement Plan**   How to adapt business processes to realize the full potential of a deployed solution

- **Knowledge Management Plan**   How to capture and harvest lessons learned while delivering a solution

- **Disaster Recovery Plan**   How to handle worst-case scenarios that might significantly affect delivering a solution

- **Purchasing and Facilities Plan**   How to acquire the necessary resources to deliver and deploy a solution

- **Security Plan**   How to identify security requirements and make sure a solution meets those requirements as well as any security policies

- **Integration Management Plan**   How to integrate the parts of a solution and integrate a solution into a deployment destination

- **Performance Management Plan**   How to assess whether value is being realized (e.g., cost performance or schedule earned value analysis [EVA])

- **Capacity Plan**   How to make sure a solution handles planned growth

- **Budget Plan**   How to deliver a solution within financial constraints and forecasting future financial needs

When a team has identified the various project management planning activities that are relevant, it is necessary to decide which team leads are responsible for the various activities and at what level of participation. Figure 4-4 is an example of one way to communicate this information. This concept scales as subteams are added to a project team. Each team lead and subteam lead is responsible for project management activities for their respective team.

Product Management Advocacy Group

The Product Management Advocacy Group acts as a managed conduit between the business world and a project team. In the beginning of a project life cycle, they drive gathering requirements, expectations, and constraints and distill them into a solution definition. As a project progresses, Product Management works with the team to clarify what has been gathered and works with stakeholders to refine expectations. As a solution starts to take form, they reverse the conduit flow to start to prepare stakeholders for the coming solution.

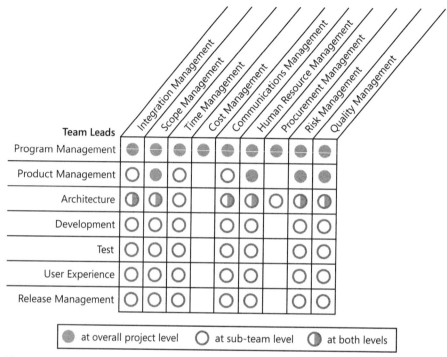

Figure 4-4   Example of various levels of team leads' project management responsibilities

Advocates

Solution definition

Constituency

Product Management team constituents include the following:

- **Stakeholders**   Anyone with a vested interest in the effort and therefore who might have requirements of a solution, including the following:
    - ❑ Project sponsor(s): Initiates, funds, and approves a solution delivery effort
    - ❑ Customer(s) (also known as business sponsors): Takes receipt of a solution and expects to gain business value from it
    - ❑ User(s): Interacts with a solution
    - ❑ Operations team: Hosts, maintains, and administers a solution

- **Internal advisory, regulatory, and/or standards group(s)**   Requires, mandates, or influences requirements, such as a technology advisory council
- **External advisory, regulatory, and/or standards group(s)**   Requires, mandates, or influences requirements, such as government regulatory agencies

Because it might be a bit confusing to understand the difference between a sponsor and a customer, here is an example scenario: an organization has five business units and an information technology (IT) department. One of the business units agrees to sponsor a line-of-business solution that all units will use. In this example, all five business units are "customers" because they will gain business value from the solution. The business unit that is paying for and approving the solution is also the project sponsor. The IT department is the Operations team. Users are employees from those five business units as well as any legacy solutions that will interact with the new solution. An example in which a project sponsor was not a customer was when organizations commissioned Y2K teams to sponsor projects to analyze and resolve "year 2000" issues. Another example is when an IT department sponsors projects for business units.

Quality Goals

The quality goals for Product Management are the following:

- Satisfy stakeholders
- Define solution within project constraints

Focus

Product Management ensures that all stakeholder expectations are understood, managed, and met throughout a project. In addition, Product Management ensures that a project sponsor is satisfied with the progress and outcome of a project. To be effective, Product Management needs to understand, communicate, and ensure success from a stakeholder perspective. To do this, they need to gain knowledge about customers' business, success factors, and key performance measures. They own and drive the definition of requirements and feature sets as well as help the team understand user profiles and how users will use a solution. As you can tell, it is a very communications-oriented group.

As discussed previously about partnering with a customer, the Product Management Advocacy Group leads this effort. They collaborate with customers to drive a solution vision and adjust both the vision and expectations as a project continues. It cannot be stressed enough how critical it is to manage customer expectations. Stuff happens—no plan is able to cover all project impacts, and as such, sharing that information in a no-fault environment is very important and healthy.

The importance of effectively managing expectations can be illustrated with an example involving the anticipated delivery of five solution features from a team to a customer by a certain date. If a team delivers only three features when a customer expects delivery of all five, a project will be deemed a failure both by the customer and by the team.

If, however, Product Management maintains constant two-way communication with the customer during a feature development and production period, changes are made with regard to customer expectations that ensure success. Product Management might include customers in the trade-off decision-making process and inform them of changing risks and other challenges. Unlike the previous scenario, customers can assess the situation and agree with the team that delivery of all five features within the specified period is unrealistic and that delivery of only three is acceptable. In this scenario, the delivery of three features now matches the customer's adjusted expectations, and both parties will consider the project a success.

Functional Areas

The Product Management Advocacy Group consists of several functional areas, including Marketing/Corporate Communications, Business Analyst, and Product Planning.

> **Clarity Point**   It is expected that some organizations may have different names for their functional areas for this and the other advocacy groups. Some functional areas may not exist within an organization. However, the key is that all responsibilities and activities identified for the various advocacy groups need to be advocated regardless of how a project team is structured.

Marketing/Corporate Communications   Before you go saying, "This is an internal project; we do not need Marketing on our project," please understand that this functional area is the process or technique of promoting, selling, and distributing a product, solution, or service. Nearly every solution needs to be introduced and promoted, even if it is a solution being rolled out internally to employees. When solution promotion is internal-facing, some organizations refer to this area as Corporate Communications.

Whether it is called a marketing plan or a corporate communications plan, this plan needs to outline how to excite the target audience. After all, not everyone will welcome change; even if it is a new and improved solution. Typical promotional efforts on a project involve launch promotions, sustained promotions, and public relations. Promotional efforts run the gamut from sending out fliers and e-mail to full advertising campaigns.

Key Responsibilities   This functional area and the others to follow have key responsibilities. Key responsibilities for this functional area include the following:

- Marketing and public relations messages to excite and positively affect the target customer and users
- Understanding the competitive landscape
- Distribution channels so target customers easily acquire a solution

- For packaged solutions, enabling customers to have a positive experience buying and using a solution

Key Activities   Each functional area has a set of key activities to help uphold its responsibilities. Some activities are done throughout a project; some are done each iteration. Key activities for this functional area include the following:

- Develop a plan to promote a solution

- Be able to highly differentiate a solution so it stands out from the competition

- Set up and prepare distribution channels

Business Analyst   A Business Analyst functional area works in conjunction with a sponsor(s) to gather, manage, and refine throughout the life cycle all the market information, all functional and operational requirements, all stakeholder expectations, and anything else that could affect the definition and delivery of a solution.

To start, a Business Analyst team forms an initial vision and conceptual understanding of a solution, given insight of business needs and opportunities as well as the competitive landscape. As a solution vision, solution road map, and constraints are worked into high-level requirements, business analysts work with product planners (discussed next) to segment a solution into projects to deliver capability incrementally.

Key Responsibilities
- Solution landscape

- Stakeholder expectations

- Quantifying a solution's return on investment (ROI)

- Sponsor relationship

Key Activities
- Perform objective cost/benefit analyses to help communicate to the team a defined stack ranking of requirements and feature priority

- Assist sponsor's development of a business case

- Define and maintain business justification for a project

- Define and measure business value realization and metrics

- Manage customer expectations and communications

- Determine business metrics and success criteria

- Provide requirements and feature trade-off decisions

Product Planning   As opposed to a Business Analyst functional area that is more externally focused, a Product Planning functional area works with the team on a tactical level, as depicted in Figure 4-5. Product planners take a vision and conceptual solution and drive a delivery strategy.

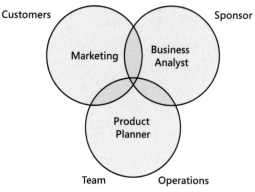

Figure 4-5   Depiction of Product Management functional areas to stakeholders and the team

As discussed in Chapter 6, "Establishing a Solution Delivery Life Cycle," MSF recommends that solutions be incrementally delivered through versioned releases. A *release* is a bundling of solution features and capabilities so that it can be shared either internally among the team or externally with stakeholders. A Product Planning functional area coordinates and manages versioned solution releases. A release can encompass one or more teams' efforts. For instance, a release might be made up of new features from some teams and updates from others with previously released features. This functional area coordinates with Product Management from each of the subteams to present an integrated solution version for release.

Product planning entails understanding the requirements of a solution completely, including what the needs of the business are, how customers will use it, what support issues will be, and what alternatives are available. It also entails working with the team to agree upon prioritization of requirements, capabilities, and feature sets; issues; risks; and so forth.

Key Responsibilities
- Shared project and solution vision
- Working with the respective teams to deliver a solution version consistent with a solution road map
- Being the authority on requirements and expectations associated with each release
- Solution definition and solution definition process

Key Activities
- Stack-rank requirements and features for a solution and for each release
- Balance and trade off requirements with project(s) constraints
- Perform market research, market demand, competitive intelligence/analysis
- Gather, analyze, and prioritize customer and business requirements
- Perform release-level requirements and feature trade-off decisions
- Identify a multiversion release plan

Program Management Advocacy Group

The Program Management Advocacy Group guides solution delivery. At the heart of it all, Program Management involves building on the past, managing the present, and forecasting the future. It involves continual balancing and optimization of known constraints as well as managing risks to mitigate what might happen. And with changes and pressures from all angles, Program Management still needs to plot a steady course to deliver a solution with the agreed-on set of features and capabilities when promised.

The MSF Team Model is based on a team of peers as discussed in Chapter 3, "Foundational Principles, Mindsets, and Proven Practices." Given that in most organizations, Program Management "owns" a project, the team-of-peers concept might seem foreign. Program Management owns part of a project but shares leadership of a project with the leads from the other advocacy groups. Not sure you get it yet? No worries—this is discussed in more detail in subsequent chapters.

Advocates

- Solution delivery

Constituency

Program Management team constituents include the following:

- **Project sponsors[3]** Initiates, funds, and approves a project and its deliverables
- **Internal governance group(s)** Requires, mandates, or influences project management practices such as Program Management Office (PMO)
- **External governance group(s)** Requires, mandates, or influences project management practices such as government regulatory agencies

Quality Goals

The quality goals for Program Management are as follows:

- Coordinate identification and optimization of project constraints
- Deliver solution within project constraints

Focus

Program Management's main mission is to balance all project constraints throughout a project life cycle while facilitating, integrating, and guiding the team to be able to deliver within those constraints.

---

3 Project Management and Product Management have a different relationship with project sponsor(s). Project Management focuses on project governance and constraints (e.g., money), whereas Product Management focuses on solution definition.

Functional Areas

The Program Management advocacy group consists of several functional areas, including Project Management, Program Management, Resource Management, Process Assurance, Project Quality Management, and Project Operations.

Project Management (PjM)   Project Management ensures that a project team works together to deliver the *right* solution at the *right* time given project constraints, where *right* is defined in agreement with stakeholders. Close coordination is necessary because what is right is subject to evolve as a project goes along. The scope of this functional area is managing one of potentially many projects needed to deliver a solution. Managing a portfolio of projects is handled by a Program Management functional area, discussed next.

Key Responsibilities

- Completely understanding project constraints and high-level requirements, and how they are allocated across the advocacy groups

- Delivering a solution that best balances project constraints

- Risk and issue management process (project level)

- A functional specification that meets project constraints

- Project Management Plan with its various subordinate plans (e.g., Deployment Management Plan)

Key Activities

- Work with the other project leads to organize project teams, sometimes referred to as *work streams* or *swim lanes*, into groupings that make sense given what needs to be done (discussed in more detail later)

- Work with architects and team leads to create a WBS

- Work with architects and team leads to staff and resource plans

- As the owner of the schedule, integrate and validate all team schedules into a master project schedule that is tracked and reported to the team and project stakeholders

- Manage master project schedule

- Manage functional specification and definition of the constraints portion of a functional specification

- As the owner of a project budget, facilitate the creation of a project budget by gathering and validating resource requirements (hardware, software, and people)

- Track and manage project budget

- Facilitate communication and negotiation within a team

- Track progress and manage project status reporting

- Manage resource allocation (project level)

- Manage project change control

- Drive critical project decisions

- Facilitate project-relevant communication

Program Management (PgM)   A Program Management functional area takes a broader view of managing solutions delivery than a Project Management functional area does. Much like how a Project Management functional area manages delivery of a project, a Program Management functional area manages solution delivery, which involves a broader set of responsibilities and often many projects. It often means working with more stakeholders and therefore involves more stakeholder analysis and coordination. Often this functional area is associated with managing at the enterprise level.

A Program Management functional area has the same key activities and responsibilities as a Project Management functional area except that the focus is at a solution level instead of at a project level. The following are additional activities and responsibilities of the Program Management functional area beyond those of the Project Management functional area:

Key Responsibilities
- Completely understanding solution constraints and high-level requirements, and how they are allocated across projects within the program

- Portfolio of projects and how to best deliver a solution

- Program Management Plan with its various subordinate plans that span across the various projects

Key Activities
- Work with project leads to coordinate and synchronize work, dependencies, and deliverables

- Work with solution architects to create and decompose solution delivery across multiple projects

Resource Management   When delivering a solution that needs unique skills, has new technology, involves creative thinking, and so forth, people are often the most valuable resource. Getting, blending, and retaining staff on a project can be a full-time job, especially when project staff are made up of customer staff, corporate staff, partner staff, and external consultants.

Other project resources that might need to be managed by the Resource Management functional area include facilities, hardware, software, and materials.

Key Responsibilities
- Completely understanding and optimally satisfying the resource needs of each project

- Skills readiness

- Furnishing a range of staffing resource (e.g., vendor, consultants, partners)

Key Activities
- Understand needed skill profiles and match them up with available resources
- Help define skill profile(s) to use for estimating, and, as staff are identified, normalize project activity estimates given staff availability and assessed capabilities
- Efficiently recruit team members
- Once candidate resources are identified, work with the respective team leads to vet the resources
- Assist team leads with skills readiness analysis
- Assist with team member skills improvement
- Work with external and internal staffing providers to secure project staff
- Understand team chemistry and team dynamics to blend assigned staff optimally

Process Assurance   What was the first thing that came to mind when you saw the words *process assurance*? Most people think "process police," which is unfortunate. If set up correctly, a Process Assurance functional area ensures that a project team adopts processes that focus on helping them meet their project quality goals, with an emphasis on minimizing issues and expeditiously resolving issues when they do arise. Process assurance can be used to help refine processes, making a team more effective.

Because people are sometimes protective of their processes and do not appreciate process refinement, it sometimes helps if Process Assurance has some degree of independence from a project team. This way they have an unbiased, external perspective. An obvious risk of moving them outside a team is that they will be viewed as outsiders and are less likely to be welcomed as refining "our" processes.

Key Responsibilities
- Process quality assurance
- Determining the team's tolerance to quality processes

Key Activities
- Understand team capabilities and abilities as well as the quality and project goals to define processes that enable and increase team quality and productivity through process definition, education, and refinement
- Provide advice and guidance on effective implementation of project processes; validate compliance with processes; undertake checkpoint reviews; recommend process improvements
- Undertake reviews to validate relevance and effectiveness of each process, recommending improvements and monitoring compliance
- Drive process enablement through tool selection and implementation

Project Quality Management   Much like how Process Assurance's mission is to improve quality and productivity through better processes, Project Quality Management's mission is to improve quality and productivity through better overall project management. This functional area takes many forms in various organizations. Sometimes it is referred to as a *Program Management Office (PMO)* and sometimes it is called *Program Quality Assurance (PQA)*. Irrespective of the name, the mission is the same: monitor project health and make improvement recommendations as needed. This team is most often an independent team, so they are able to form an unbiased perspective on how well a project is running. Most often, this team is involved with a project team on a limited basis and performs periodic reviews (e.g., quarterly). Typically, this team focuses on high-risk projects and projects critical to the success of an organization.

Key Responsibilities

- Independent validation of project health and project risks within an organization project portfolio
- Quality control
- Quality metrics

Key Activities

- Proactively monitor project health and recommend improvements as needed
- Help harvest lessons learned
- Help identify and mitigate project risks
- Conduct periodic reviews of program management practices
- Review risk and change management processes and practices
- Define and report on program-wide quality metrics
- Assist Program Management team as a sounding board

Project Operations   A Project Operations functional area makes sure that day-to-day logistics and administrative details of running a project are addressed and working smoothly. This is often the least appreciated but most valuable functional area in Program Management. If this functional area is set up and operating efficiently, it should be transparent to most people. Often, this functional area handles updating project plans; progress reporting; management and implementation of the risk, issue, and change control processes; and a number of various other project management activities.

Effective Project Operations staff requires a combination of strong administrative capability and attention to detail with sound experience in project planning and scheduling techniques, as well as a good understanding of policies and guidelines. On a larger project, this functional area provides an excellent opportunity to work alongside project managers and build experience needed to direct future projects.

Key Responsibilities

- Project management processes and support for team leads in using them
- Program/project operations

Key Activities

- Ensure that a project team operates effectively with the minimum of bureaucracy

- Support project initiation processes, such as drafting a new team member orientation guide; manage contractual arrangements; organize team facilities (e.g., space, telephones, security access, and computer accounts)

- Establish consistent planning framework; assist team leads in planning and scheduling; consolidate team input to create master plan and schedule; establish financial and progress reporting processes

- Assist team leads in progress reporting; create overall progress and financial reports; update and manage master schedule

- Perform general administrative support activities: scheduling meetings; implementing risk and issue management processes; maintaining the master risk list, action list, and issue list; generating financial and progress reports; and managing team location to enhance morale

- Gather actuals and compare to schedule to calibrate remaining estimates

- Administer project planning tools (e.g., Microsoft Project Server)

- Ensure closure of all administrative systems on project completion

Architecture Advocacy Group

The Architecture Advocacy Group drives solution design(s) and design processes. They provide a vital link between the business side of a solution (as represented by product management in conceptual designs) and the technology side of a solution (as represented by development in detailed implementation designs). Architects act as custodians of the content within the functional specification. A *functional specification* defines features necessary to satisfy solution requirements. Architects also ensure features are traceable back to requirements (and ultimately to the generation of business value) so that all features support stated requirements. This enables a team to assess the impact of any feature changes on solution value.

The Architecture Advocacy Group considers all requirements, constraints, expectations, and anything else that influences or biases a solution. They distill these requirements into design(s) for a solution. A design starts with conceptual ideas and becomes more refined and more detailed until it reaches a point when it can be implemented. An Architecture team might also work with Product Management to map out a solutions road map.

Advocates

- Solution design

Constituency

Architecture team constituents include the following:

- **Team members** building a solution according to their designs

- **Other teams** delivering a different portion of a solution (when a project is part of a program)

- **Internal advisory, regulatory, and/or standards group(s)** Requires, mandates, or influences solution designs, such as an enterprise architecture group

- **External advisory, regulatory, and/or standards group(s)** Requires, mandates, or influences solution designs, such as a security standards consortium

Focus

The Architecture team works with the team to develop a solution definition and conceptual architecture that satisfies the requirements. As part of this effort, the Architecture team provides a sanity check on the feasibility of requirements being defined by Product Management.

The Architecture team considers all requirements when designing a solution, not just technology requirements. For example, they consider environmental factors such as the services, systems, and standards with which a solution will interoperate; infrastructure in which it will be deployed; its place in business or a product family; and a road map of future versions. The Architecture group ensures that a deployed solution meets all necessary qualities of service and its business objectives, and that it will be viable in the long term.

Quality Goal

The quality goal for the Architecture team is this:

- Design a solution within project constraints

Functional Areas

The Architecture Advocacy Group consists of two functional areas: Solution Architecture and Technical Architecture.

Solution Architecture   A Solution Architecture functional area works with the rest of a team and stakeholders to form a conceptual understanding of a solution. As a solution becomes clearer, solution architects develop a conceptual design with various alternatives that emphasize different constraint trade-offs. As project requirements and constraints stabilize, solution architects work with technical architects (discussed next) to refine a design and add more detail so that it can be implemented.

Solution architects should be technically sound, with a broad base of knowledge and experience, and be able to relate to technical issues underlying business needs. Although solution architects might rely on technical architects and a development team for expertise on specific technologies used in a solution, they must be able to grasp the implications of those technical details very rapidly and understand their interrelationships and their impact on an environment into which a solution will be deployed. Solution architects must also be able to discuss those impacts with customer architects to rapidly resolve any conflicts between a proposed solution and an enterprise architecture.

Key Responsibilities

- Ensuring a solution can be used by specified users to achieve specified goals with effectiveness, efficiency, and satisfaction

- Overall solution architecture and its positioning within an enterprise architecture

- Solution definition portion of a functional specification

- High-level, top-down estimates for solution components

- Solution scope and critical trade-off decisions

- Qualities of service (e.g., design for the "–ilities")

- Major business-driven checkpoints and tasks

- Solutions road map

Key Activities

- Define conceptual solution and conceptual design, and align them with an enterprise architecture; work with technical architects to refine them into detailed implementation designs

- Review and execute plans to harvest requirements from architectural and standards groups related to interoperability; drive design process; provide a traceability map tracing features back to requirements and benefits

- Update requirements for future versioned releases; devise versioned release strategy; and define interim releases

- Create and manage changes to the technology portions of a high-level functional specification; maintain traceability map; clarify specifications to other team roles and to external stakeholders; liaise with other project teams on interoperability issues

- Participate in triage process; manage project stakeholder expectations regarding solution content

- Work with and provide updates to Enterprise Architecture team

- Help validate solution

- Work with Product Management to help quantify business value and "sell" (emphasize) the merits of a solution

- Work with Operations to design in necessary qualities of service (QoS)

- Help design for reusability (e.g., design a service-oriented architecture)

- Provide initial top-down estimates to help initial planning

- Drive high-level work breakdown structure (WBS)

- Drive high-level, top-down estimates for solution components

Technical Architecture   A Technical Architecture functional area includes technical specialists who work with a solution architecture team to further refine a design to a level that can be implemented. Usually, technical architects are very skilled in particular areas (e.g., security, databases, or messaging). Technology architects provide input into high-level designs, evaluate and validate technologies, and conduct research to mitigate technology risks early in the development process.

In coordination with a solution architect team, at the beginning of a project life cycle this functional area focuses on analyzing the requirements from an implementer's perspective. This functional area contributes to the definition of a vision/scope document by evaluating technical implications of a project for implementation feasibility. They provide guidance on pros and cons of possible implementation approaches, define implementation strategies and implementation architecture, and validate initial technology choices. In this process, this functional area might conduct research, consult with counterparts in the organization or elsewhere, and hold discussions with technology providers. For additional validation, this functional area might develop a limited-functionality prototype to serve as a proof of concept. This is particularly relevant for projects that require use of new technologies or in areas where a project team lacks experience.

Key Responsibilities

- Solution implementation design

- Detailed functional specification (also called a *technical specification*) and bottom-up estimates

- Implementation architecture

- Major implementation-driven checkpoints and tasks

Key Activities

- Validate major business-driven checkpoints and tasks

- Decompose solutions architecture into tangible, implementable components and tasks (leaving the detailed implementation decisions for a build team)

- Map the enterprise architecture to a solution's implementation architecture by providing solution-specific detail for application, data, and technology views of a solution

- Develop high-level, top-down estimates given design details and calibrated team member skills

- Expand WBS details

- Evaluate and validate technologies

- Contribute to defining technology standards for an organization

- Work with PjM on resource planning and balancing workload

- Validate top-down, high-level estimates by comparing bottom-up estimates developed when adding more design details

- Validate and quantify technology risks

Development Advocacy Group

The Development Advocacy Group (also called the Build team) is made up of the primary solution builders (i.e., solution development). They build a solution in adherence to a solution architecture and implementation architecture that, together with a function specification, form the overall specifications of a solution. This advocacy group defines low-level solution details, designs feature implementations, refines estimates required to build those features, builds a solution, and then validates that what was built is consistent with the specifications.

It is essential that a team that will be implementing a solution validates the estimates. Too many times this step is overlooked and a project suffers for it. The purpose of this effort is to achieve a higher quality of schedule, ownership of the estimates, and increased accountability for work performance.

Advocates

- Solution construction
- Solution verification

Constituency

Build team constituents include the following:

- **Internal advisory and/or standards group(s)**   Requires, mandates, or influences solution implementation, such as an enterprise coding standards group
- **External advisory and/or standards group(s)**   Requires, mandates, or influences solution implementation, such as the Extensible Markup Language (XML) standards body

Focus

The Development team focuses on building a solution in accordance with the specification(s) while verifying and refining a solution definition and design. Before building a solution, Development provides input into design and technology selection decisions, as well as constructs functional prototypes to validate decision making and mitigate development risks.

Building a solution often means developing the component parts of a solution and integrating these parts into a cohesive whole. Throughout this process, the Development team makes sure a realized solution meets its stated quality goals.

Quality Goal

The quality goal for Development is this:

- Build solution to specifications

Functional Areas

Although many functional areas are within the Development Advocacy Group such as Application Development and Infrastructure Deployment functional areas, here are some key responsibilities and key activities that span across all functional areas:

Key Responsibilities
- Detailed implementation designs
- Thoughtful technical decisions
- Clean implementations
- Validation and adoption of estimates
- Right quality solution
- A means for others to verify proper implementation (e.g., unit tests)

Key Activities
- Review implementation architecture
- Develop detailed implementation designs
- Develop features that meet design specifications
- Carry out technical testing (as opposed to functional testing and system testing, discussed later) as defined in a test plan to ensure a solution works according to its specifications
- Develop automated deployment mechanism
- Develop deployment documentation
- Decompose major checkpoints and tasks into actionable tasks
- Validate major implementation-driven checkpoints and tasks
- Address quality issues identified in a testing process
- Carry out integration of solution components to produce final deliverable
- Contribute to the definition of standards and adhere to these during solution development
- Conduct reviews to share knowledge and experience as well as to assess the quality level of solution components and features at an implementation level

Test Advocacy Group

All solutions have issues. The Test Advocacy Group drives conversations to get the team and stakeholders to reach consensus about which issues matter (i.e., which issues are significant enough to block a solution release). Subsequently, this group measures and monitors solution quality and confirms when a solution has achieved its required quality levels and is ready for release. This group is entrusted to represent solution quality fairly and accurately. They validate whether a solution works as expected from a stakeholder perspective. They define quality metrics and regularly report against them to keep the team and stakeholders abreast of quality trends and statistics.

Advocates

- Solution validation

Constituency

Test team constituents include the following:

- **Project sponsor(s)**   Initiates, funds, and approves a solution delivery effort
- **Customer(s) (also known as *business sponsors*)**   Has needs and expectations that a solution must satisfy
- **Internal advisory and/or standards group(s)**   Requires, mandates, or influences solution validation, such as an enterprise quality metrics standards group
- **External advisory and/or standards group(s)**   Requires, mandates, or influences solution validation, such as the ISO 20000 IT Service Management Standards

Focus

The Test advocacy group anticipates, looks for, and reports on any issues that diminish solution quality. To achieve this, the Test team continually assesses the status of solution quality as compared to established quality measures. They continually and thoroughly scrutinize a solution from a functional and systems perspective as opposed to making sure the technical parts work as specified, which is a responsibility of the Development team. In other words, the Development team is responsible for ensuring a solution works as specified. The Test team ensures it works as expected from a business perspective and as a whole (i.e., as a system).

Quality Goal

The quality goal for the Test team is this:

- Confirm all aspects of a solution meet or exceed their respective, defined quality levels

Functional Areas

Like other advocacy groups, the Test Advocacy Group has many functional areas primarily including functional testing and system testing, described shortly. Consistent with the MSF Governance Model (discussed in the next chapter), these testing functional areas need to plan the tests, build the tests, execute the tests, and report and track test status. Here is a brief explanation of these activities that span across all test functional areas:

- **Test planning**   How a team ensures that all solution quality issues are identified and those that matter are addressed. The Test team develops testing approaches and plans, and by doing so outlines a strategy a team will use to test a solution. These plans include specific types of tests, specific areas to be tested, test success criteria, and information on resources (both hardware and people) required to test. Specific activities include the following:

- ❑ Develop testing approach and plan

- ❑ Define test data requirements

- ❑ Develop test harnesses (i.e., automated means to test solution components)

- ❑ Participate in setting the quality bar by providing input to a project team on quality control measures and criteria for success of a solution

- ❑ Develop a test specification, a detailed description of tools and code necessary to meet the needs defined in a test plan

- **Test engineering**   Carry out activities defined in test planning. Specific activities include the following:

  - ❑ Conduct tests to accurately determine status of solution quality

  - ❑ Develop, test, and maintain test cases, tools, and scripts

  - ❑ Develop and maintain tools, scripts, and documentation to perform testing functions

  - ❑ Ensure that test procedures are performed and reported within a single frame of reference

  - ❑ Conduct tests to accurately determine the status of solution quality

  - ❑ Identify and surface issues

  - ❑ Lead the issue triage effort

- **Tracking and reporting**   Articulate clearly to a project team the current solution quality assessment. Issue tracking is performed to ensure that all identified issues of concern have been resolved before solution release. Specific activities include the following:

  - ❑ Assess quality as it relates to the quality measures

  - ❑ Provide team with data related to solutions quality

  - ❑ Track and communicate issues to ensure their resolution before solution release

Functional Testing   Functional testing focuses on making sure a solution works as expected from a user's perspective after it has been proved in development that solution components work as specified. Typically, test cases for functional testing are designed to be consistent with usage scenarios and process flows.

Key Responsibilities
- Ensuring that a solution functionally works as expected from a user's perspective (i.e., a business perspective, not a technical perspective)

■ Ensuring that a solution functionally flows smoothly from a process-flow perspective

Key Activities
■ Perform positive testing (using data within expected ranges) as well as negative testing (using data outside of expected norms). For instance, if an input field expects a value between 1 and 10, positive testing might try entering a 5 whereas negative testing might try 25 or the letter *a* to see what happens.

■ Define and gather (maybe develop) test data to perform their tests.

■ Define and develop test harnesses to perform tests.

■ Define and develop test cases using the selected testing tool (e.g., automated test tool, manual test scripts).

System Testing   System testing focuses on a solution as a whole as opposed to testing component parts of the solution. System testing can involve many types of testing, including the following:

■ **Integration testing**   Testing to see whether component parts work well together and a solution works with other solutions and legacy systems as expected

■ **Performance testing**   Performing tests and comparing timed performance tests of major components and a solution as a whole to expected design performance requirements. For instance, expected designed performance might be that a Web service takes 0.1 seconds to handle a request, transaction management takes 0.3 seconds to process the request, database management takes 0.3 seconds to execute the query and pass back the data, transaction management takes 0.1 seconds to package up the response, and the Web service takes 0.05 seconds to send out the response.

■ **Environmental testing**   Testing whether a solution operates as expected in its deployed environment. This type of testing can include ambient testing that varies with temperature, power, and moisture. It also might test that power, space, and memory consumption are within acceptable parameters.

Key Responsibilities
■ Ensuring that a solution works as expected and as specified from a holistic perspective

■ Ensuring that a solution works in the environment(s) in which it will be deployed

Key Activities
■ Perform positive and negative testing

■ Define and gather (maybe develop) test data to perform tests

■ Define and develop test harnesses to perform tests

■ Define and develop test cases using the selected testing tool (e.g., automated test tool, manual test scripts)

User Experience Advocacy Group

The User Experience Advocacy Group ensures a solution is as effective as possible from the perspective of the intended users and that users are sufficiently ready to use a solution effectively. To address this twofold responsibility, the User Experience team works with users to understand them holistically, appreciate subtleties of their needs, and develop an awareness of how best to provide users with the necessary solutions knowledge. This advocacy groups also works with the team to maximize usability from a user's perspective.

Advocates

- Solution usability
- User readiness

Constituency

User Experience team constituents include the following:

- **User(s)**   Individuals and/or systems that interact with a solution
- **Operations support team**   Individuals and/or systems that provide operations support to users
- **Internal advisory, regulatory, and/or standards group(s)**   Requires, mandates, or influences solution–human interactions, such as a human factors group
- **External advisory, regulatory, and/or standards group(s)**   Requires, mandates, or influences solution–human interactions, such as the Americans with Disabilities Act

Focus

The User Experience Advocacy Group focuses on enhancing all aspects of a solution that involve interaction with users, including training, manuals, support, user interfaces, and solution usability.

Quality Goal

The quality goals for the User Experience team are as follows:

- Maximize solution usability
- Enhance user readiness and effectiveness

Functional Areas

The various aspects of user experience are represented in these functional areas: Accessibility, Internationalization, Technical Support Communications, Training, Usability, and User Interface Design.

Accessibility   An Accessibility functional area focuses on ensuring that a solution is accessible to those with disabilities by driving accessibility concepts and requirements into a design. Accessibility is important for many reasons. Primarily, accessibility is important because a solution must be accessible and usable by all people regardless of their capabilities. A solution that does not account for accessibility falls short of full adoption. Additionally, accessibility compliance often is required to meet government regulations.

Key Responsibilities
- Driving accessibility concepts and requirements into a design
- Validation of solution accessibility with constituents

Key Activities
- Incorporate an accessibility section within each feature specification
- Integrate accessibility information into a solution help section
- Set up and conduct evaluation sessions with constituents
- Gather and distill evaluation feedback and provide it to the team
- Ensure accessibility documentation is complete and presented in accessible formats

Internationalization   An Internationalization functional area ensures the quality and usability of a solution for international markets. An Internationalization functional area is composed of both globalization and localization processes.

- **Globalization**   Process of defining and building a solution that takes into account the need to localize a solution and its content without modification or unnecessary workarounds by the localizers. In other words, a released solution that is globalized properly is ready to be localized with a minimum of difficulty.

- **Localization**   Involves modifying a solution's user interface, help files, printed and online documentation, marketing materials, and Web sites. Occasionally, these materials require changes in graphical elements for a particular language version or even content modifications.

Key Responsibilities
- Quality and usability of a solution in international markets
- Validation of solution internationalization with constituents

Key Activities
- Ensure user interfaces are encoded to support localization (e.g., not hard coded)
- Set up and conduct evaluation sessions with constituents
- Gather and distill evaluation feedback and provide it to the team

Technical Support Communications   A Technical Support Communications functional area focuses on development of solution support documentation and systems. Support systems often take the form of online tools. These tools (e.g., online, context-sensitive help) benefit both users and organizations: users benefit because they get responses to issues and questions in a timely and effective manner; organizations benefit because support costs are reduced.

Key Responsibilities

- Timely and sufficient technical support collateral and systems to maximize user effectiveness and productivity

- Validation of solution support effectiveness with constituents

Key Activities

- Design and develop support documentation for a solution, including development of installation, upgrade, and troubleshooting guides; help desk and operations manuals; help; knowledge base articles and whitepapers; and online chat support services

- Create tools to empower users to quickly resolve their own issues by providing answers to basic questions, keyword descriptions, error explanations, and frequently asked questions

- Provide help: online, context sensitive, written, and chat

- Set up and conduct evaluation sessions with constituents

- Gather and distill evaluation feedback and provide it to the team

Training   A Training functional area focuses on enhancing user performance by providing skills and knowledge needed to use a solution effectively. Skills and knowledge transfer is achieved by implementing a learning strategy followed by a training plan. The development of a learning strategy can take place within an organization, or it might be outsourced to an organization that specializes in training and development. Regardless of who actually develops a learning strategy, the approach most often consists of the following:

- Assessing current user capabilities

- Understanding organizational goals and objectives

- Establishing desired skill levels

- Developing and implementing a training plan

- Upon implementation, measuring training effectiveness and modifying the training plan as appropriate

A learning strategy might consist of one or more of the following delivery mechanisms: instructor-led training, technology-delivered training, self-study, or the use of job aids. Many organizations choose a blended approach that adapts to different individual learning styles.

Key Responsibilities

- Ensuring users have sufficient skills and knowledge to use a solution effectively

- Validation of solution training with constituents

Key Activities
- Develop and execute learning strategy (build/buy/deliver)
- Assess optimal delivery mechanism(s)
- Set up and conduct training pilot sessions
- Gather and distill pilot feedback and provide it to a team

Usability   A Usability functional area drives a design of all user interactions. This group continually provides feedback to the team by measuring and assessing user competency and solution proficiency. They work with specified users to achieve specified high-level goals of effectiveness, efficiency, and satisfaction. Often accompanying these goals is a measure of how intuitive a solution is.

Key Responsibilities
- Driving usability into a design
- Validation of solution usability with constituents

Key Activities
- Conduct usability research, which includes gathering, analyzing, and prioritizing user requirements. When time is invested early on and throughout a solution development effort to understand users, a project has a much higher likelihood of effectively meeting the needs of users.

- Assist Product Management in development of usage scenarios and use cases with a focus on usability. The key idea here is to step back and look at how an entire solution likely will be used. This effort helps the Development team understand how a user is likely to approach a solution from a conceptual and literal standpoint and often leads to design improvements that result in increased efficiency.

- Continually assess usability by providing feedback to the team and input to a solution. When the Usability group takes the time to provide user feedback to developers throughout a development cycle, a solution benefits by achieving a higher rate of user satisfaction.

- Assess and reengineer solution process flows (e.g., through listening labs) to maximize usability.

- Assist Product Management in user acceptance testing (UAT).

- Set up and conduct usability evaluation sessions with constituents.

- Gather and distill evaluation feedback and provide it to the team.

User Interface Design   A User Interface Design functional area ensures that graphical elements within a solution are designed appropriately. The major responsibility of this functional area is driving user interface (UI) design. This involves designing the objects that users interact with (and the actions applied to those objects), as well as the major screens in the interface.

Key Responsibilities
- Driving human factors best practices into a design
- Driving user interface design
- Validation of solution user interface design with constituents

Key Activities
- Develop a wire-frame user interface to help validate the UI design and process flow as well as to act as a visual specification
- Set up and conduct usability evaluation sessions with constituents
- Gather and distill evaluation feedback and provide it to the team

Release/Operations Advocacy Group

The Release/Operations Advocacy Group ensures smooth delivery and deployment of a solution. Although solutions discussed in this book are mostly referred to as being delivered and deployed into operations, other destinations are equally applicable such as commercial release of a solution through distribution channels. Irrespective of a solution's destination, this team makes sure a solution smoothly transitions from the Delivery team to the intended caretakers of the solution—referred to here as the *Operations team*. To achieve their mission, this team has many logistics and readiness activities to consider and work through. For instance, they need to make sure a solution is compatible and can be integrated with its destination.

The Release/Operations Advocacy Group works with the Operations team throughout a solution's life cycle to gather and refine operational requirements and/or constraints to provide back to the team for consideration. They work with the Operations team to help build out the production environment. And through this assistance, they are the most qualified team members to determine whether the Operations team is ready to receive a solution. Too many failed projects result from when a Delivery team builds a "great" solution only for it to be driven into the ground by an ill-prepared Operations team.

Advocates

- Solution deployment

Constituency

Release and Operations team constituents include the following:

- **Operations team**   Hosts, maintains, and administers a solution
- **Internal advisory, regulatory, and/or standards group(s)**   Requires, mandates, or influences solution operations, such as a capacity planning group
- **External advisory, regulatory, and/or standards group(s)**   Requires, mandates, or influences solution operations, such as the IT Infrastructure Library (ITIL) guidelines

Focus

The Release/Operations Advocacy Group brings an understanding of operations to a project team, and with that knowledge, they focus on making sure a solution is ready for deployment as well as readying Operations for deployment of a solution where a solution is not just technology but also the supporting activities (e.g., training) and operations material (e.g., manuals).

Quality Goal

The quality goal for a Release/Operations team is this:

- Smooth deployment and transition to operations

Functional Areas

Solutions are deployed by various means and to various destinations. Irrespective of how and where a solution is deployed, here are a few common functional areas of Release and Operations: Release Management, Delivery Infrastructure, Operations, Build Manager, and Tool Administrator.

Release Management   A Release Management functional area coordinates and manages the rollout of each solution release as defined by the Product Planner functional area. A solution might be deployed to Operations or through commercial distribution channels (e.g., shrink-wrapped products). Although deployment to an Operations data center seems nothing like deployment to commercial channels, the concept of making sure deployment goes smoothly is the same. It involves making sure a solution gets from a project team to intended users; and making sure the end users are ready to be productive.

Key Responsibilities
- Evaluating release readiness
- Handling all logistics associated with the release to Operations or media control
- Commercial release management
    - ❏ Product registration codes; registration verification process
    - ❏ Licensing management
    - ❏ Packaging
    - ❏ Managing distribution channel(s)
    - ❏ Print and electronic publication

Key Activities
- Certify release candidates for shipment or deployment
- Work with Operations to prepare for the release

Delivery Infrastructure   A Delivery Infrastructure functional area focuses on providing a team with the infrastructure necessary to deliver a solution. This team works closely with the Operations team because some of the delivery infrastructure might need to mirror production and need production-like data.

Key Responsibility

- Building and administering the infrastructure necessary (e.g., environments such as development, testing, staging, training, research) for the various solution delivery activities

Key Activities

- Build and administer support infrastructure for pilot deployment(s) and user acceptance testing

- Provide infrastructure services to a team (e.g., building servers, standard images, installing software)

- Set up and administer account and system setup controls as well as user accounts and permissions used by a team

- Assist in hardware/software procurement

- Rack and stack lab equipment

- Retrieve and administer a snapshot of operations data to use for development, testing, and training

Operations   An Operations functional area represents an organization's Operations team. Because they are the ones to work with Operations to take receipt of a solution, it is up to them to make sure that all aspects of a solution are ready for deployment from deployment and sustainability perspectives. To achieve this, they need to be engaged actively in the full life cycle.

Being a liaison to Operations teams, this team vets a solution from an operational perspective. For instance, this team reviews support systems being developed by the Technical Support Communications functional area of the User Experience Advocacy Group.

Key Responsibility

- Ensuring solution being built and deployed is operable and compatible with other services in operations

- Ensuring solution built and deployed is operationally supportable

Key Activities

- Plan and manage solution deployment into production

  - Messaging, database, telecom, and network operations

  - Systems administration, batch processing

  - Firewall management, security administration

  - Application services

❑   Host integration services

❑   Directory service operations

■   Set operations acceptance criteria for release to production

■   Participate in design, focusing on qualities of service (e.g., manageability, availability, supportability, and deployability)

■   Assist the training team in defining requirements for and execution of training for operations

■   Ensure stabilization measurements meet acceptance criteria

■   Provide a team with policies and procedures for consistent infrastructure management and standards

■   Coordinate physical environment use and planning across geographies (data centers, labs, field offices)

■   Help develop and validate "as-built" documents

■   Provide primary liaison and customer service to users

■   Support the business by managing the Service Level Agreement (SLA) with the customer and ensuring commitments are met

■   Provide incident and problem resolution; rapid response to user requests and logged incidents

■   Give feedback to build and design teams

■   Assist with capacity planning

■   Develop failover and recovery plans and procedures

Build Manager   A Build Manager functional area focuses on systematically and methodically promoting a solution from a development area, through a test area, and to staging areas in preparation for the Operations team to deploy a solution to production. As part of the set of natural checks and balances built into MSF, this team is an independent verifier of deployment activities, plans, and procedures. Many organizations make the mistake of making a development team responsible for moving a solution from a development environment to a test environment, and likewise, a test team moves a solution from a test environment to a staging environment and to a production environment. Although capable, these teams are too familiar with these activities and are likely to compensate, consciously or subconsciously, for inadequacies of deployment procedures. It is only when an independent functional area with a systems engineer perspective does a solution promotion through these environments will deployment plans and procedures really be vetted sufficiently.

Key Responsibility

■   Maturing and verifying deployment processes and procedures

Key Activities

■   Manage tool selection for release activities and drive automation optimization

■   Back up and archive collateral

Tools Administrator   With more and more emphasis placed on achieving higher productivity and efficiency while reducing costs and handling more complex technology, there is a drive to automate as much of solutions delivery as possible. Although there are obvious benefits, there are costs. Primarily, tools that are more complex are needed for this automation. The resource commitment to administer these tools sometimes exceeds that of a team. In addition, administration of these tools at the level and with the flexibility that are sometimes needed for a team to remain agile necessitates a *Tool Administrator* role. Beyond the obvious administration activities (e.g., setting up test user accounts and filling test environment databases with test data), other activities include helping a team set up and administer the following tools:

- Issue tracking tools
- Design, build, and test tools
- User feedback and survey tools
- Test environment refresh tools

Key Responsibility
- Defining and administering tools necessary to support delivery of a solution

Key Activities
- Administer users
- Build and maintain tools
- Integrate tools to provide consolidated status
- Create procedures to refresh testing systems after testing sessions

Summary

By now, hopefully you see how each advocacy group performs critical activities with built-in quality checks and balances. Although MSF was designed to be adapted, the core principles behind the Team Model should hold. Table 4-3 summarizes what each group advocates, their quality goals, constituents, and typical functional areas identified in the previous sections.

Table 4-3   Summary of Advocacy Group Attributes

Advocacy Group	Advocates	Quality Goals	Constituents	Functional Areas
Product Management	Solution definition	Satisfy stakeholders. Define solution within project constraints	Stakeholders. Internal advisory, regulatory, and/or standards group(s). External advisory, regulatory, and/or standards group(s)	Marketing/Corporate Communications. Business Analyst. Product Planning

Table 4-3   **Summary of Advocacy Group Attributes**

Advocacy Group	Advocates	Quality Goals	Constituents	Functional Areas
Program Management	Solution delivery	Coordinate identification and optimization of project constraints Deliver solution within project constraints	Project sponsor(s) Internal governance group(s) External governance group(s)	Project Management Program Management Resource Management Process Assurance Project Quality Management Project Operations
Architecture	Solution design	Design a solution within project constraints	Other teams delivering a different portion of a solution Team members building a solution according to their designs Internal advisory, regulatory, and/or standards group(s) External advisory, regulatory, and/or standards group(s)	Solution Architecture Technical Architecture
Development	Solution construction Solution verification	Build solution to specifications	Internal advisory and/or standards group(s) External advisory and/or standards group(s)	
Test	Solution validation	Confirm all aspects of a solution meet or exceed their respective, defined quality levels	Project sponsor(s) Customer(s) Internal advisory and/or standards group(s) External advisory and/or standards group(s)	Functional Testing System Testing
User Experience	Solution usability User readiness	Maximize solution usability Enhance user readiness and effectiveness	Users Operations Support team Internal advisory, regulatory, and/or standards group(s) External advisory, regulatory, and/or standards group(s)	Accessibility Internationalization Technical Support Communications Training Usability User Interface Design

Table 4-3 **Summary of Advocacy Group Attributes**

Advocacy Group	Advocates	Quality Goals	Constituents	Functional Areas
Release/ Operations	Solution deployment	Smooth deployment and transition to operations	Operations team	Release Management
			Internal advisory, regulatory, and/or standards group(s)	Delivery Infrastructure
				Operations
			External advisory, regulatory, and/or standards group(s)	Build Manager
				Tool Administrator

Another way to summarize the advocacy groups is to understand the degree of internal versus external focus as well as the degree of balance between being business focused versus being technology focused. Figure 4-6 illustrates how each advocacy group maps out across these spectrums. As depicted, each group is both internally and externally focused except for Development and Testing, which are internally focused and insulated from external communications. The relative positions should be obvious except for maybe the Test Advocacy group. Why do you think the Test team is on the "business focus" side of the figure? Most people mistakenly think of the testing team as being the ones responsible to making sure the solution works as specified. This responsibility is actually the responsibility of the Build team. As discussed previously, the Test team performs functional and system testing to verify a solution works from a business user perspective. As such, the Test Advocacy Group is much more business focused than it is technology focused.

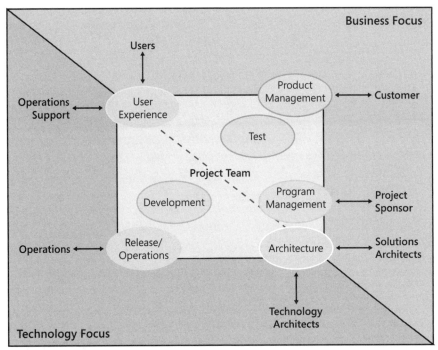

Figure 4-6 Advocacy groups focus across a technology vs. business spectrum

The figure represents a high-level perspective and offers a few constituents to provide context. Typically, teams have to coordinate with many more external groups, such as quality assurance, finance, and legal. It is important that interfaces with any external groups be explicit and understood. It is also important that development and testing continue to be insulated so that they work effectively without unnecessary disruptions. This does not mean that developers and testers should be isolated from the outside world. Contact with customer organization(s) and with real users is often invaluable to build a customer-focused mindset that MSF teams look to achieve, especially in the earlier, formative stages of a project. Such communications should not, however, replace formal communications because two-way communications would suffer badly as development and testing teams become entrenched during later stages of a project.

In addition, it is important to emphasize that, although external coordination through various groups can provide input and recommendations, neither individual team members nor teams as a whole have the authority to change priority or specifics of the project trade-offs, such as features, schedule, and resources. Those changes are at the prerogative of a project customer or sponsor and are implemented by a project team through change control.

Adapting the Team Model

The MSF Team Model was designed to be flexible enough to support various teams in how they prefer to self-organize. As long as the core principles and the set of natural checks and balances are preserved, the model can be easily adapted to match the needs of small and large as well as simple and complex projects.

This section provides guidance on how to scale the MSF Team Model. When you consider adapting the MSF Team Model, you need to understand teaming constraints imposed by the corporate structure, culture, and policies. A team structure needs to be both compatible with the corporate structure as well as represent the interests of the various corporate functional areas (e.g., the training department). Staff assigned to a team should have a healthy cross-blend of skills so that they balance out each other's competencies.

As depicted earlier, the MSF Team Model is ideally suited to support a project team of roughly 10 to 75 people spread out across the various advocacy groups (when an effort involves more staff, consider scaling this to a program-oriented team model; that is, breaking into multiple projects). However, at what point should a team adapt its structure? Most often, it is when coordination and communications among a team start to affect productivity significantly. Keep in mind that this can happen on a small team, too (e.g., 10 people), if other factors are present (e.g., globally distributed team with mixed skill levels). The goal of adapting a team is to increase subteam cohesion and minimize cross-team coupling.

Additional contributing factors to adapting a team model are the size, risk, and complexity of a project, as well as the skills required to fulfill the responsibilities of the functional areas. A goal of dividing a large team into smaller ones is to lower process, management, and communication overhead and enable faster implementation. A goal of adapting a team model to deal with risk is to help either contain or isolate risks as much as possible. In some cases, a goal is to spread risks across subteams as part of a mitigation strategy. Many types of complexity can confront a team. Like handling risk, one option is to assign more-complex efforts to a more senior subteam.

Adapting a team model does not just mean extending it; it also includes scaling it down to meet the needs of small teams. The following section discusses scaling-down strategies.

Scaling Down: Combining Advocacy Groups for Smaller Teams

Even though the MSF Team Model consists of seven advocacy groups, a team does not need a minimum of seven people. It also does not require one person per advocacy group. However, all quality goals of the advocacy groups must be championed. Typically, having at least one person per advocacy group helps to ensure that someone looks after the interests of each group, but not all projects have the benefit of filling each advocacy group in that fashion. Often, team members must share roles. On smaller teams, roles must be shared across team membership.

A guiding principle on role sharing is to try not to combine roles that have intrinsic conflicts of interest. For example, Product Management and Program Management have conflicting interests and should not be combined: Product Management wants to satisfy the customer, whereas Program Management wants to deliver on time and on budget. If these roles were combined and a customer were to request a change, the risk is that either the change will not get the consideration it deserves to maintain customer satisfaction, or that it will be accepted without understanding the impact it has on a project. Having different team members represent these advocacy groups helps to ensure that each perspective receives equal consideration. This is also true in trying to combine Testing and Development.

Combining some roles adds risk to a project. Combining other roles is unlikely as a result of intrinsic skills mismatches. But as with any teaming exercise, successful role sharing comes down to the actual members themselves and what experience and skills they bring with them. Table 4-4 advises what is perceived to be *risky* (as indicated by "Not Recommended"), *unlikely*, and *synergistic* (as indicated by "Possible") combinations of advocacy groups.

Table 4-4   Recommendations for Advocacy Group Combinations

	Product Management	Program Management	Architecture	Development	Test	User Experience	Release/ Operations
Product Management		N	N	N	P	P	U
Program Management	N		P	N	U	U	U
Architecture	N	P		P	U	U	U
Development	N	N	P		N	N	N
Test	P	U	U	N		P	P
User Experience	P	U	U	N	P		U
Release/Operations	U	U	U	N	P	U	

Key: **P** Possible   **U** Unlikely   **N** Not Recommended

By following the logic provided in Table 4-4, you can see that the smallest recommended team consists of three people in the configuration provided in Figure 4-7.

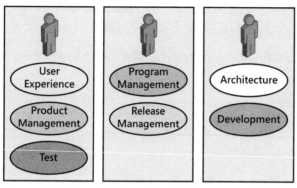

Figure 4-7   Example of combined advocacy groups for a three-person team

Scaling Up: Expanding Advocacy Groups for Larger Teams

A proven way to scale up the Team Model is to break a team into subteams using a lead team to integrate subteams and manage the overall project (i.e., a team of teams). Although this adds a bit of hierarchy to the team model, the goal remains to be as flat as possible. For example, it is preferred to decompose a large team into more subteams rather than to have an n-tiered model where n is greater than two. Of course, this too can be taken to an extreme of diminishing returns.

A lead team is composed of leads for each advocacy group. Their main responsibility is to coordinate and synchronize their counterparts on each subteam (e.g., a lead team test manager coordinates solution testing with test leads from each subteam). They might also act as arbitrators as disagreements arise between subteams. A lead team sets the overall project vision and is responsible for cross-team and integration requirements.

MSF recommends two types of subteams: feature teams and function teams. *Feature teams* are multidisciplinary subteams that are created to focus on building specific features or capabilities of a solution. *Function teams* are unidisciplinary subteams that are organized by functional role. The following sections discuss feature and function teams in more detail.

Feature Teams

Feature teams are multidisciplinary subteams organized around solution feature sets or created to focus on a particular capability (e.g., the messaging service). Each feature team is responsible for all aspects of their portion of a solution and its integration into a solution. Typically, feature teams are used in the following situations:

- A solution has highly independent components

- Members are very dispersed across organizations or geography

- There is a need to partition a solution to match organizational boundaries (e.g., outsource a portion of a delivery)

- Quick, cross-team decision making is necessary (e.g., ad hoc clarification of requirements that leads to real-time refining of a project plan)

Feature teams work best when they are colocated and have balanced representation from all advocacy groups. This is not to say that every advocacy group must be represented. A minimalist's approach to this would necessitate that each subteam contains only the minimum number of advocacy group representatives necessary to accomplish that subteam's tasks. For example, one subteam might need participation from the Release/Operations Advocacy Group whereas another subteam might not. Figure 4-8 is a team model example that includes three feature teams and a function team. There are a few things to note with this graphical example:

- It is a logical project team structure and not an organizational structure. It is expected that members of the subteams would be matrixed from various parts of an organization.

- Not all feature teams have dedicated roles in all advocacy groups (e.g., the File and Print feature team does not have a dedicated Architect role). Although there are nondedicated roles, the others on the subteam are expected to continue to champion their quality goals, responsibilities, and activities.

- The feature teams do not have dedicated user experience people. This organization has decided to group them together in a function team (discussed in more detail in the next section).

Once a team—and usually an organization's managers who have resources matrixed to the team—has agreed on how to logically structure a team, it is time to put together a staffing plan that includes how to staff a team, what skills are needed, what roles are needed, who is available, where the work location(s) are, and the many other factors needed to resource load a team properly. This type of plan is discussed further later in Chapter 8, but for now to round this out, Figure 4-9 is an example of a team structure that identifies phased solution delivery as well as named individuals filling the various roles. In this example, a solution was segmented into four phased releases. Although this team was organized by feature team, the Release/ Operations team was grouped together as a function team.

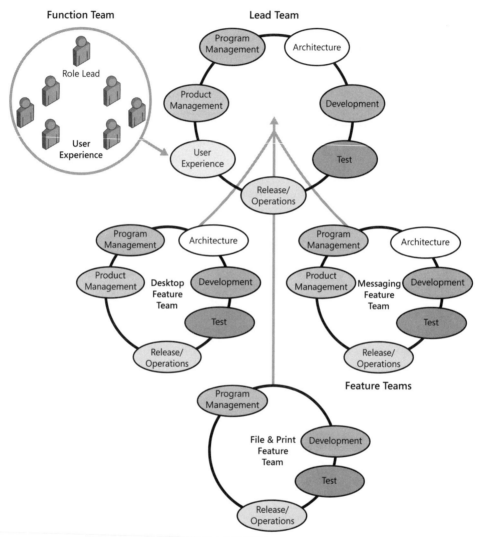

Figure 4-8   Example of a team model that includes feature teams, a function team, and a lead team

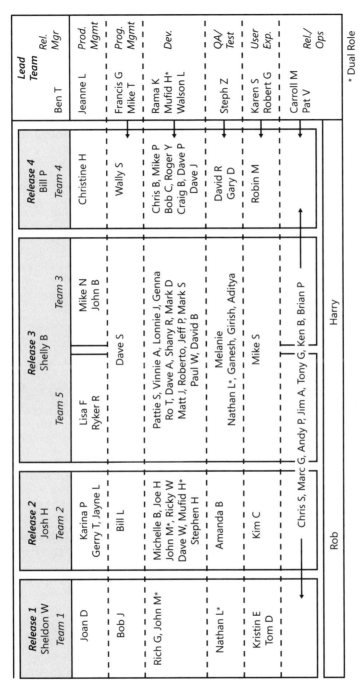

Figure 4-9   Example of large project team architecture to support versioned solution releases

Function Teams

Function teams are unidisciplinary subteams organized by functional role. Each function team is responsible for all aspects of their portion of a solution, which usually spans across the whole solution. Typically, function teams are used in the following situations:

- An organization has limited resources to perform a particular function and is unable to have those resources join each feature team. Instead, the resources are grouped into a functional team so they can centrally service all feature teams.

- A functional area is best served by being clustered together with like-minded individuals or when consistency is needed across a solution (e.g., User Interface Design, as shown in Figure 4-10).

- Distributing needed skills across feature teams is not practical (e.g., legacy systems integration).

- An organizational team is unable to be matrixed into a project team, and hence it needs to remain somewhat removed from a project team.

- Unlike a feature team that calls for balanced role representation, there exists a need for a larger concentration of effort to fulfill one or more functional areas within an advocacy group.

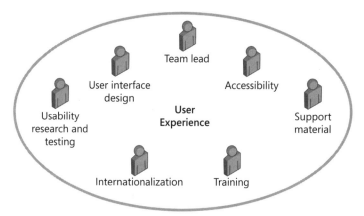

Figure 4-10   Example of a function team

Summary

Building a well-balanced and harmonious team is difficult. Therefore, the team should not spend lots of time structuring the team initially. It is something that will organically evolve over the life cycle. Where the team should initially spend time is thinking about how best to advocate for their constituencies and their quality goals. MSF believes this is best accomplished by using a team model with seven advocacy groups:

- Product Management
- Program Management

- Architecture
- Development
- Test
- User Experience
- Release/Operations

The MSF Team Model is structured to couple advocacy groups closely with their respective constituencies. This enables each advocacy group to understand more easily the totality of what they are advocating. To assist in understanding the facets of delivering a solution, the functional areas with their respective responsibilities and key activities are provided for each advocacy group.

The MSF Team Model intertwines a few different teams. It enables a team of advocates who champion different aspects of delivering a solution, namely, defining, designing, building, stabilizing, and deploying a solution. It includes a team of quality champions who each champion a different key aspect of delivering a quality solution. It includes a team of ambassadors who champion their constituencies' needs and manage their expectations. It includes a team of representatives who champion the needs of their corporate department and manage their expectations. Distilling these advocacies into the MSF Team Model enables clear team member accountability while team members share responsibility for the successful delivery of the solution.

Chapter 5
Managing Project Risks

With so many really smart and methodical people on project teams, why are there still so many projects over budget and blowing schedules? It is hard to believe this is technology related because technologies have come and gone with little difference. In discussions with project teams as to why this is likely to have occurred given their best efforts, most of them attribute it either to unplanned events disrupting progress or planned events not going as planned. Although Microsoft Solutions Framework (MSF) does not eliminate these types of things from happening, MSF does offer a means to minimize their impact through proactive management.

As do most frameworks and methodologies, MSF recommends that it is far easier to minimize project-impacting events and conditions proactively before they become project issues. Potential issues that have yet to materialize are classified as project risks. This chapter discusses how to assess risk and proactively handle it.

What Is Risk (and Why You Should Care)?

Nothing ventured, nothing gained–"You can't get anywhere unless you're willing to take a risk. The saying dates back to Chaucer (c. 1374) and is similar to the late fourteenth-century French proverb: Qui onques rien n'enprist riens n'achieva *(He who never undertook anything never achieved anything)."*

—Random House, Dictionary of Popular Proverbs and Sayings

What often confuses people is the difference between a risk and an issue. As defined in *Webster's Collegiate Dictionary*, *risk* is the "possibility of loss or injury." Risks differ from problems or issues because risks refer to anticipated problems, uncertainties, or potential for adverse outcome or loss in value, control, functionality, quality, or timely completion of a project. *Problems* and *issues*, however, are conditions or states of affairs that exist in a project at the present time. Risks can, in turn, become problems or issues if they are not addressed effectively.

Most individuals associate the concept of risk with the potential for loss; risk can adversely affect project outcomes. Inadequate handling of risk can depreciate project outcomes and likely results in the failure of a solution to achieve its full potential.

Although a risk presents the possibility of adverse project impact, when handled correctly, it also presents an opportunity for gain. As such, MSF broadly defines a *project risk* as any event or condition that can have a positive or negative impact on the outcome of a project. This wider concept of speculative risk is used by the financial industry where decisions regarding uncertainties can be associated with the potential for gain as well as loss, as opposed to the concept of pure risk used by the insurance industry where uncertainties are associated with potential future losses only.

What does it mean to handle risk correctly? How should a team handle uncertainty and what might happen? Will valuable time be wasted on what might never be realized? MSF attempts to address these questions in its risk management approach.

Managing Risks Throughout a Project

Effective handling of risk increases the likelihood of success in a project by minimizing the potential for failure and maximizing the potential to use risk for gain. Effective handling of risk involves having a good approach (i.e., risk management process) and accomplished execution of that approach (i.e., risk management discipline).

Managing risks throughout a project does not need to be hard or complicated. Risk management is a process of proactively identifying, analyzing, and addressing project risks. A goal of risk management is to maximize the positive impacts (opportunities) while minimizing the negative impacts (losses) associated with project risk. An effective policy of understanding and managing risks ensures that effective trade-offs are made between risk and opportunity.

Before discussing the *MSF Risk Management Process*, it is necessary to explore elements of risk management and how the MSF foundational principles apply to risk management.

MSF Risk Management Discipline

So what does it mean to have risk management discipline? It means successfully handling and approaching risk on a few different levels, namely, these:

- **Comprehensive**   Address all elements in a project (people, process, scope, technology, and environmental elements)
- **Systematic**   Incorporate a structured and repeatable process
- **Continuous**   Apply throughout a project life cycle
- **Proactive**   Seek to prevent or lessen impact of risk occurrences
- **Flexible**   Accommodate a wide range of quantitative and qualitative risk analysis methodologies

- **Practical**   Focus on those risks that most affect a project

- **Cost-effective**   Ensure maximum return on risk management efforts

- **Future-oriented**   Commit to individual- and enterprise-level learning

To be successful at handling risk, these characteristics of risk management need to be internalized and adapted to each project. For instance, what does it mean to handle risk proactively? It could mean anticipating problems rather than reacting to them. As part of anticipating problems, problem resolution plans are prepared before problems occur (most often for high-impact risks that are likely to occur). However, being proactive also could mean using preventative measures whenever possible to minimize and potentially avoid risks from being realized. The point being there is wide latitude for how to handle risks, and as such, a team needs to reach agreement and plan out what is appropriate for their given project constraints. The following section explores this topic further.

Risk Management Planning

At the beginning of a project, a team should develop and document how they plan to handle risk within the context of a project. Because risk management seems the least understood area, here are some questions to help you get started thinking about risk management:

- What are the assumptions and constraints for risk management?

- How will the risk management process be implemented?

- What are the process steps?

- What are the activities, roles, responsibilities, and deliverables for each step?

- Who will perform risk activities?

- What are the skill requirements?

- Is there any additional training needed?

- How does risk management at a project level relate to enterprise-level efforts?

- What kinds of tools or methods will be used to track and analyze risk?

- What definitions are used to classify and estimate risk?

- How will risks be prioritized?

- How will contingency and risk plans be created and executed?

- How will risk control activities be integrated into the overall project plan?

- What activities will team members be doing to manage risk?

- How often will risks be reassessed?

- How will status be communicated among a team and project stakeholders?

- How will progress be monitored?

- What kind of infrastructure will be used (databases, tools, repositories) to support the risk management process?

- What are the risks of risk management?

- What resources are available for risk management?

- What are the critical dates in a schedule for implementing risk management?

- Who is the sponsor and who are the stakeholders for each area of risk?

- Are resources (time, money, and people) set aside to research and address risks?

Risk management planning activities should not be viewed in isolation from the standard project planning and scheduling activities, just as risk management tasks should not be viewed as being "in addition" to tasks team members perform to complete a project. Because risks are inherent throughout a project, resources should be allocated and scheduled to manage risks actively. The next section discusses this topic further.

Integrating Risk Management in a Project Life Cycle

Risk management should be seamlessly integrated into the overall project life cycle. Risk assessment should begin at the beginning of a project as a project team and stakeholders begin to frame a project vision and begin setting constraints. With each constraint and assumption that is added to a project, additional risks will begin to emerge. A project team should begin risk identification activities as early in a project as possible. As a project continues, risk mitigation and contingency plans, discussed in detail later in this chapter, should be built directly into a project schedule and master plan. Progress of the risk plan should be monitored by the standard project management process.

In general, risk identification and risk tracking are continuous activities. Supported by the open communications principle, team members should be constantly looking for risks to a project and surfacing them for a team to consider, as well as continuously tracking the progress against specific risk plans. Analyzing and reanalyzing risks as well as modifying risk management action plans are more likely to be intermittent activities for a team, sometimes proactively scheduled (perhaps around major checkpoints or weekly project status reviews), and sometimes as a result of a unscheduled project event (discovery of additional risks during tracking and control). Learning is most often a scheduled event occurring around major checkpoints and certainly at the end of a project.

Over the course of a project, the nature of risks being addressed should change as well. Early in a project, business-, scope-, requirement-, and design-related risks dominate. As time progresses, technical risks surrounding implementation become more prominent, and then transition to operational risks. It is helpful to use risk checklists or review risk classification lists at each track transition within a project life cycle to guide risk identification activity.

Managing Risk Across a Portfolio of Projects

Not all projects have equal priority and importance. As such, risks associated with those projects are also not equally weighted. When dealing with a portfolio of projects, be it within a program or an enterprise, there needs to be a means to assess and manage risk across that portfolio. For example, how much effort should be spent on a high risk on a low-priority project as opposed to medium risk on a critical project? There is no one answer because it is situational. However, a team needs to have a clear means to resolve this. Remember, a goal is to achieve maximum return on risk management efforts across a portfolio.

But why should an organization spend extra effort managing risks across a portfolio? It seems like a lot of extra work. Yes but...many benefits at a portfolio level would not be realized unless portfolio-level management occurred. For instance, here are a few benefits:

- Resources and effort might be assigned to projects across a portfolio according to the risks they face.

- Each project's risk manager has an external escalation point to provide a second opinion on a team's assessments.

- Project teams can learn more rapidly from experience elsewhere.

- Quality assurance on the risk management processes is applied within each project.

Depending on the size of a portfolio, an organization might have resources dedicated, even if part-time, to work with project leads to manage risk across a portfolio. This dedicated team often is referred to as a *Risk Review Board*. Note that portfolio risk review complements risk assessments undertaken by each project team. A review team typically does not have enough project knowledge to help identify risks, nor does it likely have the time available to undertake risk mitigation actions. However, it can contribute to risk analysis and planning.

Because a review team normally contains more experienced practitioners, its members often call on that experience to advise a project team on the significance of certain risks, helping a team to prioritize risks. These experienced people are good resources who can recommend mitigation and contingency strategies that they have seen used effectively in the past. Based on their experience, they are well suited to help spot trends across projects that might identify an underlying problem, triggering some root-cause analysis.

The following are successful practices that have been applied in portfolio risk management:

- Secure executive support for a portfolio review process. Maintain this by regular reports on findings and lessons learned.

- Schedule meetings well in advance; ideally make meetings recurring, regular appointments on a day when many of project leads are expected to be present. Issue invitations to a review board well in advance; good reviewers have many other commitments.

■ Select projects for review carefully. Expect to review large, high-profile, mission-critical, and/or complex projects every month, but ensure that a broad cross section of other project types is also reviewed.

■ Follow a standard agenda for each project so that project leads know what to expect from the meeting. For example, have 20 minutes for presentation of a current risk assessment, followed by 20 minutes discussion of mitigation and contingency strategies, followed by a 5-minute review of any lessons learned to be shared with other project teams.

■ Use standard documents for project status reporting and risk assessment.

■ Ensure both documents are updated and distributed to all attendees in advance of a meeting; this enables a team to reduce time spent in a meeting.

■ Encourage project team leads to attend reviews, either in person or on the telephone.

■ Ensure that a project team gets value from a review. Often this is achieved by reviewing progress on issues that might not technically be risks, but where the experience of review board members can assist a project team.

■ Avoid attributing any blame for a project situation.

Creating a Risk Management Culture

Although few project delivery organizations argue against managing risks on their projects, many find it difficult to fully adopt the discipline associated with proactive risk management. What often happens is that a team initially assesses risk at the start of a project, but fails to continue to manage risks as a project proceeds. Two reasons are frequently put forward to explain this:

■ Pressure of time on a project team

■ Concern that focus on risks will undermine customers' confidence or present a negative impression

Often, a root cause for these beliefs is that managers themselves do not understand the value that risk management delivers to a project. As a result, they are reluctant to propose adequate resources necessary for risk management (and indeed other project management activities). Conversely, they might sacrifice these activities first if a project comes under pressure. It is therefore especially important to ensure that all stakeholders appreciate the importance of managing risks to establish a culture where risk management thrives. The following activities have been found to be effective in establishing risk management as a consistent discipline:

■ Secure management sponsorship.

■ Seek advice and mentorship from a risk manager who brings personal experiences and knowledge of failures.

■ Educate all stakeholders about the importance of managing risks and costs incurred from failure, much of which can be avoided through effective risk management.

- Train a core set of risk management practitioners who can provide role models and mentorship for others; an effective training approach is to combine a workshop on the theory of risk management with real exercises based on a live project.

- Invite key project stakeholders to risk review meetings and ensure that status reports are circulated to them.

- Introduce a recognition scheme for project team members who effectively identify and/or manage risks.

- Ensure that project teams consider risks in project scheduling and making key decisions.

- Seek feedback from stakeholders on the effectiveness of a risk management process and review it regularly to ensure that it is shown to add value.

Foundational Principles Applied to Risk Management

The MSF Risk Management Discipline is founded on a belief that risk must be addressed proactively, part of a formal and systematic process that approaches risk management as a positive endeavor. This discipline is based on foundational principles, mindsets, and practices that are central to MSF. The following principles are especially important for effective project risk management.

Foster Open Communications

MSF espouses an open approach toward discussing risks, within a team as well as with key stakeholders external to a team. All team members should be involved in risk identification and analysis. Team leads and management should support and encourage development of a no-blame culture to promote this behavior. Open, honest discussion of project risk leads to more accurate appraisal of project status and better-informed decision making both within a team and by executive management and sponsors.

Work Toward a Shared Vision

All aspects of delivering a solution are fraught with risks. Part of having a shared vision is making sure everyone understands how to identify, classify, communicate, and manage those risks. That way, a team makes informed decisions throughout a life cycle. Also, a team can choose to avoid risk(s) by adjusting a shared vision.

Empower Team Members

Empowering team members involves a degree of trust and personal safety. That is, any team member can raise a risk in a constructive manner without fear of retribution or distain—a blameless environment. Team members should be comfortable enough to know that raising a risk associated with their area is a sign of needed maturity. As such, the quantity of risks associated with various teams and individuals should not be used as assessment/evaluation criteria.

Establish Clear Accountability, Shared Responsibility

No one person "owns" risk management within MSF. Everyone on a team is responsible for actively participating in a risk management process. Individual team members take ownership of action items specifically addressing project risk within a project schedule and plans. Each holds personal responsibility for completing and reporting on these tasks in the same way that he or she does for other action items related to completion of a project. Activities might span all areas of a project during all tracks of a project and risk management process cycles. These activities include risk identification within areas of personal expertise or responsibility and extends to include risk analysis, risk planning, and execution of risk control tasks during a project. Within the MSF Team Model, a Project Management functional area of the Program Management Advocacy Group holds final accountability for organizing a team in risk management activities and ensuring that risk management activities are incorporated into standard project management processes for a project.

Deliver Incremental Value

Incremental delivery of value typically enables a reduction of risk. More frequent and smaller deliveries enable a team to react and respond quickly to risks. By decomposing a solution into incremental deliveries, a team and stakeholders reduce risk on many fronts. They reduce risks associated with technology because they continually are building and refining a deployed solution. They reduce risks that a solution will not meet stakeholders' needs and expectations. They reduce risks that what is being delivered does not provide value to stakeholders. They reduce risks associated with team member skills readiness because incremental builds of a solution can be used to hone and assess team member skills.

Stay Agile, Expect and Adapt to Change

> *Murphy was an optimist!*
>
> —*O'Toole's commentary on Murphy's Law*

Prospect of change is one of the main sources of uncertainty facing a project team. Risk management activities should not be limited to any one portion of a project life cycle. All too often, teams start out a project with the good intention of applying risk management principles, but fail to continue the effort all the way through project completion under pressures of a tight schedule. Agility demands that a team continuously assess and proactively manage risks throughout all tracks of a project life cycle because continuous change in all aspects of a project means that project risks are continuously changing as well. A proactive approach enables a team to embrace change and turn it into an opportunity to prevent change from becoming a disruptive, negative force.

Invest in Quality

Investing in quality typically translates into reduced risk and better management of risk. Managing risks effectively usually means a team has more time to focus on their efforts rather than spending time reacting to realized risks (i.e., issues). How many times have you been on a project that has had to "drop everything" to deal with an issue that could have been prevented? Most likely too many times!

Learn from All Experiences

MSF assumes that keeping focus on continuous improvement through learning leads to greater success. Knowledge captured from one project decreases uncertainty surrounding decision making with inadequate information when it becomes available for others to draw upon in the next project. MSF emphasizes the importance of organizational or enterprise-level learning from project outcomes by incorporating a step into a risk management process. Focusing directly on capturing project outcome experiences encourages team-level learning (from each other) through fostering open communications among all team members.

Partner with Customers

As discussed, risks are not necessarily caused by the failings of a team. Rather, risks are usually generated when a team takes calculated steps to accelerate solution delivery. This type of risk, if handled correctly, typically means a windfall for customers. As such, partnering with customers to gauge how much risk should be assumed is essential to the success of a project.

MSF Risk Management Fundamentals

In this section, important concepts about risk and risk management central to understanding the MSF Risk Management Discipline are discussed.

Risk Is Inherent in Any Project or Process

Although different projects might have more or fewer risks than others do, no project is completely free of risk. Projects are initiated so an organization is able to achieve a goal that delivers value in support of an organization's purpose. Uncertainties always surround a project and the environment that can affect the success of achieving this goal. By always keeping in mind that risk is inherent and everywhere, MSF practitioners seek ways to continuously make the right trade-off decisions between risk and opportunity and do not become too focused on minimizing risk to the exclusion of all else.

Proactive Risk Management Is Most Effective

MSF adopts a proactive approach to identifying, analyzing, and addressing risk by focusing on the following:

- Anticipate problems rather than just reacting to them when they occur
- Address root causes instead of just dealing with symptoms
- Have problem resolution plans ready ahead of time—before a problem occurs

- Use a known, structured, repeatable process for problem resolution

- Use preventative measures whenever possible

Effective risk management is not achieved by simply reacting to problems. A team should work to identify risks in advance and to develop strategies and plans to manage them. Plans should be developed to correct problems if they occur. Anticipating potential problems and having well-formed plans in place ahead of time shortens the response time in a crisis and can limit or even reverse the damage caused by an occurrence of a problem.

Defining characteristics of proactive risk management are risk mitigation and risk impact reduction. Mitigation can occur at the level of a specific risk and target the underlying immediate cause, or it can be achieved by intervention at a root-cause level (or anywhere in the intervening causal chain). Mitigation measures are best undertaken in the early stages of a project when a team still has the ability to intervene in time to affect project outcome.

Identification and correction of root causes has high value for the enterprise because corrective measures can have far-reaching positive effects well beyond the scope of an individual project. For example, absence of coding standards or machine naming conventions can clearly result in adverse consequences within a single development or deployment project and thus be a source of increased project risk. However, creation of standards and guidelines can have a positive effect on all projects performed within an enterprise when these standards and guidelines are implemented across an entire organization.

Treat Risk Identification as Positive

Effective risk management depends on correct and comprehensive understanding of risks facing a project team. As the variety of challenges and the magnitude of potential losses become evident, identifying and managing risks can become a discouraging activity for a team. Some team members might even take the view that to identify risks is actually to look for reasons to undermine the success of a project. In contrast, MSF adopts the perspective that the very process of risk identification enables a team to manage risks more effectively by bringing them out into the open, and thereby increases the prospects for success by a team. Open, documented discussion of risk frees team members to concentrate on their work by providing explicit clarification of roles, responsibilities, and plans for preventative activities and corrective measures for problems.

A team (and especially team leaders) should always regard risk identification in a positive way to ensure contribution of as much information as possible about the risks they face. A negative perception of risk causes team members to feel reluctant to communicate risks. The environment should be such that individuals identifying risks do so without fear of retribution for honest, constructive expression of tentative or controversial views. Examples of negative risk environments are easy to find. For example, in some environments reporting new risks is viewed as a form of complaining. In this setting, a person reporting a risk is viewed as a troublemaker, and reaction to a risk is directed at a person rather than at the risk itself. People generally become wary of freely communicating risks under these circumstances and then begin to selectively present the risk information they decide to share to avoid confrontation with team members. Teams that create a positive risk management environment by actively rewarding team members who surface risks are more successful at identifying and addressing risks earlier than those teams operating in a negative risk environment. There also should be a reward for team members who propose ways to address these risks.

To achieve a goal of maximizing positive gains for a project, a team must be willing to take risks. This requires viewing risks and uncertainty as means to create the right opportunity for a team to achieve success.

> **Lesson Learned**   How risks are reported to a team and to stakeholders can have a big effect on morale. Although project risks should be available to everyone in keeping with the foundational principle of open communications, it is also in keeping with this principle that the right information should be shared with the right people at the right time. Accordingly, it is advantageous, especially on large, complex projects, to provide a means to filter a risk log when reporting on risks. That way, subteams can focus on their risks (and issues) and not get distracted by what might not be relevant to them.

Continuous Assessment

Many people misperceive risk management as, at best, a necessary but boring task to be carried out at the beginning of a project or only at the introduction of a new process. However, actively managing risk can provide team members with the confidence to be able to take risks.

Continuing changes in project and operating environments require project teams to reassess the status of known risks regularly and to reevaluate or update plans to prevent or respond to problems associated with these risks. Projects teams should also be constantly looking for the emergence of new project risks. Risk management activities should be integrated into an overall project life cycle in such a way as to provide appropriate updating of risk control plans and activities without creating a separate reporting and tracking infrastructure.

Maintain Open Communications

Although risks are generally known by some team members, this information is often poorly communicated. Often, it is easy to communicate information about risks down an organizational hierarchy, but difficult to pass information about risks up the hierarchy. At every level, people want to know about project risks but are wary of communicating this information upward. Restricted information flow regarding risks is a potent contributor to project risk because it forces decision to be made about those risks with even less information. Managers and key influencers need to encourage and exhibit open communications about risk and ensure that risks and risk plans are well understood by everyone.

Specify, Then Manage

Risk management is concerned with decision making in the face of uncertainty. Generic state-ments of risk leave much of the uncertainty in place and encourage different interpretations of a risk. Clear statements of risk aid a team in the following:

■ Ensuring that all team members have the same understanding of a risk

■ Understanding the cause or causes of a risk and the relationship to problems that might arise

■ Providing a basis for quantitative, formal analysis and planning efforts

■ Building confidence by stakeholders and sponsors in a team's ability to manage a risk

MSF advocates that risk management planning be undertaken with attention to specific infor-mation to minimize execution errors in a risk plan that render preventative efforts ineffective or interfere with recovery and corrective efforts.

Don't Judge a Situation Simply by the Number of Risks

Although team members and key stakeholders often perceive risk items as negative, it is important not to judge a project or operational process simply on the number of communi-cated risks. Risk, after all, is the possibility, not the certainty, of a loss or suboptimal outcome. As explained in the next section, the MSF Risk Management Process advocates the use of a structured risk identification and analysis process to provide decision makers with informa-tion on the presence of risks and the importance of those risks as well.

MSF Risk Management Process

As discussed at the beginning of this chapter, MSF Risk Management consists of two things: the MSF Risk Management Process and the discipline to use it efficiently, effectively, systemat-ically, and repetitiously. This section bundles it all together into a process that enables proactive risk management, continuous risk assessment, and integration into decision making through-out a project or operational life cycle. A project needs just enough rigor to make sure that risks are continuously assessed, monitored, and actively managed until they are either resolved or turn into issues to be handled.

Although the MSF Risk Management Process draws upon the well-known Software Engineer-ing Institute (SEI) Continuous Risk Management process model[1,2] for technical project risk,

---

1 Audrey J. Dorofee, Julie A. Walker, Christopher J Alberts, et al., *Continuous Risk Management Guidebook* (Pittsburgh, PA: Carnegie-Mellon University, 1996).

2 Ronald P. Higuera, "Team Risk Management: A New Model for Customer-Supplier Relationships," SEI Techni-cal Report CMU/SEI-94-SR-5 (Pittsburgh, PA: Software Engineering Institute–Carnegie Mellon University, 1994).

MSF seeks to interpret this model in view of Microsoft's extensive product development experience and the software development and deployment project experience derived from Microsoft Consulting Services (MCS) and Microsoft partners.

The MSF Risk Management Process consists of the following six steps, as depicted in Figure 5-1:

1. Identify risks. *Risk identification* allows individuals to surface risks so that a team becomes aware of a potential problem. As the input to a risk management process, risk identification should be undertaken as early as possible and repeated frequently throughout a project life cycle.

2. Analyze and prioritize risks. *Risk analysis* transforms estimates or data about specific project risks that developed during risk identification into a form that a team uses to make decisions around prioritization. *Risk prioritization* enables a team to commit project resources to manage the most important risks.

3. Plan and schedule risk handling. *Risk planning* takes information obtained from risk analysis and uses it to formulate strategies, plans, and actions. *Risk scheduling* ensures that these plans are approved and then incorporated into the standard day-to-day project management process and infrastructure to ensure that risk management is carried out as part of the day-to-day activities of a team. Risk scheduling explicitly connects risk planning with project planning.

4. Track and report risk status. *Risk tracking* monitors status of specific risks and the progress in their respective action plans. Risk tracking also includes monitoring probability, impact, exposure, and other measures of risk for changes that could alter priority or risk plans and project features, resources, or schedule. Risk tracking enables visibility of a risk management process within a project from a perspective of risk levels as opposed to a task-completion perspective of the standard operational project management process. *Risk reporting* ensures that a team, sponsors, and other stakeholders are aware of the status of project risks and the plans to manage them.

5. Control risk mitigation and project change activities. *Risk control* is a process of executing risk action plans and their associated status reporting. Risk control also includes initiation of project change control requests when changes in risk status or risk plans could result in changes in project features, resources, or schedule.

6. Learn from risk resolutions. *Risk learning* formalizes lessons learned and relevant project artifacts into knowledge for reuse within a team and by an enterprise.

Note that these steps are logical steps and that they do not need to be followed in strict chronological order for any given risk. Teams often cycle iteratively through the identification-analysis-planning steps as they develop experience on a project for a class of risks and only periodically visit a learning step for capturing knowledge for an enterprise.

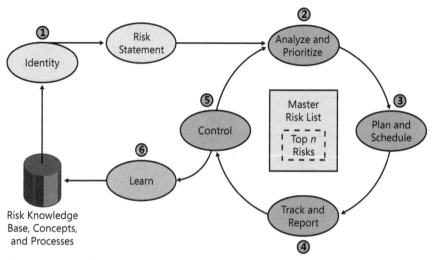

Figure 5-1   MSF Risk Management Process

It should not be inferred from the diagram that all project risks pass through this sequence of steps in lockstep. Rather, MSF advocates that each project define during project planning when and how a risk management process will be initiated and under what circumstances transitions between the steps should occur for individual or groups of risks. For example, a project team might deem that all risks that have significant financial implications need to be reviewed by project sponsor(s) before being incorporated into a project schedule. Another example is when a cursory review of risks is performed to determine a tentative priority. After assessment of the impact on the schedule, more analysis might be required (i.e., bouncing risks between step 2 and step 3).

The following sections explain each step of the MSF Risk Management Process.

Step 1: Identify Risks

Risk identification is the initial step in the MSF Risk Management Process. Risks must be identified and stated clearly and unequivocally so that a team comes to consensus and moves on to analysis and planning. During risk identification, a team focus should be deliberately expansive. Attention should be given to learning activity and directed toward seeking gaps in knowledge about a project and its environment that might adversely affect a project or limit its success. Figure 5-2 depicts graphically the inputs, outputs, and activities for a risk identification step.

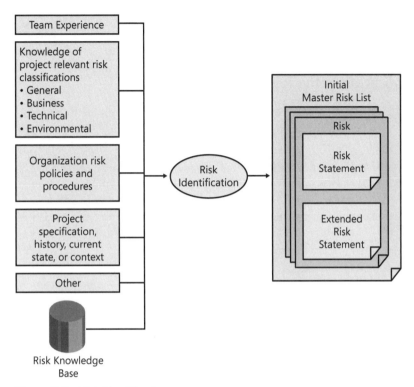

Figure 5-2   Risk identification

Goals

The goal of a risk identification step is for a team to identify project risks and, from them, produce a comprehensive, consensus list of these risks, covering all areas of a project in clear and unambiguous stated form.

Inputs

The inputs to a risk identification step are the available knowledge of general and project-specific risk in relevant business, technical, organizational, and environmental areas. Additional considerations are the experience of a team; the current organizational approach toward risk in the forms of policies, guidelines, templates, and so forth; and information about a project as it is known at that time, including history and current state. A team can choose to draw upon other inputs—anything that a team considers relevant to risk identification should be considered.

At the start of a project, it is useful to employ group brainstorming, facilitated sessions, or even formal workshops to collect information on project team and stakeholder perceptions on risks and opportunities. Industry classification schemes such as the SEI Software risk taxonomy,[3] project checklists,[4] previous project summary reports, and other published industry sources and guides can also be helpful in assisting a team in identifying relevant project risks.

Risk Identification Activities

During risk identification, a team seeks to create an unambiguous statement or list articulating risks that they face. At the start of a project, it is easy to organize a workshop or brainstorming session to identify risks associated with a new situation. Unfortunately, many organizations regard this as a one-time activity, and never repeat the activity during a project or operations life cycle. MSF Risk Management emphasizes that risk identification should be undertaken at periodic intervals during a project. Risk identification might be schedule-driven (e.g., daily, weekly, or monthly), checkpoint-driven (associated with a planned checkpoint in a project plan), or event-triggered (forced by significant disruptive events in the business, technology, organizational, or environmental settings). Risk identification activities should be undertaken at intervals and with scope determined by each project team. For example, a team might complete a global risk identification session together at major checkpoints of a large development project, but might choose in addition to have individual feature teams or even individual developers repeat risk identification for their areas of responsibility at interim checkpoints or even on a weekly scheduled basis.

During the initial risk identification step in a project, interaction between team members and stakeholders is very important because it is a powerful way to expose assumptions and differing viewpoints. For this reason, MSF advocates involvement of as wide a group of interests, skills, and backgrounds from a team as is possible during risk identification. Risk identification also can involve research by the team or involvement of subject matter experts to learn more about risks within a project domain.

The two main areas of activity during an identification step are risk classification and risk statement formation.

Risk Classification   Risk classifications, sometimes called *risk categories* and *risk taxonomies*, serve multiple purposes for a project team. Risk classification provides a basis for standardized risk terminology needed for reporting and tracking. During risk identification, they stimulate thinking about risks arising within different areas of a project as well as providing a ready-made list of project areas to consider from a risk perspective that is derived from previous similar projects or industry experience. During brainstorming, risk classifications also ease complexities of working with large numbers of risks by providing a convenient way for grouping similar risks together. Finally, risk classifications are critical for establishing and maintaining working industry and enterprise risk knowledge bases because they provide a

---

3 Ronald P. Higuera and Yacov Y. Haimes, "Software Risk Management," SEI Technical Report CMU/SEI-96-TR-012 ESC-96-012 (Pittsburgh, PA: Software Engineering Institute–Carnegie Mellon University, 1996).

4 For example, Steve McConnell, *Software Project Survival Guide* (Redmond, WA: Microsoft Press, 1998).

basis for indexing new contributions and searching and retrieving existing work. Table 5-1 illustrates high-level classifications for sources of project risk.

Table 5-1   Risk Classifications and Respective Risk Sources

Risk Classification	Risk Sources
People	Customers, end users, sponsors, stakeholders, personnel, organization, skills, politics, morale
Scope	Mission, goals, assumptions, constraints, requirements
Process	Decision making, project characteristics, budget, cost, schedules, design, building, testing
Technology	Security, supporting environment, tools, deployment, support, operational/production environment, availability
Environmental	Legal, regulatory, competition, economic, technology, business

There are many taxonomies or classifications for general software development project risk. Well-known and frequently cited classifications that describe the sources of software development project risk include Barry Boehm,[5] Caper Jones,[6] and the SEI Software Risk Taxonomy.[7]

Lists of risk areas covering limited project areas in detail are also available. Schedule risk is a common area for project teams, and a comprehensive, highly detailed list for assisting software development project teams with risk identification around schedules has been compiled by Steve McConnell.[8]

Different kinds of projects (e.g., infrastructure or packaged application deployment), projects carried out with specialized technology domains (e.g., security, embedded systems, safety critical, EDI), vertical industries (e.g., health care and manufacturing), or solution-specific projects can carry well-known project risks unique to that area. Within the area of information security, risks concerning information theft, loss, or corruption as a result of deliberate acts or accidents are often referred to as threats.[9,10] Projects in these areas will benefit from a review of alternative risk (threat) classifications or extensions to well-known general-purpose risk classifications to ensure breadth of thinking on the part of a project team during a risk identification step.

---

5 Barry W. Boehm, *Software Risk Management* (New York: IEEE Press, 1989).

6 Capers Jones, *Assessment and Control of Software Risks* (Englewood Cliffs, NJ: Prentice Hall, 1994).

7 Ronald P. Higuera and Yacov Y. Haimes, "Software Risk Management," SEI Technical Report SEI/CMU-96-TR-012 (Pittsburgh, PA: Software Engineering Institute–Carnegie Mellon University, 1996).

8 Steve McConnell, *Rapid Development* (Redmond, WA: Microsoft Press, 1996), 87–91.

9 Thomas R. Peltier, *Information Security Risk Analysis* (Boca Raton, FL: Auerbach Publications, 2001).

10 Donald L. Pipkin, *Information Security: Protecting the Global Enterprise* (Upper Saddle River, NJ: Prentice Hall, 2000).

Other sources for project risk information include industry project risk databases such as the Software Engineering Information Repository (SEIR)[11] or internal enterprise risk knowledge bases.

Risk Statements   A *risk statement* is a natural language expression of a causal relationship between a real, existing project state of affairs or attribute and a potential, unrealized second project event, state of affairs, or attribute. The first part of a risk statement is called the *condition* and provides a description of an existing project state of affairs or attribute that a team feels might result causally in a project loss or reduction in gain.

The second part of a risk statement is called the *consequence* and describes an undesirable project attribute or state of affairs. The two parts of a statement are linked by a term or phrase such as "therefore" or "and as a result" that implies an uncertain (in other words, less than 100 percent sure) but causal relationship. This is depicted schematically along with an example in Figure 5-3.

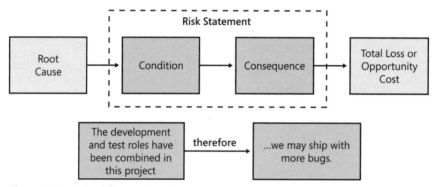

Figure 5-3   MSF risk statement

The two-part formulation of risk statements has the advantage of coupling risk consequences with observable (and potentially controllable) risk conditions within a project early in a risk identification stage.[12,13] Use of alternative approaches where a team focuses only on identification of risk conditions within a project during a risk identification stage usually requires that a team back up to recall a risk condition later on in a risk management process when they develop management strategies.

Although commonly done, it is not recommended that risk statements be written initially as "if-then" statements. Instead, it is recommended that risk statements be left loosely defined for later refinement during an analysis step. Similar to brainstorming where a goal is to get everything on the proverbial table without refinement or judgment, the goal of risk identification is to identify as many risks as possible, deferring what-if analysis for a Plan Track

11 Software Engineering Information Repository, http://seir.sei.cmu.edu/.

12 Dorofee et al., *Continuous Risk Management*.

13 Linda H. Rosenberg, Theodore Hammer, and Albert Gallo, *Continuous Risk Management at NASA*, 1999, http://satc.gsfc.nasa.gov/support/ASM_FEB99/crm_at_nasa.html (accessed June 19, 2006).

(discussed in Chapter 8, "MSF Plan Track: Planning a Solution"). During risk identification, it is not uncommon for a team to identify multiple consequences for the same condition. Sometimes a risk consequence identified in one area of a project can become a risk condition in another. These situations should be recorded by a team so that appropriate decisions are made during risk analysis and planning to take into account causal dependencies and interactions among risks.

> **Lesson Learned**   For people new to risk analysis, sometimes it is easier to grasp risk statements if they are phrased as "if-then" statements. Although not optimal, it is better to start with something a team understands, and then gradually mature their risk management capabilities.

When formulating a risk statement, a team should consider both the cause of the potential, unrealized less desirable outcome as well as the outcome itself. A risk statement includes the observed state of affairs (condition) within a project as well as the observable state of affairs that might occur (consequence). As part of a thorough risk analysis (a step that is often overlooked), team members should look for similarities and natural groupings of the conditions of project risk statements and backtrack up the causal chain for each condition, seeking a common underlying root cause.[14] It is also valuable to follow the causal chain downstream from a condition–consequence pair in a risk statement to examine effects on an organization and environment outside a project to gain a better appreciation for the total losses or missed opportunities associated with a specific project condition.[15]

Depending on the relationships among risks, closing one risk might close a whole group of dependent risks and change an overall risk profile for a project. Documenting these relationships early during the risk identification stage provides useful information for guiding risk planning that is flexible, comprehensive, and that uses available project resources efficiently by addressing root or predecessor causes. Benefits of capturing such additional information at an identification step should be balanced against rapidly moving through the subsequent analysis and prioritization and then reexamining the dependencies and root causes for the most important risks during a planning and scheduling step.

Outputs

The minimum output from risk identification activities is a clear, unambiguous set of risk statements faced by a team, recorded as a *risk list*. A risk list in tabular form, as exemplified in Table 5-2, is the main input for the next stage of the risk management process—analysis. The risk identification step frequently generates a large amount of other useful information,

---

14 One effective brainstorming technique for root cause identification is called "Five Whys." In this approach, the group should ask the question "Why is that?" of the risk condition, provide an answer, and then repeat the "why is that?...Because of..." cycle up to five times.

15 This can be accomplished by a variant of the "Five Whys" technique in which the team cycles through the "so what?...Because of..." question and answer sequence five times.

including the identification of root causes and downstream effects, affected parties, owner, and so forth.

Initial Master Risk List   A master risk list is the compilation of all risk assessment information at an individual project list level of detail. It is a living document that forms a basis for an ongoing risk management process and should be kept up-to-date throughout the cycle of risk analysis, planning, and monitoring. A master risk list is a fundamental document for supporting active or proactive risk management. It enables team decision making by providing a basis for the following activities:

- Prioritizing effort

- Identifying critical actions

- Highlighting dependencies

An example of an initial master risk list resulting from an identification step is depicted in Table 5-2.

Table 5-2   Example of Initial Master Risk List

Classification	Root Cause	Condition	Consequence	Downstream Effect
People	Organization	Development team is divided between London and Boston.	Communication among team members will be difficult.	Delays in solution shipment with additional rework
Scope	Inadequate requirements management	Informal requirements management.	Team members will have an inconsistent understanding of requirements.	Prolonged integration and stabilization efforts
Process	Inadequate staffing	The roles of development and testing have been combined.	We might ship with more bugs.	Reduced customer satisfaction Increased support costs
Technology	Technology change	Developers are to work with new shipping technology.	Development time will take longer because of the need for developers to learn.	Later to market Lost market share to competitors
Environmental	Regulatory	New legislation is likely to be approved.	Some solution requirements will need to be changed to comply with new policy.	Delays in solution shipment with additional rework

Extended Risk Statements   When identifying individual project risk, it is beneficial to record additional information with a risk statement to provide context to assist others in better understanding a risk.[16,17,18] Although not part of a risk statement, this information coupled with a risk statement is often referred to as an *extended risk statement* or *risk statement form*. Note that given the potential verbose nature of this additional information, it is sometimes easier to retain it as a separate document from a master risk list. This information also helps classify risks (by project area or attribute)—especially when using project risk information to build and use an enterprise risk knowledge base. Risk context information that some project teams might choose to record during risk identification to capture team intent includes the following:

- Environmental and project conditions
- Context
- Constraints
- Circumstances
- Assumptions
- Contributing factors
- Dependencies among risks
- Related issues
- Business asset owner
- Originator
- Team concerns

It is typical that this information might not be fully known during an identification step. This information can also be added during subsequent steps.

Step 2: Analyze and Prioritize Risks

Risk analysis and prioritization make up the second step in the MSF Risk Management Process. Risk analysis involves conversion of risk data into a form that facilitates decision making. Risk prioritization ensures that team members address the most important project risks first.

Selecting the "right" risk analysis method or combination of methods depends on making the right trade-off decision between expending effort on risk analysis or making an incorrect or indefensible (to stakeholders) prioritization choice. Risk analysis should be undertaken to support prioritization that drives decision making and should never become analysis for the sake of analysis. The results from quantitative or semiquantitative approaches to risk prioritization should be evaluated within the context of business goals, opportunities, and sound

---

16 L. H. Rosenberg et al., *Continuous Risk Management*.

17 Elaine Hall, *Managing Risk. Methods for Software Systems Development*, SEI Series in Software Engineering (Reading, MA: Addison-Wesley, 1998), ch. 4.

18 Dorofee et al., *Continuous Risk Management*.

management practices and should not be considered an automated form of decision making by itself.

During this step, a team examines an initial list of risk items produced in the risk identification step and prioritizes it for action, within a master risk list. A team determines to which top risks they will commit resources for planning and executing a specific strategy. A team also identifies which risks, if any, are of such low priority for action, and not likely to increase in priority, that they can be dropped from a list. As a project moves toward completion and as project circumstances change, risk identification and risk analysis will be repeated and changes made to a master risk list. New risks might appear and old risks that no longer carry a sufficiently high priority might be removed or deactivated. The inputs and outputs to this step are depicted in Figure 5-4.

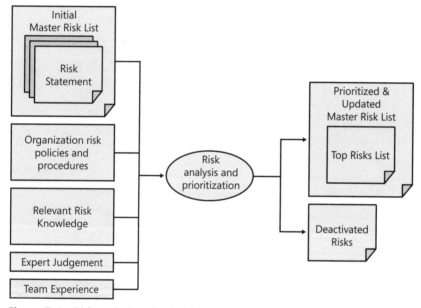

Figure 5-4   Risk analysis and prioritization

Goal

The goal of this step is to perform just enough analysis of each risk to be able to prioritize items on a risk list and determine which of these risks warrant commitment of resources for planning—typically for the highest priority risks.

Lesson Learned   Risk analysis should initially be done very quickly to keep risk analysis from becoming a major schedule risk. The risk ratings assigned will be revised as more information is discovered throughout a project, so it is not usually worth having lengthy discussions about them up front. If no consensus is quickly found, use an average of the ratings given by the team members involved.

Inputs

During the risk analysis and prioritization step, a team draws upon its own experience and information derived from other relevant sources regarding risk statements produced during risk identification. Relevant information to assist the transformation of an initial master risk list into a prioritized master risk list can be obtained from an organization's risk policies and guidelines, industry risk databases, simulations, analytic models, business unit managers, and domain experts, among others.

Risk Analysis Activities

Risk analysis is the process of transforming estimates or data about specific project risks into a form that the team uses to make decisions around prioritization. Many qualitative and quantitative techniques to accomplishing prioritization of a risk list exist. One easy-to-use technique for risk analysis is to use consensus team estimates of two widely accepted components of risk: *probability* and *impact*.

Risk Probability   Risk probability is a measure of the likelihood that the state of affairs described in the risk consequence portion of a risk statement will actually occur. Whatever measure is used to indicate priority, it must be clearly understood across the team and all stakeholders. Typically, a team will use ratings in numerical form or natural language expressions (e.g., high, medium, low). Which one used is often dictated by the way in which probability is determined. For instance, if probability is mathematically calculated, a numerical rating is often used. If communicating with stakeholders and users, natural language ratings are more intuitive and therefore are used. However, an obvious downside of using natural language ratings not based on numeric values is that level determinations are subjective and therefore prone to inconsistent leveling. This issue increases as the number of levels used increases.

Probabilities are notoriously difficult for individuals to estimate and apply, although industry or enterprise risk databases can be helpful in providing known probability estimates based on samples of large numbers of projects. Most project teams, however, verbalize their experience, interpret industry reports, and provide a spectrum of natural language terms. If necessary, these terms are mapped back to numeric probability ranges. This can be as simple as mapping "low-medium-high" to discrete probability values (e.g., 17%, 50%, 84%) or as complex as mapping different natural language terms, such as "highly unlikely," "improbable," "likely," and "almost certainly." So, how many levels are recommended? A rule of thumb is to use the simplest means necessary to adequately represent the degree of precision needed. Table 5-3 demonstrates an example of a three-value division of risk likelihood expressed in probabilities. Table 5-4 demonstrates a seven-value division.

Note that the probability values used for calculation in the tables represent a midpoint of each range. With the aid of these mapping tables, an alternative method for quantifying

Table 5-3   Example of Three Probability Levels

Probability Range	Probability Value Used for Calculations	Natural Language Rating	Numeric Score
1% through 33%	17%	Low	1
34% through 67%	50%	Medium	2
68% through 99%	84%	High	3

Table 5-4   Example of Seven Probability Levels

Probability Range	Probability Value Used for Calculations	Natural Language Rating	Numeric Score
1% through 14%	7%	Extremely unlikely	1
15% through 28%	21%	Low	2
28% through 42%	35%	Probably not	3
43% through 57%	50%	50-50	4
58% through 72%	65%	Probably	5
73% through 86%	79%	High likelihood	6
87% through 99%	93%	Almost certainly	7

probability is to map a probability range or natural language rating agreed upon by the team to a numeric score. No matter what technique is used for quantifying uncertainty, a team needs to agree on a consistent rating approach for risk probability that represents their consensus view regarding each risk.

Also provided in the tables for each level of probability is a numeric score. This is just another way to represent a range of probability. Typically, the numeric score used for each probability range is a linear progression of values starting from 1.

Risk Impact   Risk impact is an estimate of the severity of adverse effects, or the magnitude of a loss, or the potential opportunity cost should a risk be realized within a project. It should be a direct measure of the risk consequence as defined in a risk statement. Like probability, impact might be represented either in numerical terms or as natural language expressions. Unlike probability, more flexibility is afforded to define what is meant by "impact." For instance, impact might be represented in various terms, such as financial loss, schedule slippage, or market share.

In addition to natural language ratings often used for probability, an additional level is used with impact (e.g., critical) to emphasize catastrophic impact to a project. As such, an artificially high score is assigned. This ensures that a risk with even low probability will rise to the top of a risk list and remain there if the impact is serious.

A scoring approach for estimating impact often matches the complexity of how impact is determined (i.e., simple impact assessments lead to simple scoring). An impact score should reflect a team's and organization's values and policies. For instance, if impact is measured financially, a $10,000 monetary loss that is tolerable for one team or organization might be unacceptable for another. Hence, the former team might assign a low impact score whereas the latter team will likely score the impact higher. Table 5-5 is an example of natural language ratings for impact and their respective scores.

Table 5-5   Example of Impact Ratings and Their Respective Scores

Rating	Score
Critical	10
High	3
Medium	2
Low	1

The following two sections provide a bit more insight on impact scoring. They discuss impact scoring based on a single attribute and on multiple attributes.

Single-Attribute Impact Scoring   The simplest form of determining risk impact is to use only one attribute. Often, using only one attribute makes it easier and more intuitive to quantify the magnitude of loss or opportunity cost. It also helps when communicating to stakeholders and users to relate impact in their terms. For instance, financial impact can be agreed to represent long-term costs in operations and support, loss of market share, short-term costs in additional work, or opportunity cost.

Once a team reaches agreement on what "impact" means, the same people need to agree on quantifying the magnitude of the impact. It is helpful to create translation tables relating specific units such as time or money into values that can be compared to subjective units used elsewhere in the analysis, as illustrated in Table 5-6. This approach provides a highly adaptable means for comparing the impacts of different risks across multiple projects and at an enterprise level.

Table 5-6   Example of Quantized Impact Levels

Score	Monetary Loss
1	Under $100
2	$100–$1,000
3	$1,000–$10,000
4	$10,000–$100,000
5	$100,000–$1 million
6	$1 million–$10 million
7	$10 million–$100 million
8	$100 million–$1 billion
9	$1 billion–$10 billion

Table 5-6   Example of Quantized Impact Levels

Score	Monetary Loss
10	Over $10 billion

Multiattribute Impact Scoring   At times, it is challenging to assess impact using only one attribute. Often, impact results from a confluence of factors. As such, a team might need to assess impact based on multiple attributes. Table 5-7 provides an example of determining impact based on multiple attributes.[19]

Table 5-7   Example of Multiattribute Impact Ratings

Rating	Cost Overrun	Schedule	Technical
Low	Less than 1%	Slip 1 week	Slight effect on performance
Medium	Less than 5%	Slip 2 weeks	Moderate effect on performance
High	Less than 10%	Slip 1 month	Severe effect on performance
Critical	10% or more	Slip more than 1 month	Mission cannot be accomplished

If possible, try to use attributes that are not too project specific because assessing risk at the program, portfolio, and/or enterprise level will be challenging.

Risk Prioritization Activities

Risk prioritization is the process of ranking risks in order of their overall threat to an organization and, therefore, their priority for action. Because a goal of risk analysis is to prioritize risks and to drive decision making regarding commitment of project resources toward risk control, it should be noted that each project team should select a method for prioritizing risks that is appropriate to a project, a team, stakeholders, and risk management infrastructure (tools and processes). The simplest form of common quantitative means to prioritize risk is to sort them by a single calculated value, called *risk exposure*, derived by multiplying risk probability by risk impact. Like impact scoring, other more advanced means of prioritization are based on multiple attributes.

Risk Exposure: Simple Prioritization Approach   Risk exposure measures the overall threat of a risk, combining information expressing the likelihood of actual loss (i.e., probability) with information expressing the magnitude of a potential loss (i.e., impact) into a single rating estimate. Risk exposure can be represented either in numerical terms or as natural language expressions.

When nonnumeric scores are used to quantify probability and impact, it is sometimes convenient to create a matrix that considers the possible combinations of scores to determine a resultant exposure rating. For example, Table 5-8 is a common assignment of exposure given natural language expressions of probability and impact. In this arrangement, it is easy to

19 Elaine Hall, *Managing Risk*, 101.

classify risks as low, medium, high, and critical depending on their position within the diagonal bands of increasing score.

Table 5-8   Example of Exposure Rating Based on Nonnumeric Ratings

Probability/Impact	Low	Medium	High	Critical
High	M	M	H	C
Medium	L	M	M	H
Low	L	L	M	M

Multiattribute Prioritization Approach   In addition to risk exposure, some projects can benefit from use of other attributes in determining risk priority. Commonly, weighted multiattribute techniques are used to factor in other components that a team wishes to consider in a ranking process such as required time frame, magnitude of potential opportunity gain, or reliability of probability estimates and physical or information asset valuation. An example of a weighted prioritization matrix that factors in not only probability and impact but critical time window and cost to implement an effective control is shown in Table 5-9, where ranking score is calculated using this formula:

Ranking value = 0.5 (Probability × Impact) − 0.2 (when needed) + 0.3 (Control cost
× Probability control will work)

Table 5-9   Example of Multiattribute Exposure Scoring and Prioritization

Probability	Impact (thousands of dollars)	When Needed (weeks)	Cost to Implement (thousands of dollars)	Likelihood of Control Working	Resultant Ranking Score
0.50	500	1	2	0.50	125.1
0.84	200	4	4	0.33	83.6
0.66	150	3	12	0.50	50.7
0.33	200	2	20	0.84	37.6

This method enables a team to factor in risk exposure and schedule criticality (when a risk control or mitigation plan must be completed to be effective), and to incorporate the cost and efficacy of the plan into the decision-making process. This general approach enables a team to rank risks in terms of the contribution toward any goals that they have set for a project and provides a foundation for evaluating risks both from the perspective of losses (impact) and opportunities (positive gains).

Deactivating Risks   Risks can be deactivated or classified as inactive so that a team concentrates on those risks that require active management. Classifying a risk as inactive means that the team has decided that it is not worth the effort needed to track that risk. A decision to deactivate a risk is made during risk analysis.

Some risks are deactivated because their probability is effectively zero and likely to remain so, that is, they have extremely unlikely conditions. Other risks are deactivated because their impact is below a threshold where it is worth the effort of planning a mitigation or contingency strategy; it is simply more cost-effective to suffer the impact if a risk is realized. Note that it is not advisable to deactivate risks above this impact threshold even if their exposure is low, unless the team is confident that the probability (and hence the exposure) will remain low in all foreseeable circumstances. Also, note that deactivating a risk is not the same as resolving one; a deactivated risk might reappear under certain conditions and the team might choose to reclassify a risk as active and initiate risk management activities.

Outputs

Risk analysis provides a team with a means to prioritize a master risk list to guide the team in risk planning activities. Because a master risk list can include many risks, a team should focus only on the highest priority risks, collectively called the *top risks list*.

Prioritized Master Risk List   A master risk list was introduced during the risk identification step. The analysis step enables a team and stakeholders to mutually agree on a means to prioritize risks in a master risk list. Table 5-10 is an example of a prioritized master risk list in tabular form using a two-factor (i.e., probability and impact) estimate approach.

Table 5-10   **Example of Prioritized Master Risk List**

Condition	Consequence	Probability	Impact	Exposure	Priority
Long project schedule	Loss of funding at end of year	80%	High	2.4	1
No coding standards for new programming language	Ship with more bugs	45%	Medium	0.9	2
No written requirements specification	Some solution features will not be implemented	30%	Medium	0.6	3

Note: Low impact = 1, medium impact = 2, high impact = 3.

Top Risks List   Risk analysis weighs the threat of each risk to help a team decide which risks merit action. Managing risks takes time and effort away from other activities, so it is important for a team to do only what is necessary to manage them.

A simple but effective technique for monitoring risk is to list risks and establish a cut-off for ones that are considered high priority (i.e., top risks list). The top risks list is externally visible to all stakeholders and often is included in critical reporting documents, such as the vision/scope document, project plan, and project status reports.

Typically, a team identifies a limited number of high-priority risks that must be managed (usually 10 or fewer for most projects) and allocates project resources to address them. If it becomes necessary to address more than the top 10 risks, the list should be segmented and the higher priority risks addressed before moving to less critical risks. After ranking risks, a team should focus on a risk management strategy and how to incorporate risk action plans into the overall plan.

Additional Analysis Methods

Some teams might choose to perform additional levels of analysis to clarify their understanding of project risk. Alternate techniques performed by the team to provide additional clarification of project risk are discussed in standard project management and risk management textbooks.[20],[21] Techniques such as decision tree analysis, causal analysis, Pareto analysis, simulation, and sensitivity analysis have all been used to provide a richer quantitative understanding of project risk. These techniques provide good root cause analysis that can help identify issues not apparent by analyzing individual risks. The decision to use these techniques should be based on value that a team feels these tools bring in either driving prioritization or in clarifying the planning process to offset resource costs.

Step 3: Plan and Schedule to Manage Risks

Risk planning and scheduling is the third step in the risk management process. Planning involves developing detailed strategies and actions for each of the top risks, prioritizing risk actions, and creating an integrated risk management plan. Scheduling involves the integration of the tasks required to implement risk action plans into a project schedule by assigning them to individuals and actively tracking their status. The inputs and outputs of this step are depicted schematically in Figure 5-5.

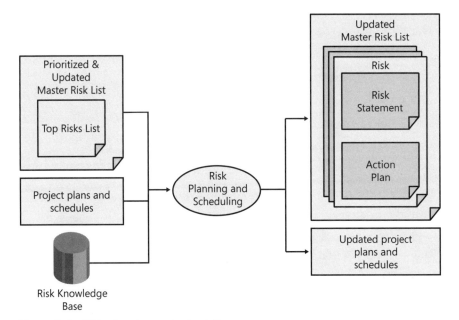

Figure 5-5   Risk planning and scheduling

20 Project Management Institute, *A Guide to the Project Management Body of Knowledge 2000 Edition* (Newtown Square, PA: Project Management Institute, 2000), ch. 11.

21 Elaine Hall, *Managing Risk.*

Goals

The goals of the risk planning and scheduling step are to develop detailed plans for addressing the top risks identified during risk analysis and to integrate these plans with project plans using standard project management processes to ensure that they are completed.

Inputs

MSF advocates that risk planning be tightly integrated into the standard project planning processes and infrastructure. Inputs to the risk planning process include not only a master risk list and information from the risk management knowledge base, but also project plans and schedules.

Risk Planning Activities

Risk planning is a process of trying to reduce risk exposure of the top risks and developing action plans for those that remain top risks. The first step in the process is to attempt to reduce exposure for each risk (i.e., reduce probability and/or impact). If not reduced sufficiently, action plans need to be formed to handle a risk should it be realized.

Exposure Reduction   Consistent with the proactive philosophy of MSF, it is better to mitigate a risk before it is realized. In support of this, a team should first seek to reduce risk exposure, starting with the top priority risks and working down in priority. The following are a few risk reduction approaches to consider:

- Address the condition to reduce the probability.

- Address the consequences to minimize the impact.

- Look for root causes as opposed to symptoms.

- Determine the root cause, and then look for similar situations in other areas that might arise from the same cause.

- Be aware of dependencies and interactions among risks.

- For those risks a team is able to control, apply the resources needed to reduce a risk.

- For those risks outside the control of a team, find a workaround or transfer (escalate) a risk to individuals that have the authority to intervene.

Risk Action Planning   So now that the risks have been identified, a team needs to do something about those pesky risks—but what? If exposure reduction activities have not yielded sufficient results, action plans need to be developed to deal with the potential realization of the risks deemed worthy of redress, typically the top risks.

The first step in formulating an action plan is for the team to consider which of the following six approaches to handling risk best fit the needs of a project (explained further in subsequent sections). Based on which approach is selected, plan details need to be worked out. This includes planned adjustments in committed resources, schedule, and feature set, resulting in a set of *risk action items* specifying individual tasks to be completed by team members. A team should also understand how these tasks will be integrated into standard project plans and schedules, should it be necessary.

- **Research**   Does a team know enough about this risk? Is there a need to study a risk further to acquire more information and better determine characteristics of a risk before deciding what action to take?

- **Accept**   Should a team live with the consequences if a risk was realized? Is a risk acceptable with no further action required?

- **Avoid**   Should a team avoid a risk by changing scope?

- **Transfer**   Should a team avoid a risk by transferring it to another project, team, organization, or individual?

- **Mitigation**   Should a team do anything to reduce the probability or impact of a risk?

- **Contingency**   Can the impact be reduced through a planned reaction?

Research   Much of a risk that is present in projects is related to uncertainty surrounding incomplete information. Risks that are related to lack of knowledge can often be resolved or managed most effectively by learning more about a domain before proceeding. For example, a team might choose to pursue market research or conduct user focus groups to learn more about user baseline skills or willingness to use a given technology before completing a project plan. If the decision by a team is to perform research, a risk plan should include an appropriate research proposal, including hypotheses to be tested or questions to be answered, staffing, and any needed laboratory equipment.

Accept   Some risks are such that it is simply not feasible to intervene with effective preventative or corrective measures, so a team elects to accept a risk to realize an opportunity. Acceptance is not a "do nothing" strategy, and a plan should include development of a documented rationale for why a team has elected to accept a risk and not develop mitigation or contingency plans. It is prudent to continue monitoring such risks through a project life cycle in the event that changes occur in probability, impact, or the ability to execute preventative or contingency measures related to this risk. These ongoing commitments to monitor or watch a risk should have appropriate resources committed and tracking metrics established within an overall project management process.

Avoid   On occasion, a risk is identified that is easily controlled by changing the scope of a project in such a fashion as to eliminate the risk altogether (e.g., remove activities that have unacceptable risk). The risk plan should then include documentation of the rationale for a change, and the project plan should be updated and any needed design change or scope change processes initiated.

Transfer   Sometimes it is possible for a risk to be transferred so that it can be managed by another entity outside of a project. Examples where risk is transferred include these:

- Insurance

- Using external consultants with greater expertise
- Purchasing a component instead of building it
- Outsourcing services

Risk transfer does not mean risk elimination. Rather, it means a reduction to an acceptable level of risk. In general, these risks still require proactive management and might even generate new risks. For instance, using an external consultant might transfer technical risks outside of the team, but can introduce risks in project management and budgetary areas.

Mitigation   Risk mitigation involves actions and activities performed ahead of time either to prevent a risk from occurring altogether or to reduce the impact or consequences of its occurring to an acceptable level. For example, using redundant network connections to the Internet reduces the probability of losing access by eliminating a single point of failure. In cases where mitigation is not available, it is essential to consider effective contingency planning instead.

Because of project constraints (e.g., financial pressures), sometimes it is not possible to mitigate a risk even though the risk might be in the top risk list. In this situation, a team might need to postpone implementing risk mitigation until more definitive effects of a risk are evident. To facilitate this, a team can choose to use a *mitigation trigger*. A trigger is a defined event, situation, or condition that, when it occurs, invokes a respective plan or action. A mitigation trigger invokes the start of the respective mitigation efforts. A team establishes mitigation triggers based on the type of risk or the type of impact that will be encountered. There are three types of triggers:

- *Point-in-time triggers* are built around dates, generally the latest date by which something has to happen (e.g., missed planned checkpoint completion date)
- *Threshold triggers* rely on things that can be measured or counted (e.g., bug count reaches 75)
- *Events triggers* rely on specific events to occur (e.g., team members are reassigned or resign)

> **Lesson Learned**   It is very important to define crisp, irrefutable triggers. Many times, because of loosely defined triggers, teams get stuck arguing over whether a risk has been realized.

Contingency   Risk contingency planning involves creation of one or more fallback plans that are activated if efforts to prevent the adverse event fail. Contingency plans are necessary for as many risks as is prudent, including those that have mitigation plans. They address what to do if a risk is realized. This means focusing on the consequence and minimizing its impact. To be effective, a team should make contingency plans well in advance.

Each contingency plan is invoked by satisfying criteria defined within an associated contingency trigger. It is important for a team to agree on contingency triggers and their values with the appropriate stakeholders as early as possible so that there is no delay committing budgets or resources needed to carry out a contingency plan.

Risk Scheduling Activities

Risk scheduling is the process of integrating risk management plan tasks into a project schedule. Scheduling risk management and control activities does not differ from the standard approach recommended by MSF toward scheduling project activities in general. It is important that a team understand that risk control activities are an expected part of a project and are not an additional set of responsibilities to be done on a voluntary basis. All risk activities should be accounted for within project scheduling and status reporting processes.

Outputs

The outputs from risk planning and scheduling should include specific *risk action plans* employing one of the six approaches discussed earlier at a step-by-step level of detail. A master risk list should be updated to reflect the additional information included in mitigation and contingency plans. It is convenient to summarize risk management plans into a single document.

Updated Master Risk List   Top risks within a master risk list are updated with additional information derived from risk exposure reduction efforts as well as action plan development. Because risk action plans are sometimes complex and detailed, they are often put in a separate document.

Risk Action Plan   A risk action plan outlines an approach (e.g., avoid a risk) and tasks necessary to handle a stated risk. Table 5-11 lists examples of simple action plans associated with risk statements, where a selected approach is mitigation with contingency as the backup approach should mitigation not work.

Table 5-11   Example of Risk Action Plans

Risk Statement		Risk Action Plan			
Condition	**Consequence**	**Mitigation**	**Contingency**	**Trigger**	**Owner**
Developers to work with new shipping technology	Development time will take longer because of the need for developers to learn.	Provide technical training to developers	Revert back to previous version	Developers have not passed related technology exam by project plan approval	Kim Akers
Development team is divided between London and Los Angeles	Communication among the team will be difficult.	Hold a weekly team meeting by teleconferencing between London and Los Angeles	Establish an Internet-based communication portal for posting important project information	Lack of communication results in schedule slippage	Don Hall

Should the selected approach be mitigation with contingency as backup (which is the most common approach), a team should consider including the following information when developing their action plans:

- **Risk mitigation strategy**   A paragraph or two of text describing a team strategy for mitigating a specific risk, including any assumptions that have been made

- **Risk mitigation strategy metrics**   Metrics a team will use to determine whether planned risk mitigation actions are achieving the desired results

- **Risk action items**   A list of actions a team is taking to implement a strategy for a specific risk, including the due date for completion and the person responsible

- **Risk contingency strategy**   A paragraph or two describing a team strategy in the event that the actions planned to manage a risk do not work (A team would execute a risk contingency strategy if a risk contingency trigger was satisfied.)

- **Risk contingency strategy metrics**   Metrics used by a team to determine whether a contingency strategy is working

Updated Project Schedule and Project Plan   Planning documents related to risk should be integrated into the overall project planning documents. A master project schedule should be updated with new tasks generated by the action plans.

Step 4: Track and Report Risk Status

Risk tracking and reporting is the fourth step in the MSF Risk Management Process. Risk tracking and reporting is the *proactive* process of managing risk prevention (e.g., mitigation plan execution) and reporting associated status. Risk tracking is the monitoring function of a risk action plan. It also ensures that assigned tasks implementing preventative measures are completed in a timely fashion within project resource constraints. Risk reporting provides updated status on risk metrics and provides notification of triggering events. Risk tracking and reporting is depicted schematically in Figure 5-6.

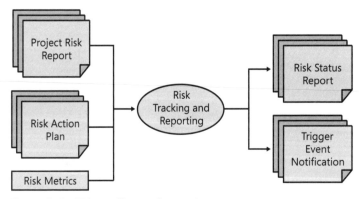

Figure 5-6   Risk tracking and reporting

Goals

The goals of the risk tracking and reporting step are these:

- Track and report status of a preventative portion of risk action plan execution

- Monitor and report project risk metrics

- Provide notification when contingency plan triggers are met so that a risk's respective contingency plan is initiated

Inputs

The principal inputs to the risk tracking and reporting step are the following:

- Risk action plans that contain specific preventative measures and which specify project metrics and trigger values are to be monitored

- The relevant project status reports that are used to track progress within the standard project management infrastructure

Depending on specific project metrics being tracked by a team, other sources of information such as project tracking databases, source code repositories or check-in systems, or even human resources management systems can provide tracking data for a project team.

Risk Tracking Activities

Risk tracking activities include monitoring risk metrics and triggering events to ensure that planned risk actions are working. A team executes the actions in a mitigation plan as part of the overall team activity. Progress toward these risk-related action items and relevant changes in trigger values are captured and used to create specific risk status reports for each risk.

Risk Reporting Activities

Risk status reporting provides a project team and stakeholders with regular, detailed updates of project risks. The particulars of who, what, when, and how to report risks should be encompassed in a project communications plan. At a minimum, risk status reports should consider four possible risk management situations for each risk:

- A risk is resolved, completing a risk action plan.

- Risk actions are consistent with a risk management plan, in which case risk plan actions continue as planned.

- Some risk actions differ from a risk management plan, in which case corrective measures should be defined and implemented.

- A situation has changed significantly with respect to one or more risks and will usually involve reanalyzing risks or replanning an activity.

For external reporting, a team should report the top risks and then summarize the status of risk management actions. It is also useful to show the previous ranking of risks and the number of times each risk has been on the top risks list. As a project team takes actions to manage risks, the total risk exposure for a project (i.e., the cumulative exposure of the top risks) should begin to approach acceptable levels.

Outputs

The main outputs from this step are regular, detailed risk status reports and notifications of any contingency trigger conditions that have been met, which subsequently invoke a risk's contingency plan (i.e., a risk has been realized).

Risk Status Report   The purposes of a risk status report are to communicate changes in risk status and report progress of mitigation planning activities. Typically, a communications plan calls for a project team status report and a higher-level summary for people outside of a project team. Information that is useful in a project team risk status report includes the following:

- Risk name
- Risk classification
- Probability, impact, and exposure at identification
- Current probability, impact, and exposure
- Risk rating
- Summary of mitigation and contingency plan(s)
- Status toward completion of mitigation plans
- Readiness of contingency plans
- Trigger criteria
- Planned actions
- Risk owner

Another type of risk status report is for people external to a project team (e.g., executives and stakeholders). Useful information to include in this summary risk status report includes the following:

- Project name
- Risk level by project area—typically colored red, yellow, green to visually represent high, medium, and low risk ratings
- Risk trend (e.g., getting better [+], staying the same [=], getting worse [−])
- Summary of mitigation and contingency plan activity

> **Lesson Learned**   A summary risk status report is most effective when it contains few words and many visuals so a reader can get a quick, intuitive grasp of the overall risk status.

Step 5: Control Risk

The fifth step in the MSF Risk Management Process is risk control. Risk control is the *reactive* process of managing risk contingency plan execution and reporting associated status. Risk control also includes initiation of project change control requests when changes in risk status or risk plans could result in changes in project features, resources, or schedule. The inputs and outputs of this step are depicted in Figure 5-7.

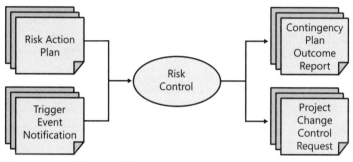

Figure 5-7   Risk control

Goals

The goals of the risk control step are these:

- Minimize impact of realized risk by successful execution of contingency plans

- Keep project collateral current with initiation of project change control requests when changes in risk status or risk plans could result in changes in project features, resources, or schedule

Inputs

The inputs to the risk control step are notifications of what triggers have involved their respective contingency plans and risk action plans that detail contingency plan activities to be carried out by project team members.

Risk Control Activities

Risk control is the process of executing risk contingency plans for realized risks and providing updated status for affected risks and overall changes to risk analyses, priorities, plans, and schedules. Risk control also includes initiation of project change control requests when changes in risk status or risk plans could result in changes in project features, resources, or schedule.

Risk control activities should use standard project management processes for initiating, monitoring, and assessing progress along a planned course of action. Specific details of risk plans vary from project to project, but a general process for task status reporting should be used. It is important to maintain continuous risk identification to detect secondary risks that might appear or be amplified because of the execution of a contingency plan.

Outputs

The outputs from a risk control step are project change control requests and contingency plan outcome reports.

Change Control Request   A change control request is documentation of and a request for permission to change a solution or delivery of a solution. A change might be necessary as part of contingency plan execution.

Contingency Plan Outcome Report   A contingency plan outcome report documents the results, status, and lessons learned from contingency plan execution. This information likely will become part of a project and enterprise risk knowledge base and will be rolled into a risk status report, as discussed previously. It is important to capture as much information as is possible about problems when they occur or about a contingency plan when it is invoked to determine the efficacy of such a plan or strategy on risk control.

Step 6: Learn from Risks

Learning from risks from a strategic, enterprise, and organizational perspective is the sixth and last step in the MSF Risk Management Process. This step extracts, documents, and communicates project risk lessons learned and captures relevant project artifacts in an enterprise-wide risk knowledge base. This step, sometimes referred to as *risk leverage*, emphasizes the value that is returned to an organization by increased capabilities and maturing at team, project, and organizational levels and improvement of a risk management process. Risk learning should be a continuous activity throughout the MSF Risk Management Process and can begin at any time. It focuses on three key objectives:

- Providing quality assurance on current risk management activities so that a team gains regular feedback

- Capturing lessons learned, especially around risk identification and successful mitigation strategies, for the benefit of other teams; this contributes to a risk knowledge base

- Improving a risk management process by capturing feedback from a team

Risk review meetings provide a forum for learning from risk. They should be held on a regular basis, and, like other MSF reviews, they benefit from advance planning; development of a clear, published agenda in advance; participation of all participants; and free, honest communication in a "blame-free" environment. Figure 5-8 depicts a learning step.

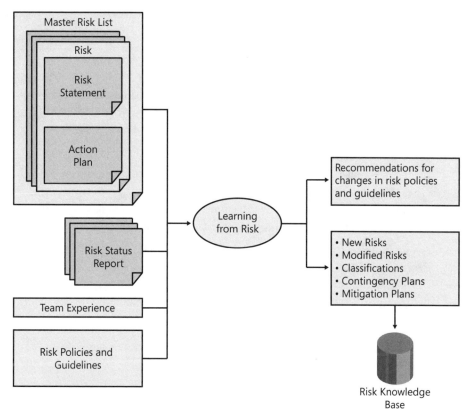

Figure 5-8   Learning from risk

Goals

The goals of the learning step are these:

- Provide quality assurance on current risk management activities
- Extract lessons learned to use in future projects
- Capture relevant project artifacts for a risk knowledge base
- Improve risk management process

Inputs

Learning comes from and as a result of a combination of many inputs. Basically, learning comes from all aspects of risk management.

Risk Learning Activities

Learning spans the range from tangible improvements in a risk management process to less tangible personal team member growth. Learning needs to be captured, managed, and retained in such a way that others are able to draw meaning later.

Capturing Learning About Risk   How does a team capture learning because learning comes in so many forms and with so many levels of learning? How do they enable personal learning, which is very different from institutional learning?

One of the tangible areas of experiential refinement is risk classifications. Refining risk classification is a powerful means for ensuring that lessons learned from previous experience are made available to teams performing future risk assessments. Two key aspects of learning associated with risk classifications are as follows:

- **New risks**   If a team encounters an issue that has not been identified earlier as a risk, they should review whether any signs (leading indicators) could have helped to predict a risk. It might be that the existing risk classifications need to be updated to help future identification of a risk condition. Alternatively, a team might have identified a new project risk that should be added to an existing risk knowledge base.

- **Successful mitigation strategies**   Another key learning point is to capture experiences of strategies that have been used successfully (or even unsuccessfully) to mitigate risks. Use of a standard risk classification provides a meaningful way to group related risks so that teams are easily able to find details of risk management strategies that have been successful in the past.

Managing Learning from Risks   Organizations using risk management techniques often find that they need to create a structured approach to managing project risk. Otherwise, lessons learned identified by team members quickly fade away as teams refocus on the next project. Experience has shown that elements of successful learning management include the following:

- An individual should be given ownership of a specific risk classification area and responsibility for approving changes.

- Risk classifications should balance the need for a comprehensive coverage of risks against complexity and usability. Sometimes creating different risk classifications for different project types improves usability dramatically.

- A risk knowledge base should be set up to maintain risk classifications, definitions, diagnostic criteria, and scoring systems and to capture feedback on a team's experience with using them.

- A risk review process should be well managed to ensure all learning is captured. For a project team, reviews can be held at a project closure review, when the results of risk management should be apparent to all.

Retaining Learning from Risks   Most often, retaining lessons learned includes a knowledge base. It is one form of knowledge repository that can range from a simple collection of risk collateral (e.g., action plans) to a complex collaboration server that helps categorize and index the knowledge for faster identification and retrieval. Sometimes knowledge retention is as simple as the shared experience among a team. Like what has been said before about other parts of MSF, with risk knowledge management, keep it simple and do only as much as provides a compelling return on investment of time and effort.

Outputs

Just as there might be areas within risk management that team members learn from, those same areas might also benefit and be refined based on those lessons learned. For instance, a risk management process should be refined and matured to better fit an organization. Part of this maturation is typically getting better at retaining knowledge, usually within a knowledge base. The process of identifying and quantifying risk greatly benefits from risk lessons learned. As discussed at the beginning of this chapter, using risk classification is a great way to stimulate a team's thinking and to make sure a team considers enough risk areas.

Risk Knowledge Base   A risk knowledge base is a key driver of continual improvement in risk management. It is a formal or informal mechanism by which an organization captures learning to assist in future risk management. Without some form of knowledge base, an organization might have difficulty adopting a proactive approach to risk management. A risk knowledge base differs from a risk management database, which is used to store and track individual risk items, plans, and status during a project.

Context-Specific Risk Classifications   Risk identification might be refined by developing risk classifications for specific repeated project contexts. For example, a project delivery organization might develop classifications for different types of projects. As more experience is gained on work within a project context, risks can be made more specific and associated with successful mitigation strategies.

Please keep in mind that making risk classifications more specialized increases the potential that these classifications might not be applicable outside of a project.

Levels of Risk Management Maturity

At the lowest level of risk management maturity, project and process teams have no form of knowledge base. Each team has to start fresh every time it undertakes risk management. In this environment, an approach to risk management is normally reactive, but can transition to the next higher level of active risk management. However, a team does not manage risks proactively.

The next level of maturity involves an informal knowledge base, using implicit learning gained by more experienced members of an organization. This is often achieved by implementing a risk board where experienced practitioners review how each team is performing. This approach encourages active risk management and might lead to limited proactive management through the introduction of policies. An example of a proactive risk management policy is "before approval to proceed all projects of more than 20 days need a risk review."

The next level of maturity and the first level of formality in knowledge management come through providing a more structured approach to risk identification. MSF advocates the use of risk classifications for this purpose. With formal capture and indexing of experience, an organization is capable of much more proactive management as the underlying causes of risks start to be identified.

Finally, mature organizations record not only the indicators likely to lead to risk, but also the strategies adopted to manage those risks and their success rate. With this form of knowledge management, the identification and planning steps of a risk process are based on shared experience from many teams, and an organization starts to optimize its costs of risk management and return on project investment.

When contemplating implementation of a risk knowledge base, experience has shown that:

- The value of a risk knowledge base increases as more of the work becomes repetitive (such as organizations focusing on similar projects, or for ongoing operational processes)

- When an organization has dissimilar projects, a less complex knowledge base is suggested and easier to maintain

Risk management should not become an automatic process that obviates the need for a team to think about risks. Even in repetitive situations, the business environment, customer expectations, team skills, and technology are always changing. A team, therefore, must assess appropriate risk management strategies for their specific project situation.

Summary

Risk is inherent in every aspect and at all levels of an endeavor. Therefore, a solution team needs to have a comprehensive and flexible approach to handle risk proactively. This includes managing risk across projects, should multiple projects be necessary to realize a solution. The same holds true for handling risk at an organizational level, should multiple solutions be required to implement a business initiative or strategy. Handling risk does not need to be cumbersome, but the process of handling risk needs to be well thought out and structured to enable the team to remain agile and able to mitigate a risk quickly should it be realized.

In the spirit of that approach, MSF provides the Risk Management Discipline. It is a systematic approach to handling risk on many levels. In this chapter, a matching risk management process was also discussed. The MSF Risk Management Process consists of six logical steps: identification, analysis, planning, tracking, controlling, and learning. The goals, inputs, activities, and outputs for each step were discussed. To handle risk effectively, a project team should cycle through these steps continuously during a project life cycle. Once the team has a reasonable mastery of handling risks, they will realize that risks are not a sign of negligence or failure. Conversely, a healthy risk management culture will turn risk into opportunity.

Chapter 6
Establishing a Solution Delivery Lifecycle

Hundreds, if not thousands, of books describe and define solutions delivery and its processes. The reasons so many books are written on the subject is because no one delivery model or process has yet met the needs of all projects. Each method provides a different perspective on how to balance team member productivity with team delivery predictability. Too little process might enable high initial productivity, but at the expense of low predictability and quality. Too much process might ensure predictability, but at a severe cost in productivity. So, what is the right balance for a project and for an organization?

As discussed in this chapter, a project team should select and adapt a solution delivery life cycle that best fits their needs within the bounds of their organizational guidelines. This involves their not only adapting life cycle guidance, but also understanding and adapting workflow, policies, templates, reports, permissions, and so forth. This, of course, is much easier for a project team if an organization has tools, templates, and guidance preconfigured and ready for adapting. Other factors that need to be considered include process maturity and tolerance of a team as well as maturity of technology being used. To start to determine which solution delivery life cycle will work best, a team needs to understand the environment(s) in which they must deliver their solution.

> **Clarity Point**   The difference between *project life cycle* and *solution delivery life cycle* is scope. Project life cycle is focused on a project to deliver some or all of a solution; whereas solution delivery life cycle is focused on a solution, which can encompass a few projects to deliver a solution. Taking an even broader perspective, a team might need to consider using an *enterprise life cycle* in which many solutions are needed to deliver on a business strategy.

Solution Delivery Environment

Understanding a solution delivery environment is an ever-changing challenge. Challenges come from every aspect of solutions delivery and will likely seem overwhelming at first. They might manifest from within and externally to a project, including externally to an organization. They might come from gathering requirements or dealing with conflicts among project constraints.

With so many imposing constraints and challenges, where does a team start? As depicted in Figure 6-1, commonly a team starts by trying to understand business pain point(s) to derive a set of business needs. As the needs are better understood and quantified, a team is better enabled to build and deliver a solution that meets those needs.

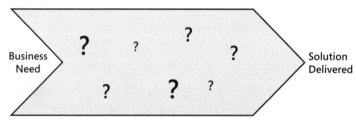

Figure 6-1   How does a team get from business need to delivered solution?

Many good ways might exist to handle these solution delivery challenges. Following is Microsoft's approach.

The Microsoft Solution Delivery Lifecycle

Experience has shown that solution delivery challenges are easier to manage if a team segments them into workable pieces, starting with two parts as shown in Figure 6-2. The first part deals with challenges associated with defining and building a solution. The second part deals with challenges associated with keeping it up and running.

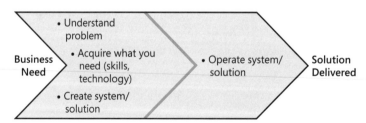

Figure 6-2   Decomposition of solution delivery

Rather than providing another limited-scope methodology, Microsoft offers two interrelated frameworks to address these two parts, as depicted in Figure 6-3. Both frameworks use proven practices from Microsoft, its partners, its customers, and industry expertise. Whereas the Microsoft Solutions Framework (MSF) addresses solution definition and development, the

Microsoft Operations Framework (MOF) addresses solution operations and sustainment. Although very important to the successful delivery of a solution in that a team designs a solution to address the qualities of service (e.g., availability) optimally, MOF is only lightly addressed in this book. For more information on MOF, please see the sidebar titled "MSF and Microsoft Operations Framework" that follows.

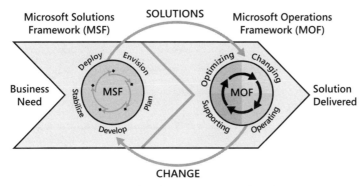

Figure 6-3 The Microsoft Solution Delivery Lifecycle

MSF and Microsoft Operations Framework

Whereas MSF is focused on defining, building, and deploying solutions, Microsoft Operations Framework (MOF), a related framework, is focused on making sure a solution operates optimally (i.e., use MSF to build it right and MOF to run it right).

MOF provides operational guidance that enables organizations to achieve mission-critical system reliability, availability, supportability, and manageability of Microsoft products and technologies. MOF is based on an internationally accepted set of IT service management best practices called the *IT Infrastructure Library* (ITIL) from the U.K. government's Office of Government Commerce (OGC). MOF is best viewed as a superset of the ITIL standards.

MOF provides operational guidance in the form of white papers, operations guides, assessment tools, best practices, case studies, templates, support tools, courseware, and services. This guidance addresses the people, process, technology, and management issues pertaining to complex, distributed, and heterogeneous technology environments.

Microsoft created MOF by using lessons learned through the evolution of MSF, building on top of ITIL's best practice for organizational structure and process ownership, and modeling the critical success factors used by partners, customers, and Microsoft's internal Operations and Technology Group (OTG).

MSF and MOF share foundational principles and core disciplines. They differ in their application of these principles and disciplines, each using unique Team and Governance Models and proven practices that are specific to their respective domains. MSF presents team structure and activities from a solution delivery perspective, whereas MOF presents team structure and activities from a service management perspective. In MSF, the emphasis is on projects; in MOF, it is on running the production environment. MSF and MOF provide an interface between a solution development domain and a solution operations domain.

MSF and MOF are designed to be used in conjunction throughout the technology life cycle to provide business-driven technology solutions successfully—from inception to delivery through operations to final retirement. MSF and MOF are intended for use within the typical organizational structures that exist in businesses today; they collectively describe how diverse departments work together to achieve common business goals in a mutually supportive environment.

For more information on MOF, see *http://www.microsoft.com/mof.*

Foundational Principles Applied to Solution Delivery Lifecycle

The Microsoft Solution Delivery Lifecycle is grounded in MSF's foundational principles. Adherence to these principles enables the Microsoft Solution Delivery Lifecycle to provide the right guidance to the right people at the right time. An understanding of these principles enables customization of the life cycle to fit an organization and its inherent processes optimally.

Foster Open Communications

As discussed, the Microsoft Solution Delivery Lifecycle contains two symbiotic frameworks that are based on openly sharing design, development, deployment, and sustainment information. This open flow of information helps to deliver a solution that not only meets stakeholder needs but also is operationally viable, sustainable, and supportable.

Work Toward a Shared Vision

The structure of the life cycle is established to reach a shared vision incrementally through input and consensus from all advocacy groups. It is expected that initially the vision of a solution might not be complete and perfect. A shared vision is something that is initially defined and then evolves as a better understanding of a solution and how to deliver it unfolds through an iterative approach. What is important is that it is clearly and commonly understood, regardless of its completeness.

Empower Team Members

Typically, empowerment needs to be earned. Incrementally delivering a solution provides repeated opportunities to demonstrate reliability and dependability—key ingredients for empowerment. It also provides opportunities to learn and grow. This minimizes readiness gaps that might have hindered others from empowering specific team members.

Once team members have been empowered, the Microsoft Solution Delivery Lifecycle provides many areas of self-governance. Activities and deliverables are coordinated by using checkpoints as opposed to low-level management of team member activities.

Establish Clear Accountability, Shared Responsibility

As discussed in detail in later chapters, each aspect of the Solution Delivery Lifecycle has singular accountability supported by shared responsibility. Supporting this concept, MSF instills checkpoint-driven accountability. Although one advocacy group is accountable for the successful achievement of each checkpoint, achieving success takes a coordinated effort and shared responsibility with the other advocacy groups.

Deliver Incremental Value

The incremental approach built into the Microsoft Solution Delivery Lifecycle provides for incremental delivery of value. Each enactment track is focused on incrementally evolving a solution while maximizing business value. Further supporting this idea, each track involves multiple solution iterations to enable rapid and agile replanning should what is being delivered not meet stakeholder needs and expectations. Having a shippable solution at every iteration is an important part of helping validate a solution and its requirements and to gain support from stakeholders.

Stay Agile, Expect and Adapt to Change

The Microsoft Solution Delivery Lifecycle and subordinate MSF Governance Model are structured to provide just enough process and guidance to help teams deliver successfully. Given that no two solutions, projects, teams, subteams, and so forth are alike, the Solution Delivery Lifecycle and Governance Model were designed to allow a team to adapt them to provide the necessary level of process formality and rigor.

The integration of the MSF Governance Model with the MSF Team Model makes a formidable combination for project success if effectively instilled into an organization. Collectively, they provide flexible but defined road maps for successful project delivery that takes into account the uniqueness of an organization's culture, project types, and personnel strengths.

Invest in Quality

Although it might seem counterintuitive that an agile approach to solution delivery such as MSF should have so many checkpoints and deliverables, the Solution Delivery Lifecycle is structured to be lightweight and flexible. Should something become too overtaxing or burdensome, adapt it to be more amenable. Continue to improve portions of the life cycle that provide value and either "fix" or eliminate portions that do not. With an incremental delivery approach, many opportunities to refine project processes and solution quality exist.

Learn from All Experiences

Teams that commit time in the schedule for learning and reviews create an environment of ongoing improvement and continuing success. In addition, one of the ways Microsoft is successful in creating a culture that is willing to learn is by adding learning and knowledge sharing as part of individual review goals.

An iterative approach to solution delivery provides many opportunities to learn and experiment. It also enables team members to hone their skills to improve their readiness.

Partner with Customers

The iterative nature of the Microsoft Solutions Delivery Lifecycle provides many opportunities to collaborate with customers and solicit their feedback. Each checkpoint provides an opportunity to review progress against planned work as well as review and provide feedback on what was built thus far. It is unfortunate that sometimes project teams wait to engage with customers well into a life cycle.

An iterative approach also enables customers to refine and even change their minds as to what is required of a solution. Sometimes they might also redefine "value." Too often, project teams are not agile enough to be able to respond to these types of customer feedback.

Solution Delivery Lifecycle Fundamentals

Every project needs some means to identify, govern, and guide all project activities needed to translate business needs into a deployed solution. As a team better understands their solution delivery life cycle, they are able to identify how their project needs to be governed given organizational and project constraints. Working through project particulars, they are able to define their governance and project process activities as well as the order in which the activities are performed (i.e., a governance model). An appropriate governance model provides many benefits, including the following:

- Streamlines a project
- Guides and coordinates the flow of activity
- Helps drive a project closer to successful completion
- Accelerates orderly production of project deliverables
- Keeps solution aligned with business objectives
- Provides a means of keeping projects on track
- Increases predictability and visibility
- Provides a phased transition to operations

The following sections discuss a few key aspects of a solution delivery life cycle.

How Much Governance Is Needed? How Much Is Too Much?

To answer the questions about how much governance is required, how much is healthy, how much is helpful, and so forth, try to understand what works for each team member up through what works for the enterprise. The trick is to find a dynamic way to balance between formality and unconstrained thinking at all levels of an organization with the goal being to optimize team productivity and delivery predictability. Because each team is different, each team needs to find their optimum in concert with defining what is best for the enterprise.

Another aspect to consider in determining how much governance is needed is to think about the costs associated with the degree of governance. Consider not only the cost of implementing governance but also its impact on the costs of delivery enactment and change management. For example, light governance might enable a team to be more agile but might require more mature enactment, which typically involves more senior staff (i.e., higher labor costs). It also likely involves more change. Conversely, governance that is more rigorous might extend the schedule but might lessen the demands on enactment and minimize change.

Start Working and Delivering as Soon as Possible

Regardless of whether a team tends to be more agile-oriented or more plan-oriented, MSF espouses that stakeholders like to see progress and like solutions delivered as soon as possible with the expected features and within budget. In understanding what solution delivery life cycle and corresponding governance model is right for a team, try to understand team member capabilities, project constraints, and a realistic sense of process maturity for both an organization and a team.

> **Clarity Point**   The goal is not to deliver a partial solution quickly. The goal is to start validating all aspects of a solution quickly through incremental delivery.

Good Implementation Is Essential

You can lead a horse to water, but you can't make him drink.

Defining a great life cycle and governance model is nothing without successful implementation of various activities embodied within a governance model. In other words, a well-crafted life cycle is useless if a team is not able to execute. This is why it is essential to have a life cycle and governance model that fit a team's abilities and are adaptable to the changing delivery landscape. Keep in mind that it is possible to implement a solution successfully without a good governance model—the converse is unfortunately not true (i.e., a good governance model does not ensure a successful implementation).

MSF Governance Model

A key component of the Microsoft Solution Delivery Lifecycle is the *MSF Governance Model*. The Governance Model is structured to allow a team to deliver key portions of a solution faster than would otherwise be possible if they focused on the highest priority features first and moved less critical ones to subsequent releases. The model is structured to help drive a team quickly to a shared consensus on how to deliver on the various aspects of a solution. The Governance Model is a flexible component of MSF that has been used successfully to improve project control, minimize risk, improve solution quality, and increase development speed. Because MSF is fully customizable, it is expected that an organization adapts the Governance Model to fit its business processes and existing solution delivery approaches.

As mentioned earlier, MSF is designed to provide the right guidance to the right people at the right time. To help achieve this, the MSF Governance Model couples project governance with process enactment, as depicted in Figure 6-4. Project governance focuses on optimizing a solution delivery process and efficient and effective use of project resources. Process enactment focuses on defining, building, and deploying a solution that meets the needs and expectations of the stakeholders.

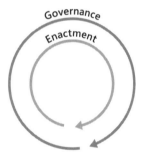

Figure 6-4   MSF Governance Model, which consists of enactment and governance

From a different perspective, the one depicted in Figure 6-5, the core of the MSF Governance Model is orienting team members to how they should approach solution delivery (i.e., mindsets). The model then layers on principles to guide how a team should work together to deliver a solution. Next, the model calls for a team to define and complete a set of activities to realize a solution (i.e., process enactment). Finally, the model adds how to use project resources optimally, balance project constraints, and organize and perform project work to deliver a solution (i.e., project governance). Additional governance layers can be added if a project is part of a program or if it is necessary to reflect organizational governance.

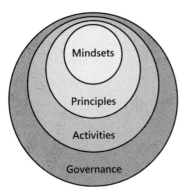

Figure 6-5   How governance, activities, principles, and mindsets relate

The following sections as well as the next six chapters discuss key elements of the MSF Governance Model, namely, tracks, checkpoints, and the iterative approach to completing the work necessary to deliver a solution.

Tracks

At one level, tracks are overlapping, coordinated groupings of certain activities aimed at producing relevant deliverables for each track. However, MSF tracks are more than this; each has a distinct mission and represents a change in the pace and focus of a project. Tracks use reviews and synchronization points (called *checkpoints*–discussed next) throughout each track to assist in determining whether track objectives are being met. Additionally, major checkpoints are used to bring closure to each track, which enables a shift of responsibilities for directing many activities and encourages a team to take a new perspective more appropriate for the goal(s) of the next track. Track closure is demonstrated by delivery of all required track deliverables and by the team and customer reaching a level of affirmative consensus around those deliverables. These deliverables, developed throughout a track, are used to initiate the next track. Note that this is likely a phased influence on the next track because it probably started before the end of the current track.

The MSF Governance Model consists of five overlapping enactment tracks and a persistent governance track that spans across the enactment tracks. Within each track, activities are further decomposed and regrouped into subtracks, called *work streams*. Work streams might be further decomposed and regrouped into *swim lanes*. The next three sections provide a high-level understanding of enactment tracks, what each advocacy group needs to focus on during these tracks, work streams, and swim lanes.

> **Clarity Point**   So why are they called "tracks" and not "phases," the word used by other frameworks and methodologies? It is an attempt to distinguish the fact that tracks are groupings of activities that, although they are started sequentially, might be completed quickly and run concurrently, as opposed to phases, which are more often associated with larger efforts and frequently need to be completed linearly before moving on to the next phase.

Enactment Tracks

Process enactment is the detailed sequence of steps by which a solution is defined, built, and deployed. The five overlapping enactment tracks are conceptually shown in Figure 6-6. Essentially, the enactment tracks help a team reach a high-level agreement on what is envisioned and create approach options to deliver on that vision (i.e., Envision Track); assess those options and plan out the selected option (i.e., Plan Track); build the solution (i.e., Build Track); make sure the solution is delivered as expected (i.e., Stabilize Track); and ultimately, deploy that solution (i.e., Deploy Track). From a simpler perspective, the enactment tracks are effectively: (1) *think* about what to do; (2) *plan* it out; (3) *do* it; (4) *verify* it was done right; and (5) *wrap up*.

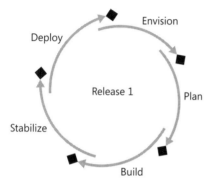

Figure 6-6   Conceptual view of enactment tracks within MSF Governance Model

When you look at the enactment tracks from a time perspective, as exemplified in Figure 6-7, one track starts well before its predecessor track has finished. As depicted, multiple tracks of activity are running in parallel.

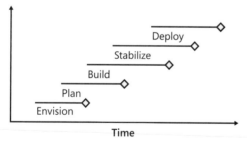

Figure 6-7   Enactment tracks splayed out over time

Figure 6-8 adds changes in risk, knowledge, and solution completion to this perspective. As shown, as a project proceeds, a solution moves ever closer to completion. A team's knowledge about a solution and how to deliver it increases. In addition, as more of a solution is built, typically the amount of risk decreases because riskier aspects of a solution should have been built in earlier releases. It is not intended to convey that the passage of time alone increases knowledge and drives down risk.

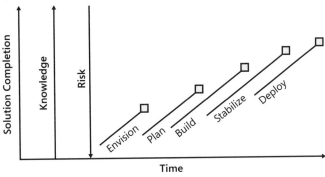

Figure 6-8   Conceptual view of MSF Governance Model applied to changes in risk, knowledge, and solution completion

Although all advocacy groups have specific responsibilities and deliverables for each track, their level of effort in each track varies. It is not that each advocacy group is not busy; it is just that the "spotlight" is on different advocacy groups at different times throughout the life cycle. For instance, solution architects are very busy defining a solution during a Plan Track, supporting a build team during a Build Track, and helping to troubleshoot a solution during the Stabilize and Deploy Tracks. So, for solution architects, their time in the spotlight is during planning. Table 6-1 contains a representative set of focal areas for each advocacy group across all tracks.

Table 6-1   Example of MSF Team Focal Areas for Each Enactment Track

Advocacy Group	Envision	Plan	Build	Stabilize	Deploy
Product Manage-ment	Overall goals Customer needs Requirements Vision/scope definition Customer acceptance criteria	Conceptual design Business require-ments analysis Communications plan Requirements prioritization	Clarifying scope, require-ments, and stakeholder expectations Market chan-nels and sales aids	Communica-tions plan execution Launch planning Scope trade-off prioritization	Customer feedback, assessment, signoff for each site deployment
Program Manage-ment	Project structure Project constraints Constraint trade-offs	Master project plan Master project schedule Functional specification management Budget	Project tracking Plan updating	Project tracking Constraint and scope trade-offs	Deployment plan and schedule updates Stabilization manage-ment

Table 6-1   Example of MSF Team Focal Areas for Each Enactment Track

Advocacy Group	Envision	Plan	Build	Stabilize	Deploy
Architecture	Design goals and strategies Solution concept Feasibility analysis Build and technology options	Conceptual and logical design Technology evaluation Functional specification content Initial build estimates	Architectural validation Clarifying design details	Issue triage	Solution/scope comparison
Development	Build needs and strategies	Logical and physical design Build plan/schedule Build estimates Prototypes	Solution construction Infrastructure development Configuration documentation	Issue resolution Solution optimization	Issue resolution Escalation support
User Experience	User performance needs and implications User acceptance criteria	Usage scenarios/use cases User requirements Localization/accessibility requirements User documentation, training plans and schedules for usability testing Training	Training Usability testing Graphic design Support tools and manuals	User documentation stabilization Training materials User acceptance Usability assessments Training pilot users, operations, and support teams	Training User readiness
Test	Testing strategies, approach, and metrics	Design evaluation Testing requirements Test plan and schedule Test scenarios	Technology and limited functional testing Issues identification Documentation testing Test plan updates	Functional, system, and integration testing Issue reporting and status Configuration testing	Issue triage Deployment stabilization

Table 6-1   Example of MSF Team Focal Areas for Each Enactment Track

Advocacy Group	Envision	Plan	Build	Stabilize	Deploy
Release/ Operations	Deployment implications Operations management and supportability Operations acceptance criteria Qualities of service	Design evaluation Operations requirements Pilot and deployment plan and schedule Define and build various project environments	Rollout checklists Rollout and pilot plan updates Site preparation checklists	Pilot setup and support Deployments Operations and support readiness	Site deployment management Change approval

Governance Track

As mentioned earlier, MSF is designed to provide the right guidance to the right people at the right time (i.e., governance). As discussed in Chapter 12, "MSF Governance Track: Guiding the Solution Delivery," the Governance Track focuses on balancing efficient and effective use of project resources and delivery of a solution with adherence to a set of potentially changing project constraints. In addition, the Governance Track espouses continuous process improvement.

Work Streams and Swim Lanes

Most solution delivery approaches segment work into smaller and smaller work packages (e.g., activities), and ultimately into work items (e.g., tasks). However, there is a wide variance in what to call these groupings and the subteams performing the work. Whatever nomenclature or taxonomy is selected, it should be applied consistently across an organization. One common taxonomy is to segment activity into *work streams* and each work stream into *swim lanes*. Work streams are synchronized by using checkpoints but otherwise are independent, parallel efforts. Swim lanes tend to be within a subteam, and as such, it is up to teams to self-manage and synchronize. Keep in mind that, typically, work streams proceed at their own pace, and as such, checkpoints need to be structured to support this.

For example, a project involves three distinct domains of activity segmented into work streams: application development, infrastructure, and operational readiness. Because application development can be such a big area, it is often further segmented into functional-oriented swim lanes such as presentation layer, business logic layer, and database layer swim lanes; and/or capability-oriented swim lanes such as financial, messaging, and reporting.

It is that simple: segment the work into groups and assign it to teams so that it makes sense for an organization. For instance, the U.S. Army calls its progressively smaller teams: Army, Corps, Division, Brigade, Battalion, Company, Platoon, and finally, Squad. In this organization, team names have definitive meanings, work capacity, and attributes that are commonly understood throughout the organization.

Checkpoints

Checkpoints, a central theme in MSF, are used to plan and monitor project progress and call out completion of deliverables and activities. Checkpoints are used to provide explicit opportunities for a team and the customer(s) to reconfirm project scope, or adjust project scope to reflect changing customer or business requirements or to accommodate risks and issues that might materialize during the course of a project. Checkpoints are used for many reasons, namely, these:

- Help to synchronize work elements

- Provide external visibility of progress and quality

- Enable midcourse corrections

- Focus reviews on goals and deliverables

- Provide approval points of work before moving forward

> **Clarity Point**   So, why are they called *checkpoints* instead of *milestones*? Same reason as given for why tracks are called tracks instead of phases. Checkpoints signify the conclusion of activities or a planned point during an activity to cross-coordinate with the team and with stakeholders. A milestone, sometimes called a toll gate, more often refers to a bigger or more formal event. As such, milestones are just one type of checkpoint. The real driver is that, within MSF, synchronizing with team members should be a regular event not to be shied away from because it is surrounded with pomp and circumstance.

MSF distinguishes between two types of checkpoints: major checkpoints and interim checkpoints. Major checkpoints mark the completion of major activities and major deliverables, including the end of planned activities for a given track. Interim checkpoints are defined by the team to indicate progress within a track and to segment large efforts into workable pieces.

Major Checkpoints

The alignment of team advocacy groups with each of the six major checkpoints clarifies which advocacy group is primarily responsible for achieving each checkpoint. Table 6-2 shows which advocacy groups drive each major checkpoint. This creates clear accountability. Although the completion of each checkpoint is driven by an advocacy group, all advocacy groups contribute in this achievement.

Table 6-2   Primary Driver for Each Major Checkpoint

Major Checkpoint	Marks Track Ending	Primary Driver
Vision/scope approved	Envision	Product Management
Project plans approved	Plan	Program Management
Scope complete	Build	Development
Release readiness approved	Stabilize	Test
Deployment complete	Deploy	Release/Operations
Customer acceptance	Governance	Product Management

Interim Checkpoints

Interim checkpoints vary depending on project type. In subsequent chapters, MSF provides a set of suggested interim checkpoints for each track. However, it is up to a team to adapt these checkpoints so they make sense for the project.

Defining interim checkpoints early on in a Plan Track helps to frame and focus team thinking when defining work packages without getting caught up in the details. Teams often have a strong sense of what needs to be accomplished but often struggle to identify tasks, schedules, and interim checkpoints. It is important not to worry about any dates at this time but instead to make sure the teams understand how their tasks and checkpoints interrelate. To help with this, a team maps out the logical relations using predecessor associations between the work streams and the swim lanes, as exemplified in Figure 6-9, which is an example of interim checkpoints for a Stabilize Track of a software development effort. Notice that the interim checkpoints are relative to each other and to the major checkpoints (e.g., Testing's 1st Pass Functional Testing Complete interim checkpoint occurs one week after Development's Code Complete major checkpoint). This way, it is clearly understood early on how teams rely on each other. Please note that the dates are included in the figure only for ease of understanding the figure.

Checkpoint Reviews

Each checkpoint provides an opportunity for learning and reflection through checkpoint reviews as well as an opportunity to review deliverables and synchronize expectations between customer, stakeholders, sponsors, and team. Checkpoint reviews used to identify and share lessons learned among a team are sometimes called *postmortems* or *after-action reviews*. These reviews are also occasions to gain agreement on project decisions, secure go/no-go decisions to move forward, or course-correct as needed.

For checkpoint reviews to be effective and valuable, open communications among the participants (e.g., project team, users, and stakeholders) must be established. As stated previously, open communications relies upon a no-blame culture.

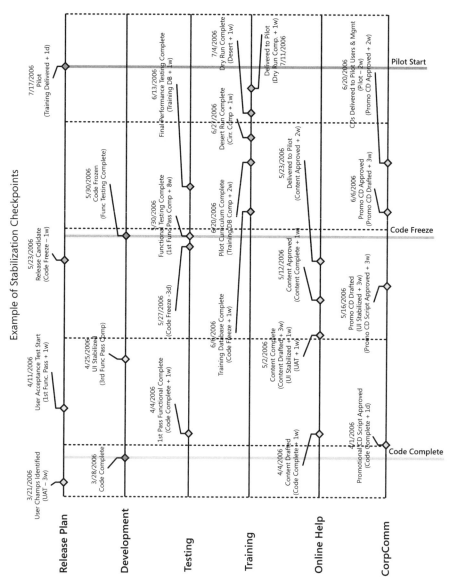

Example of Stabilization Checkpoints

Figure 6-9   Example of major and interim checkpoints for software Stabilize Track

Iterative Approach

How do you swallow an elephant?...One bite at a time.

—An old adage

A solution does not provide business value until it is deployed into production and used effectively. For this reason, the life cycle of the MSF Governance Model includes incremental development and deployment of a solution into production, thereby ensuring realization of business value and of a team's overall strategic vision and goal(s). The combination of a strong multidimensional business representation on a team with explicit focus on impact to the business throughout the process is how MSF ensures that projects fulfill the promise of technology.

The practice of iterative development is a recurrent theme in MSF. Documents, designs, plans, and other deliverables are developed in an iterative fashion. As you would expect, the MSF Governance Model is an iterative approach. There are many highly compelling arguments across many disciplines for taking an iterative approach to solution delivery[1]:

1. **Risk management:** If the desired result is not known in advance or the technology used is unproven, a solution should be incrementally implemented, starting with the highest risk elements, to prove or disprove the requirements and design assumptions.

2. **Economics:** In an uncertain business climate, it is important to review priorities frequently and treat investments as though they were financial options. The more flexibility gained through early payoff and frequent checkpoints, the more valuable the options.

3. **Focus:** People retain only so much information. By batching activities into small work packages, team members better grasp and deliver on the work at hand.

4. **Motivation:** The most energizing phenomenon on a delivery team is seeing users interacting with a solution, even if the solution is in a limited operational capacity.

5. **Control theory:** Small iterations allow a reduction in the margin of error for estimates and provide fast feedback about the accuracy of project plans.

6. **Stakeholder involvement:** Stakeholders see results quickly and become more engaged in a project, offering more time, insight, and funding.

7. **Continuous learning:** The entire team will learn and mature with each iteration, improving the accuracy, quality, and suitability of the finished solution.

Although delivery methodologies vary in how they approach iterative development, the concept of incrementally developing component parts to realize a solution is fundamental. An example of this concept for software development is shown in Figure 6-10. The elements of the iterative approach start with the individual (i.e., check-in) and incrementally roll up to a portfolio of projects to deliver a solution (i.e., program). Before talking about each of these elements in this figure, a few guiding principles regarding the MSF iterative approach are discussed next.

---

1 Sam Guckenheimer, *Software Engineering with Microsoft Visual Studio Team System* (Upper Saddle River, NJ: Addison-Wesley Professional, 2006), 30.

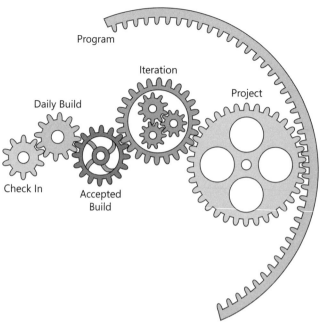

Figure 6-10   Elements of an iterative approach

Iterative Approach Fundamentals

The MSF iterative approach has two key guiding principles: *creating living documents* and *baselining early and freezing late*. Each of these is discussed next.

Create Living Documents   MSF project documents are "living documents" that are developed iteratively to keep documentation consistent with project changes. An example of a living project document is a planning document. Planning documents often start out as a high-level "approach." These are circulated for review by the team and stakeholders during an Envision Track. As a project moves into a Plan Track, these are developed into detailed plans. Again, these are reviewed and modified iteratively. The types and number of these plans vary with the size of a project. To avoid confusion, planning documents that are started during an Envision Track are referred to as *approaches*. For example, a brief test approach is written during envisioning that evolves into a test plan in later tracks.

Baseline Early, Freeze Late   The phrase "baseline early, freeze late" literally means complete an activity as soon as possible to solicit feedback from others regarding output of that activity; but do not be too quick to declare the output final because project changes might alter the output. Basically, *baselining* is the end of the planned activity, and *freezing* is "last call" for changes after others have had a chance to validate the solution is what is needed and expected.

One way to instill this iterative approach in members of a team is to establish that every activity and deliverable taking longer than three days to complete needs to have iterative interim checkpoints, identified in Figure 6-11. As shown in the figure, shortly after starting a task or drafting a deliverable, the team responsible needs to get sign-off on task strategy or deliverable outline. Iterative interim drafts are submitted and reviewed as time permits. A team reaches a "completion" checkpoint when the team believes they finished their required work. Only after successfully passing a review, be it a peer review or formal review, is an effort *baselined*, meaning an independent group concurs that the team is complete. This marks the end of planned activity for that task or deliverable until such time that enough time has passed (sometimes months later) that there is little chance for additional change, and as such the effort is declared done (i.e., frozen checkpoint achieved).

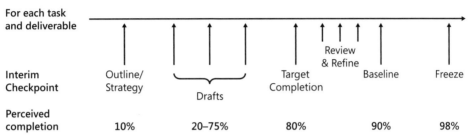

Figure 6-11   Iterative task and deliverable life cycle

By completing and baselining project deliverables early in the process, team members are empowered to proceed with follow-on work without delay. By making the deliverable life cycle flexible by freezing checkpoints late within their corresponding tracks, changes are more likely to be accommodated. Note that the cost of this flexibility is paying careful attention to the change control process. It is essential to track changes and ensure that no unauthorized changes occur.

Check-In

Although a software development concept, the concept of *check-in* has universal appeal if you consider it an activity performed by a team member to deliver incrementally, at the lowest level, on his or her portion of a solution. It is a "public" acknowledgment of a degree of completion. For example, this could be a messaging engineer sharing a design draft among infrastructure peers. Work items are not checked in until they have a degree of completeness and correctness. Each check-in needs to progress a solution and not disrupt or "break" it. For example, software developers do not check-in code until they have validated that what they are checking works both as a component part of a solution and with the other component parts already checked in.

Daily Builds

MSF advocates frequent integration of all solution components for testing and review purposes, rather than waiting until the end of solution construction to do integration testing. This iterative approach enables maturity of the total solution to be well understood, with ample test data, before a solution is released into production.

Larger, complex projects are often split into multiple segments, each of which is developed and tested by separate subteams or feature teams, and then consolidated into the whole. In projects of this type, typical in Microsoft product development, the "daily build" approach is a fundamental part of the process. A *build* is a periodic assembly of all solution elements that are sufficiently complete to be included. Typically, core functionality of a solution or product is completed first, and then additional features are added. Development and testing occur continuously and simultaneously in parallel tracks. The daily build provides independent verification that all solution components are compatible and viable in a production-like environment, and enables the various subteams to continue their development and testing iterations. Builds that pass predetermined quality levels are called *accepted builds*.

Note that these iterative builds are not deployed in a live production environment. Only when builds are well tested and stable are they ready for a limited pilot (or beta) release to a subset of the production environment. Rigorous configuration management is essential to keeping these builds in sync.

Another advantage of daily builds is that they enable a team to mature their skills. This is especially needed for the nondevelopment roles (e.g., training role). These teams are dependent on the output of a build team to get their tasks and deliverables done. For instance, a deployment team uses frequent builds to hone their skills. Otherwise, there could be an unacceptable delay in portions of a solution (e.g., training material).

> **Clarity Point**   Daily builds are not always done literally daily. In some approaches, they occur once a week as development starts, and the frequency increases as a project progresses. Toward the middle to end of an iteration, the frequency of builds could be continuous—kicked off by each check-in. This is not to say that builds are pushed to a test environment continuously with each build. Builds are usually pushed to a test environment when the quality is sufficient.

Iteration

An *iteration* is a predetermined logical stopping point in a delivery life cycle. Typically, it is either a predetermined period (i.e., time-boxed; for example, 4 weeks), a predetermined set of features, or a predetermined capability. Regardless of approach, there is a predetermined level of quality that must be achieved. A graphical depiction of a set of iterations leading up to a release is provided in Figure 6-12.

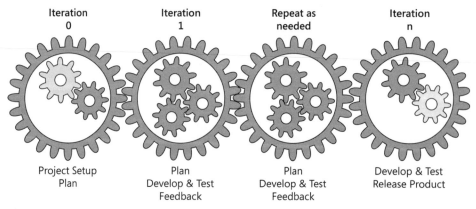

Figure 6-12   Iterations leading to a release

Versioned Releases

MSF recommends that solutions be incrementally delivered by using versioned releases. A *release* is a bundling of solution features and capabilities so that it can be shared either internally among the team or externally with stakeholders. The initial release is typically a bundled set of core solution features and capabilities. Subsequent releases build upon prior releases by either adding new features and capabilities or adding onto the existing ones. This is known as a *version release strategy*. It is true that some small projects might need only one version. Nevertheless, it is a recommended practice to look for opportunities to break a solution into a multiple versions. Figure 6-13 conceptually shows versioned releases.

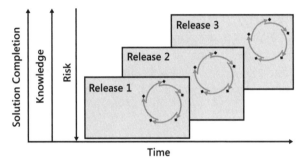

Figure 6-13   Example of versioned releases

As depicted in Figure 6-13, versioned releases are not necessarily developed linearly. Mature solution delivery organizations often have multiple version teams working with overlapping release cycles. The time between versions varies depending on the size and type of project, as well as customer needs and strategy.

Experience shows that versioned releases improve a team's relationship with the customer and ensure that the best ideas are reflected in a solution. It also shows that customers will be more receptive to deferring features until a later release if they trust the team to deliver the initial and subsequent solution releases in a timely fashion. Otherwise, they will overload the team with feature requests. Other benefits of using versioned releases include the following:

- Manages uncertainty and changes in scope
- Encourages continuous and incremental improvement
- Enables shorter delivery time
- Sets clear and motivational goals for team members
- Forces closure on project issues
- Minimizes risks by breaking large projects into multiple versions

Note that successfully implementing a versioned release strategy adds significant coordination overhead to an organization. For instance, scope and schedule must be coordinated across versions. The following are considerations for adopting versioned releases, each of which is discussed in subsequent sections:

- Create an incremental release strategy
- Deliver core functionality first
- Prioritize using risk-driven scheduling
- Cycle through iterations rapidly
- Establish configuration management
- Establish change control

Create an Incremental Release Strategy   Timeless wisdom recommends that the best way to approach accomplishing a large effort is to decompose it into smaller, more manageable parts (i.e., swallowing-the-elephant approach referenced earlier). Consistent with an iterative approach, an incremental release strategy describes how a solution will be delivered incrementally through a series of releases. This strategy maps out which components, features, functions, and services will be delivered in each release. It might contain a few alternate approaches.

Thinking beyond the current version enhances a team's ability to make good decisions about what to build now and what to defer. By providing a timetable for future feature development, a team is able to make the best use of available resources and schedule constraints, as well as to minimize unwanted scope expansion.

Deliver Core Functionality First   A basic, solid, and usable solution in the customer's hands is of more immediate value than a deluxe version that will not be available for weeks, months, or years. By delivering core functionality first, a team has a solid foundation upon which to build and benefits from customer feedback that will help drive feature development in subsequent iterations.

Prioritize Using Risk-Driven Scheduling   Risk assessment by a team identifies which features are riskiest. Based on experience, it is best to schedule the riskiest features for completion first. Problems requiring major changes to the architecture should be handled earlier in a project, thereby minimizing the impact on schedule and budget.

Cycle Through Iterations Rapidly   A significant benefit of versioning is that it quickly delivers usable solutions to the customer and improves the solutions incrementally. If this process stalls, customer expectations for continual solution improvement suffer. Maintain a manageable scope so that iterations are achievable within acceptable periods.

Establish Configuration Management   Configuration management is often confused with project change control, which is discussed next. The two are interrelated, but are not the same. *Configuration management* is the formalized tracking and controlling of the state of various project elements (e.g., deliverables and documents). These elements include version control for code, documentation, user manuals, and help files, schedules, and plans. It also includes tracking the state of hardware, network, and software settings of a solution. A team must be able to reproduce or "roll back" to an earlier configuration of the entire solution if needed.

Configuration management provides the baseline data that a team needs to make effective change control decisions. An example of configuration management is the recording of settings selected and tracking their changes as they are made during development and testing. For organizations using MOF, configuration management processes and procedures already used for operations should be adapted.

Establish Change Control   Once specifications are baselined, all features and functionality of a solution should be considered to be under change control. *Change control* is the process of requesting, reviewing, approving, documenting, and distributing changes. If a change is approved, it alters the scope of a solution. An example of change control is as follows. To conform to new government regulations, someone has proposed adding a new electronic data interchange (EDI) mapping schema. Key team members meet with sponsor(s) funding a project and members of the operations staff to review the proposed change, its technical risk, and impact on cost and schedule. After considering all impacts of the change, the approvers (typically called a *change board*) decide either to approve or disapprove the change. Note that disapproving the change can still leave it open for consideration in a later release of the solution.

It is essential that the customer and entire team understand the change control process. MSF does not prescribe a specific set of change control procedures. Procedures can range from simple to elaborate, depending on the size and nature of the project. However, effective change control must have the following elements:

- Features are not added or changed without review and approval by both the team and customer.

- To facilitate review, requests to change features are submitted in writing. This enables groups of change requests to be tracked. At Microsoft, these are known as *design change requests* (DCRs).

- Each feature request is analyzed for impact, feasibility, and priority. Dependencies with other features are considered, including user and operational documentation, training materials, and the operating environment.

- The impact on cost and schedule for each change request is estimated.

- Individuals (including the customer, program management, and some combination of stakeholders and other team members) to serve on a change control board to authorize changes are specified. Such a group takes many forms, as long as it is authorized to approve changes to cost, schedule, and functionality.

- Changes are tracked and made easy to access. For example, it is a good practice to maintain change requests and their respective status in a team collaboration site using tools such as the Microsoft SharePoint and Visual Studio Team Systems products.

- Change control requires effective configuration management to be effective.

Adapting the Microsoft Solution Delivery Lifecycle

The Microsoft Solution Delivery Lifecycle and its subordinate MSF Governance Model represent a grouping of activities to enable incremental delivery. It is expected that track and checkpoint names might need to be changed to be consistent with an organization's existing process. Accompanying the adaptation of the MSF Team Model, it is also expected that the activities outlined for each track by advocacy groups might also be adapted. As with adapting the MSF Team Model, as long as the core principles and set of natural checks and balances are preserved, the MSF Governance Model can be easily adapted to match the needs of both small and large as well as agile and more formal projects.

Summary

It is critical for a solution delivery team to be able to define the important drivers of their solution delivery life cycle. As discussed, Microsoft decomposes the life cycle into two symbiotic frameworks, namely, MSF and MOF. Each supports and augments the other.

This chapter highlights the fact that a delivery team should define a solution delivery life cycle that best fits their needs and the constraints of the organization. This involves balancing team member productivity with team delivery predictability. Based on what the team decides, they need to convert this thinking into how much process and governance is therefore needed.

This chapter introduces the MSF Governance Model. The model contains dynamic and integrated elements, such as the following:

- Overlapping tracks of activity, for both enactment and governance
- Checkpoints, major and interim ones to synchronize work
- An iterative approach to incrementally delivering value to the customer

It is unlikely that a solution delivery team will initially be able to define an ideal solution delivery life cycle and governance model. As such, the team should plan to evolve these as they learn what works best for the team and for the organization.

Part II
Inner Workings of Solution Delivery

Chapter 7

MSF Envision Track: Defining a Solution

An Envision Track addresses one of the most fundamental requirements for project success—unification of a project team behind a common vision. A team must have a clear vision of what it wants to accomplish and be able to state it in terms that motivate the entire team and the customer. Envisioning, by creating a high-level view of a project's goals and constraints, is an early form of planning; it sets the stage for the more detailed planning process that takes place during a project's Plan Track.

The primary activities accomplished during envisioning are the formation of the core team and the preparation and delivery of a vision/scope document. The delineation of a project vision and the identification of a project scope are distinct activities; both are required for a successful project. *Vision* is an unbounded view of what a solution might be. *Scope* identifies the part(s) of the vision to be accomplished within project constraints.

Risk management is a recurring process that continues throughout a project. During an Envision Track, a team prepares a risk document and presents the top risks along with the vision/scope document.

> **Lesson Learned**   How the team and sponsors approach envisioning is often driven by who and how quickly a conceptual solution can be formed. Typically, this concept is represented in how an organization finishes this statement: "We, the organization, have a problem/ opportunity and...

- ■ no one knows how to solve the problem."
- ■ an external provider knows how to solve the problem."
- ■ we know how to solve the problem."

Projects starting from situation 1 typically have elongated envisioning. Projects starting from situation 2 typically spend more time defining and documenting a solution as well as more time structuring a project. Projects starting from situation 3 typically have a short envisioning.

Goals

The goals for an Envision Track are to develop a clear understanding of what is needed within context of project constraints and to assemble the necessary team to envisage solution(s) with options and approaches that best meet those needs while optimally satisfying those constraints.

Team Focus

Typically before a team is formed, a few core individuals go through the early stages of working with project sponsor(s) to quantify the problem or opportunity and establish an initial vision for a solution. As more information is learned and the effort seems worthy of pursuing, other key individuals join the team to refine the vision while constricting it into an achievable project scope. As the initial solution concept(s) becomes clearer, additional resources are solicited to help further refine project goals, assumptions, risks, and constraints. The team starts to form initial high-level requirements and puts forth a few options and approaches to implementing a solution.

At this point, all advocacy groups should be represented on the team. The team is starting to work through defining detailed roles and responsibilities for the team as well as identifying any skills gaps that would necessitate bringing on additional people or that might justify replacing existing team members. Overall roles and responsibilities for the team during an Envision Track are described in Table 7-1.

Table 7-1   Team Focal Areas During Envisioning

Advocacy Group	Focus
Product Management	Overall goals, identify customer needs, requirements, vision/scope definition, customer acceptance criteria
Program Management	Project structure, project constraints, constraint trade-offs
Architecture	Design goals and strategies, solution concept, feasibility analysis, build and technology options

Table 7-1   Team Focal Areas During Envisioning

Advocacy Group	Focus
Development	Build needs and strategies
User Experience	User performance needs and implications, user acceptance criteria
Test	Testing strategies, approach, and metrics
Release/Operations	Deployment implications, operations management and supportability, operations acceptance criteria, qualities of service

Key Deliverables

The key deliverables for an Envision Track are the following:

- Vision/scope document
- project structure document
- Initial risk assessment document

Each of these is discussed in detail in the following sections.

Key Checkpoints

Key checkpoints consist of a major checkpoint for the track and a few interim checkpoints.

Major Checkpoint

The major checkpoint concluding an Envision Track is *Vision/Scope Approved.*

Vision/Scope Approved

Lead Advocacy Group: Product Management

The major checkpoint that concludes an Envision Track is getting approval of a solution vision and scope. This checkpoint signifies that the team and stakeholders agree on the description of the problem or opportunity and with the conceptual solution and delivery approaches. This checkpoint also serves to validate other aspects of a project and conceptual solution.

Interim Checkpoints

The interim checkpoints for an Envision Track are *core team organized* and *vision/scope baselined*, as depicted in Figure 7-1.

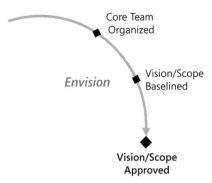

Figure 7-1   Envision Track checkpoints

Core Team Organized

Lead Advocacy Group: Program Management

This checkpoint signifies key team members have been assigned to a project. Typically, the full team is not assembled yet. The initial team often might be playing multiple roles until all members are in place. To make sure it is clear as to who has what role, this information is recorded in a project structure document. A project structure document includes information on how a team is organized and who plays which roles and has specific responsibilities. A project structure document also clarifies the chain of accountability to the customer and designated points of contact that a project team has with the customer. These vary depending on the circumstances of a project.

Vision/Scope Baselined

Lead Advocacy Group: Product Management

At this interim checkpoint, the team believes they have completed the vision/scope document and have circulated it among the extended team, customers, and stakeholders for review and concurrence that it is complete. With such an important document, it usually takes many rounds of iterative discussions to reach concurrence. As defined in Chapter 6, "Establishing a Solution Delivery Life Cycle," once the reviewers concur that the document is complete, the document is baselined and put under change control. This means that there is no further planned activity to modify this document.

Understanding Stakeholders

Lead Advocacy Group: Product Management

Stakeholder analysis is a process to identify key people and organizations that have a vested interest in a project. As defined in Chapter 4, "Building an MSF Team," the following people might be stakeholders:

■ **Project sponsor(s)**   Initiates, funds, and approves an effort

- **Customer(s) (also known as business sponsors)**   Takes receipt of a solution and expects to gain business value from it

- **User(s)**   Interacts with a solution

- **Operations team**   Hosts, maintains, and administers a solution

With potential for such a wide collection of people and organizations, it is important to understand who the key stakeholders are and have a general understanding of the rest. So, how does a team find out who are the stakeholders? How do they make sure they understand stakeholder interests, motivations, and drivers? How does a team work with stakeholders throughout the life cycle? It is hard but possible. Basically, a team can follow the MSF Governance Model in that it goes through tracks of activities in conceptually understanding who stakeholders are; plan out how to refine the team's understanding and start to represent that understanding in a stakeholder map that shows what and how they relate to a solution and project team; start to meet with stakeholders to develop the team's understanding; test that understanding on a few "friendly" ones; and wrap up stakeholder analysis with "delivering" a list of stakeholders and a stakeholder map. These deliverables are used in subsequent tracks to continue working with stakeholders.

Stakeholder analysis involves three key activities:

- Identify them
- Prioritize them
- Understand them

Identifying Stakeholders

When the core project team first starts mapping out the conceptual solution, people and organizations external to a project team associated with these conceptual components start to surface. These are a team's initial batch of stakeholders. This list of stakeholders grows as solution components become clearer and new groups and key people associated with these components are added to the list. Typically, this list grows as solution usage scenarios and/or use cases are developed to flush out the system wherein stakeholders are identified. Keep in mind that stakeholders are also members of the extended project team.

Prioritizing Stakeholders

With potentially so many stakeholders, a team must come up with a means to sift through this list to identify which stakeholders have the most impact and influence on a project (i.e., prioritize the list). Going forward, a team should concentrate their efforts on only this "short list" of key stakeholders.

There are many ways to prioritize stakeholders. One means to achieve this is to map the long list into quadrants where the axes are differentiating qualities (e.g., domain knowledge, availability, constituency backing, and new technology acceptance). Figure 7-2 is one such example using *impact* and *influence* as the axes to indicate the type of relationship with the stakeholder. In this example, key stakeholders are those placed in the three identified quadrants:

- **Managed Relationship**   Very influential with significant impact on a project. The relationship with these stakeholders needs to be well managed.

- **Informed Relationship**   Very influential but low to moderate impact on a project. These stakeholders should be kept apprised of project status but do not need to be closely managed.

- **Coordinated Relationship**   Low to moderate influence but significant impact on a project. These stakeholders often are users who should continually be included in discussions with a project team throughout the life cycle.

Stakeholders with little influence and little impact on a project should be considered, but often there is little time to expend to maintain a relationship with them.

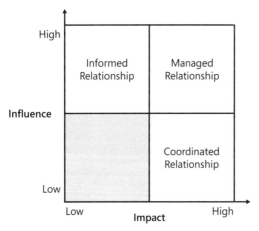

Figure 7-2   Example of types of stakeholder relationships to reflect priority

Understanding Key Stakeholders

Understanding key stakeholders means knowing what motivates them and drives their involvement with a project with the goals of gaining commitment and support from them. Not all stakeholders will be supporters; some will be "anchors" that are seemingly bent on hindering a project but because of their position and influence are necessary stakeholders. Other stakeholders might seem neutral and apathetic.

A team needs to understand the key stakeholders to facilitate their continual involvement. This includes making sure they are involved and interested in participating in major checkpoint reviews. It also means knowing how, what, and when to communicate with the stakeholders.

Selecting and Preparing a Project Team

The goal of selecting and preparing a project team is to deliver the right resources, against the right projects, at the right time. To achieve this, a project should be carefully staffed with team members ready to contribute at the needed skill levels for the given roles. This does not happen magically, it takes careful preparing and continual adjusting.

Staffing a project team should be a fluidic process of adding and removing people as needed throughout the life cycle. It typically involves gradually adding appropriately skilled people as a project gets defined; making personnel changes as different skills and abilities are needed over the course of the various tracks; and rolling off team members as they complete their planned work.

Typically, a team starts with a few key individuals as the core team. A few senior staff are added to help plan out a solution. These folks often continue as team leads of the various sub-teams. Additional staff are usually brought on to help develop a solution and are phased off a project typically when there is a high degree of confidence that a solution works and it is subsequently a matter of refining a solution (e.g., typically after the first full functional test in stabilization). By the end of stabilization, a team is typically backed down to the core people plus a deployment team. Some of the people who help develop a solution transition over to other projects to handle subsequent releases/versions of a solution whereas some transition to Operations to help support the deployed solution.

Selecting who to bring on a project and when is based on many tangible as well as subjective factors. The tangible factors include budgetary constraints (we all wish we could afford a whole team of the best and brightest); matching needed skills and proficiencies with available personnel; an organization's desire to provide mentoring or on-the-job training necessitating a mix of senior and junior skilled personnel; and technology complexity. Subjective factors include team cohesiveness, team chemistry, resultant team readiness, development style (e.g., best suited for efforts that are more formal), and leadership.

For the staffing process to be fluidic, a team needs to adopt a means to easily ramp-up and transition personnel onto a project as well as capture lessons learned and collateral from personnel rolling off a project. To do this, a team and each successive subteam need to decide what is the right level of planning and documentation necessary to ensure smooth transitions. Too little transitional material likely means the new personnel will lose time because of a slow start. Too much transitional material likely means the overall project will suffer under the burden of updating and managing this material. Keep in mind that the optimal mix often changes as the teams evolve.

Another intertwined aspect of preparing a project team is assessing their readiness to perform their given tasks, both current and future, as well as their ability to adapt to the changing project environment. The next section discusses a means, called the *MSF Readiness Management Discipline*, to fine-tune individual readiness up through readiness at the enterprise level.

MSF Readiness Management Discipline

An organization can expend great effort readying a team. Readiness has two components: *technical readiness* and *psychological readiness* (e.g., willingness and mental preparedness). As defined within MSF, technical readiness is a measurement of the current state versus the desired state of knowledge, skills, and abilities of individuals and teams within an organization. This measurement is the real or perceived capabilities at any point during the ongoing process of planning, building, and managing solutions.

The MSF Readiness Management Discipline, a core component of MSF, addresses technical readiness. It provides guidance and processes in the areas of assessing and acquiring knowledge, skills, and abilities necessary for solution delivery. It is based on MSF foundational principles and provides guidance for a proactive approach to readiness throughout a solutions life cycle. Together with proven practices, this discipline provides a foundation for individuals, their project teams, and up to the enterprise level to manage readiness, as depicted in Figure 7-3. The additional organizational readiness examples shown in the figure (i.e., process improvement and organizational change management) should be proactively addressed but are outside the focus of this discipline.

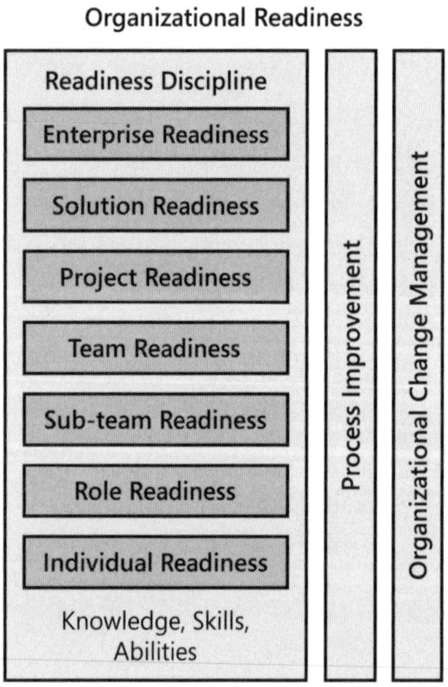

Figure 7-3   MSF Readiness Management Discipline related to organizational readiness

As shown in this figure, there are many levels of readiness to consider. Each level builds off another—starting with individual readiness that focuses on knowledge, skills, and abilities needed to meet the responsibilities required for each role. As each successive level is traversed, readiness evolves into making sure an organization is poised for strategic initiatives and successful adoption and realization of its technology investments. Given this additive nature, organizations should start by first focusing on addressing individual readiness to assess and affect change to readiness.

The foundational principles, mindsets, and proven practices of MSF as applied to the MSF Readiness Management Discipline are outlined in the following sections. The primary ideals of effective readiness management are highlighted in this section and are referenced throughout this book.

Foundational Principles Applied to Readiness

The MSF foundational principles are cornerstones of the framework's approach. Those principles relating to successful readiness management are highlighted in this section.

Foster Open Communications   By establishing an open learning environment that encourages individuals to take ownership of their skills development, acknowledge and commit to rectifying skill deficiencies, and participate in setting their goals for their learning plans, individuals tend to take greater pride and have a higher drive to succeed and help others. Groups successful in creating this type of open learning environment often have periodic team training sessions where knowledge and learning are both shared and received.

Work Toward a Shared Vision   An understanding of individual team member readiness enables a shared vision to be framed in a context such that every team member grasps what is envisioned for a solution. It also allows for a more realistic understanding of what a team is able to accomplish—enabling a more realistic vision and matching expectations.

Empower Team Members   When team members have requisite skills, they are better able to perform their role. As such, they feel more empowered to contribute successfully to delivering a solution. This feeling often leads to higher productivity and creativity as well as team harmony. Typically, if an organization has a good understanding of skills readiness and how it directly benefits an organization, an organization is more willing to provide additional training and skills enhancement activities.

Establish Clear Accountability, Shared Responsibility   Similar to the benefits of empowering team members, better alignment of team member proficiency and role competency usually leads to more accountability (i.e., it is easier to be accountable when you know what you are doing). Good alignment usually also leads to a high degree of confidence across a team. As such, team members are typically more willing to be jointly responsible for a solution.

Deliver Incremental Value   With readiness gaps identified and actively being minimized, team members are able to focus on delivering business value instead of fretting about role mismatches. With role alignment, team members are well suited to understand what needs to be delivered for customers to realize value.

Frequent deliveries mean that smaller portions of a solution are being delivered more often. This provides more learning opportunities for a team to increase their skills. It also helps team leads quickly calibrate team member skills and abilities as well as role and task skill assumptions, and if necessary, make staffing changes early on in the life cycle.

Stay Agile, Expect and Adapt to Change   Changes in project direction, operational procedures, or individual resources do occur unexpectedly and with significant impact. Being adept at successfully facing change means having individuals and project teams committed to readiness. *Readiness agility* refers to having a defined readiness management process, doing proactive readiness management, and providing incentives that encourage individuals and project teams to gain the appropriate level of knowledge, skills, and abilities swiftly through training, mentoring, or hands-on learning to successfully meet their defined goals. Leaving out any of these aspects of the Readiness Management Discipline increases the likelihood of risks and failure. Without the agility achieved from having a readiness management process in place and quickly being able to obtain the appropriate skills necessary for success, organizations sometimes miss opportunities and find themselves behind their competition.

Invest in Quality   Obtaining the appropriate skills for a project team is an investment. Because they take time out of otherwise productive work hours, the funds for classroom training, courseware, mentors, or consulting can certainly be a significant monetary investment. However, investing time and resources to obtain or develop the right people with the right skills generally results in higher quality output and greater chances of success. Projects that fail do not supply a positive return on investment. Projects that succeed with low quality result in lowered satisfaction and adoption, which in turn might have significant cost impact in areas such as support. Up-front investment in staffing teams with the right skills generally leads to greater success and higher quality.

Learn from All Experiences   Capturing and sharing both technical and nontechnical best practices are fundamental to ongoing improvement and continuing success by ensuring the following:

- Allowing team members to benefit from the success and failure experiences of others

- Helping team members to repeat successes

- Institutionalizing learning through such techniques as checkpoint reviews

Checkpoint reviews help teams to make midcourse correction and avoid repeating mistakes. Additionally, capturing and sharing this learning creates best practices out of the experiences that went well.

Partner with Customers   Partnering with customers is a mutually beneficial means to improve team readiness and validate customer readiness to use a solution. It is great way to engage customers in their environment. A team should use this opportunity to better understand how customers use their current solutions and how they might use a solution being developed. While engaging customers, a team might use this opportunity to calibrate their assumptions about customer readiness. A team can also use this to informally validate alternative solution implementation approaches and options.

MSF Readiness Management Fundamentals

In this section, important concepts about readiness that are central to understanding the MSF Readiness Management Discipline are discussed.

Understand the Experience Within Each Team Member   Individual knowledge and experience are assets that offer dual value. The individual who possesses the knowledge and experience benefits personally, and the organization as a whole benefits when the individual applies knowledge and experience to projects. The value of this knowledge is diminished for both an individual and an organization without a collective understanding and measurement. For example, an individual might possess knowledge that an organization does not currently recognize, or an organization can lack a method to access that knowledge. Consequently, knowledge assessment and knowledge management are key concepts of a readiness effort. An organization should promote readiness through the capture and utilization of knowledge. A defined knowledge management program takes the idea from concept to reality. The benefit of a knowledge management program is its identification of knowledge lacking in both individuals and an organization.

Readiness Must Be Continuously Managed   Learning must be made an explicit and planned activity—for example, by dedicating time for it in the schedule—before it will have the desired effect.

Carry Out Readiness Planning   As with any aspect of a project, planning for readiness is the key to success. Knowing up front the required level of readiness creates a proactive approach to assembling the appropriate resources, defining budgetary needs for training or obtaining the appropriate expertise, and building training time into the schedule. Readiness plans for each role are rolled up to create an overall readiness plan for a project team. Without planning, readiness management is likely to be overlooked until a significant gap in skills causes a project to be challenged, leading to significant risk of failure.

Measure and Track Skills and Goals   Successful readiness management includes assessing and tracking skills and the goals of individuals. This includes taking into account current abilities versus the desired knowledge levels so that the appropriate matching of skills can happen at both individual and project levels during resource allocation. Tracking and measuring the information help ensure project teams have the capability of doing readiness planning. Through the process of planning, project teams select members with both the desire to participate and skills required. The most effective way to accomplish this is by using a mandatory skills-reporting database and requiring all individuals to keep the data up to date.

Treat Readiness Gaps as Risks   After completing assessments and determining proficiency gaps—essentially finding the current versus desired state—project teams should identify readiness gaps as risks and treat them as such. Gaps in areas of key knowledge, such as the skills and abilities needed to complete a project successfully, can have profound effects on the schedule, budget, and resources needed to fill those gaps. Depending on the type of project, readiness risks can delay project initiation or indicate a need to obtain resources with the appropriate skills. When gaps are treated as risks, there is generally a more proactive approach to readiness management and subsequent mitigation of these risks.

Avoid Single Points of Failure in Skills Coverage   It is not good to have single points of failure, including team skills. Therefore, a team should have a primary and secondary for every skill set deemed important to the success of a project.

Readiness and the MSF Team and Governance Models

As the size and complexity of solutions tend to become greater, so does the importance of establishing and maintaining proactive readiness activities throughout a solution life cycle. Readiness goals should be expressed as activities and deliverables produced throughout a project life cycle intended to achieve those goals. Each advocacy group performs activities and produces deliverables that relate to project readiness goals for their constituency. When readiness is seen as a component of project goals, readiness deliverables are completed at various levels within each track and checkpoint of a project. Thus, mapping of readiness activities and deliverables to the MSF Governance Model tracks is useful, but teams will need to adjust their activities (and when these activities occur) according to the size and type of project.

The focus is on preparing a team with the knowledge, skills, and abilities to deliver a project effectively. In the early stages of the MSF Envision Track, this includes documenting a project approach to readiness. This approach documentation might contain information such as follows:

- The individuals that are to perform assessments, priorities, and budgets for training existing staff or obtaining the needed skills

- Determination of project scenarios and desired proficiency levels

- The ways in which these activities will be accomplished

During the MSF Plan Track, the high-level activities and deliverables identified during envisioning are taken to a greater level of detail, with estimates and dependencies applied for the tasks and integrated into the overall project plan and schedule. This helps determine the true cost and feasibility of a project beyond a development effort alone. This is the time when team assessment should be conducted to produce information on skills gaps so analysis and planning for bridging that gap move forward.

Because the needs of a team precede operational needs, many of the gaps identified for a team are filled during planning. This improves a design and determines readiness of a team for development.

Effectively prepared, Development and Test teams focus on project deliverables during a Build Track. Release/Operations, User Experience, and Product Management often begin to be involved in the early stages of preparation for final release. Incremental exposure of a solution to external constituencies and gradual involvement in later stages of testing enable a team to assess efficacy of organizational readiness activities of the eventual solution owners.

In the last stages of a project, most of the readiness activities have been or are being executed as the training and preparation of users and support and operations staff are done, and a solution is released and/or deployed.

At the end of a project, team effort relative to readiness is evaluated by a team and an organization so that subsequent projects are able to repeat successes and learn from areas that require improvement.

Deliberate outputs for readiness are often embedded in regular checkpoint deliverables but can be itemized separately to highlight or manage them with individual attention. If large readiness gaps exist, Program Management needs to make sure readiness activities and deliverables are not relegated to the background or assumed to occur indirectly. Readiness activities are people-centric, and therefore require constant vigilance.

MSF Readiness Management Process

Lead Advocacy Group: Program Management

The MSF Readiness Management Discipline includes a readiness management process to help prepare for the knowledge, skills, and abilities needed to build and manage projects and solutions. It is considered a systematic, ongoing, iterative approach to readiness and is adaptable to both large and small projects. The MSF Readiness Management Process, graphically depicted in Figure 7-4, is composed of four steps:

- **Define**   Identify and match up required team competencies and individual proficiency levels needed to plan, build, and manage a solution successfully.

- **Assess**   Compare actual individual readiness with required readiness to identify readiness gaps.

- **Change**   Take steps to improve readiness in an attempt to minimize readiness gaps.

- **Evaluate**   Assess effectiveness of readiness improvement activities.

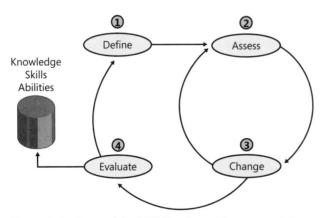

Figure 7-4   Steps of the MSF Readiness Management Process

The most basic approach is simply to assess skills and make appropriate changes through training and assessment. On projects that are small or have short time frames, this streamlined approach is quite effective. However, performing the steps of defining needed skills, evaluating the results of change, and keeping track of knowledge, skills, and abilities allows for the full realization of readiness management. It is also typically where organizations reap rewards from investments in readiness activities.

Step 1: Define

During envisioning, a team aligns its business and technology goals to create a shared vision of what a solution will look like. A team uses this to define environmental factors under which the team needs to perform (i.e., called *scenarios*). An example of a scenario is a high-risk infrastructure effort with tight deadlines. Using this information, a team defines a set of skills (i.e., *competencies*) needed in the various advocacy groups to achieve that vision successfully. The collective set of skills defined for each advocacy group can be further decomposed into required skill sets for each functional area. Scenarios are also used when assessing team member abilities (i.e., *proficiencies*). All of this is encompassed in the first step of the MSF Readiness Management Process called *Define*.

As just explained, the three components of defining readiness include the following:

- Scenarios
- Competencies
- Proficiencies

Outputs from this step include the following:

- Competencies identified with desired proficiency levels
- Competencies and proficiencies mapped to the appropriate scenario

Scenarios   Skill proficiency is greatly influenced by a solution delivery environment. A person with a given ability to perform a task will have varying degrees of success given different environmental factors. For example, some people are not fazed by a work environment with uncertainty and ever-changing requirements. Conversely, others lose productivity in this type of environment. Therefore, a person with an aversion to change put in a changing environment will not do as well as if that person were put in an environment with little change. This exemplifies how the same person with the same skills might exhibit different amounts of productivity because of environmental factors.

The description and classification of the different types of environments and situations in which teams operate within an organization are called *scenarios*. Scenarios generally fall into one of four categories as shown here and in Figure 7-5:

- **High potential**   Planning and designing to deploy, upgrade, and/or implement a new solution, technology, or service in its organization. These are typically research type situations or situations in which an organization is reactively responding to competitor actions.

- **Strategic** Developing and exploiting new technologies, solutions, or services for strategic advantage or to capture a potential opportunity. These are typically market-leading solutions, which could lead to business transformation defining the next generation, long-term architecture.

- **Key operational** Deploying, upgrading, and/or implementing a new solution, technology, or service that has to coexist or continue to interact seamlessly with legacy software and systems. These are typically today's business-critical systems, aligned with the as-is technology architecture.

- **Support** Extending a solution to fit the needs of a customer's environment. These are typically valuable but not business-critical solutions, and they often involve legacy technology.

Figure 7-5 Typical scenario categories for solution delivery[1]

By categorizing projects within an organization into appropriate scenarios, readiness planning is done according to the unique nature of that project. Different scenarios require distinct approaches to obtaining the appropriate resources and skills for that project type. By first defining the scenario best classifying a project, the appropriate competencies and proficiencies can then be mapped.

Differing scenario types can also drive decisions for outsourcing or using consulting to obtain the skills needed. For example, staffing for a *high-potential* project scenario might include specialized vendor-trained consultants versus a project scenario where readiness planning

---

1 John Ward and Joe Peppard, *Strategic Planning for Information Systems*, 3rd ed. (West Sussex, England: John Wiley & Sons, 2002), 41.

typically includes courseware training and certification of in-house staff. Following are a few approaches to obtain the appropriate levels of readiness for each scenario in terms of knowledge, skills, and abilities.

- **High potential**   Need to have a high degree of agility, be able to investigate and evaluate new technologies, and be prepared to obtain (for a short period) the best expertise available.

- **Strategic**   Need in-house, in-depth expertise at a solution architect level and be able to bridge skills across technology to the business.

- **Key operational**   Quality of technical knowledge and process are critical as is ready availability of the right skills. Typically, outsourcing occurs to obtain quality skills and knowledge or to develop strong in-house capabilities.

- **Support**   The cost of delivery becomes paramount, and an organization might decide to rely on external skills (particularly for legacy) on a reactive basis.

With projects and their associated scenarios defined, it is then time to identify the competencies and subsequent proficiencies associated with these project scenarios.

Competencies   Competencies define a level of adeptness with which teams are able to perform given tasks given a particular scenario. Being adept means having the requisite knowledge and skills to perform the given role and associated tasks at an expected proficient level of performance (i.e., needed ability to perform a task). Competencies are commonly associated with task types or roles. A skills profile is associated with each task type or role such that an individual with the requisite skills should be able to perform. With roles, it is expected that competency in a few different areas is required. For example, on a particular project, the Infrastructure Architect role requires expertise in designing solutions that involve the Microsoft Active Directory and Exchange Server product lines.

Proficiencies   Proficiency is a measure of an individual's ability to execute tasks or demonstrate skill or capability within a given scenario. To make sure the difference between competencies and proficiencies is clear, consider that proficiencies are an assessment of a team member's abilities to perform in various capacities in various scenarios, whereas competencies define the abilities necessary to be able to perform a respective task type or role in a specific scenario.

The proficiency is designated by the level at which individuals are assessed or assess themselves. A proficiency level provides a benchmark, or starting point, for analyzing the gap between the individuals' current skills set and the necessary skills for completion of the tasks associated with the given scenario.

During the *Define* step of the MSF Readiness Management Process, the level at which individuals should be performing for each role in given scenarios is determined using either self-assessment or assessment testing. Individual proficiency levels are then associated with required project competencies so that when assessments are completed, the output is measured and analyzed to determine proficiency gaps. A proficiency gap is when performance is at a lower level than that of the expected proficiency level for a role or task type. Table 7-2 shows a sample proficiency rating scale used in proficiency assessments.

Table 7-2   Example of a Proficiency Rating Scale

Numerical Rating	Natural Language Rating	Description
0	No Experience	Not applicable.
1	Novice	*Familiarity:* Skill in formative stages, has limited knowledge. Not able to function independently in this area.
2	Intermediate	*Working knowledge:* Good understanding of skill area, and is able to apply it with reasonable effectiveness. Functions fairly independently in this area, but periodically seeks guidance from others.
3	Experienced	*Strong working knowledge:* Strong understanding of skill area, and is able to apply it very effectively in position. Seldom needs others' assistance in this area.
4	Expert	*Expert:* Has highly detailed, thorough understanding of this area, and is able to apply it with tremendous effectiveness in this position. Often sought out for advice when others are unable to solve a problem related to this skill area.

Step 2: Assess

The *Assess* step of the MSF Readiness Management Process measures individual proficiencies, and identifies and plans to mitigate readiness gaps. Two types of readiness gaps are assessed:

- Are the stated project needs, be it at a solution, team, subteam, or role level, actually what are needed?

- Are the teams, subteams, roles, and individuals able to deliver at their assessed skill level given their actual delivery environment?

By measuring these readiness gaps, learning plans are assembled to start to minimize these gaps.

Activities during this step include the following:

- Measure individual knowledge, skills, and abilities

- Revisit readiness needs

- Identify and analyze readiness gaps

- Create learning plans

Outputs from this step are as follows:

- Assessment output/gap analysis

- Learning plans

Measure Individual Knowledge, Skills, and Abilities   Two options are available for performing individual assessments: self-assessment and standardized tests. Self-assessment is a procedure whereby individuals assess their own level of ability. This includes responding to a list of questions such as: "How well are you able to perform x?"

Self-assessment requires individuals to measure their own abilities using a scale such as that shown in Table 7-2. This technique is effective in learning how individuals perceive their own levels of ability. Although it might not always be an accurate assessment of the individual's abilities, it is a quick way to get some measurements. In addition, it helps later in forming personalized learning plans to know where individuals think they are with their abilities.

Standardized testing is the other method of assessing an individual's abilities. It enables calibration of an individual's skills as compared to a given baseline. This type of test requires individuals to respond to specific, often technical, questions to show their knowledge; to perform specific tasks; and to demonstrate analytical abilities.

Revisit Readiness Needs   Teams are assembled based on an estimated level of competency needed for the various roles. As teams gain experience with delivering, each team should revisit their readiness needs. In addition, readiness needs should be regularly revisited corresponding with changes in the business environment and changes in technology.

Although it is expected that project readiness needs will flux over the course of a solution delivery life cycle, if the variance is big enough, this should be treated as a readiness gap (if the need increases) or a potential staffing change (if the need decreases).

Identify and Analyze Readiness Gaps   A *readiness gap* is when an individual has demonstrated lower proficiency for a specific, required competency than the defined required level for his or her role (identified during the *Define* step). As mentioned previously, individual readiness gaps roll up through the various levels and can lead to a readiness gap at the enterprise level. Usually, this is not the case because part of the staffing process would make sure that selected team members complement each other's proficiencies and competencies so as to not have readiness gaps. However, in many cases when facing a new project, organizations do not have the internal capabilities or experience to assess correctly the skills and abilities needed. Providers such as Microsoft Certified Technical Education Centers (CTEC) or consulting organizations are able to assist with this essential step.

Create Learning Plans   Once readiness gaps at all levels have been analyzed, the information gathered is used to formulate learning plans. A learning plan consists of both formal and informal learning activities and guides individuals through the process of moving from one proficiency level to the next. A learning plan must go beyond traditional training delivery, such as instructor-led and self-study, and account for how to begin to apply the learned information to the job. This is usually reinforced with on-the-job mentoring or coaching. An effective learning plan takes into account the following:

- Different learning styles of individuals, and it accommodates those differences to efficiently use time and resources

- Appropriate resources such as training materials, courseware, white papers, computer-based training, mentoring, and on-the-job or self-directed training

It is critical that an organization and project team support its members as they execute their learning plans. Identifying a readiness gap is meaningless unless an organization is ready to mitigate it.

Step 3: Change

The *Change* step of the MSF Readiness Management Process implements the learning plans in an attempt to minimize readiness gaps and tracks progress to make sure the efforts are effective.

As just identified, activities during this step include the following:

- Implement learning plans
- Track progress

Outputs from this step include the following:

- Knowledge gained from training
- Progress tracking data

Implement Learning Plans   Activities and tasks outlined in an individual's learning plan should be incorporated into that person's respective project schedule. Otherwise, these activities and tasks are at great risk of being overwhelmed by the other planned activity.

Track Progress   It is important not just to facilitate learning but also to understand the effectiveness of the readiness efforts. Because learning is more involved and subjective than training is, it is challenging to track progress against the learning plans. The approach to track progress does not have to be complex. It might be as simple as having the individual report completed training.

Step 4: Evaluate

The *Evaluate* step of the MSF Readiness Management Process determines whether the learning plans were effective and whether lessons learned are being successfully implemented. During evaluation, a determination is made if the desired state, as described during the *Define* step and measured during the *Assess* step, was achieved during the *Change* step. In addition, a team should harvest lessons learned to help make the next project more successful.

This *Evaluate* step could be the end of the process. But because learning is an ongoing need for continued success, evaluation should be viewed as input to the next iterative cycle through the process.

Activities during this step include the following:

- Review results
- Manage knowledge

Outputs from this step include the following:

- Feedback
- Certifications
- Knowledge management system

Review Results   A real-world test of learning activities success is the effectiveness of the individual back on the job. A benefit of reviewing the results with each individual is the capability not only to guide individuals through their first exposure to new concepts, but also to enable the expert (mentor or coach) to assess training effectiveness. Using verbal and written feedback, the expert highlights the areas where individuals are performing well and are demonstrating understanding of the given concepts. Likewise, the mentor or coach is able to provide feedback on the areas where individuals are struggling or appear weak in their understanding and application of the new learning. This review helps to identify whether the knowledge transfer approach taken was the most effective and those areas that might need to be readdressed and where further training might be necessary. This also enables an organization, at any time in the life cycle, to analyze overall readiness to make necessary adjustments to readiness plans.

The individuals' activities in this step can include some introspection and self-assessment to determine whether the learning was effective before putting those new competencies to work. Individuals might also decide it is a good time to become certified because they have done the learning, performed the key tasks, and assimilated the knowledge.

Manage Knowledge   A natural side effect of training individuals is that the knowledge they acquire becomes intellectual capital that the individual is able to capture and disseminate throughout an organization. As learning plans are completed and applied on the job, individuals discover key learning that their training provided. Sharing this information with others throughout an organization enhances the collective knowledge and fosters a learning community. One objective of the Readiness Management Discipline is to encourage development of a knowledge management system to better enable the sharing and transfer of proven practices and lessons learned, as well as to create a skills baseline of the knowledge contained within an organization.

Individuals in an organization carry with them a body of learning, expertise, and knowledge that, however extensive or expansive, encompasses less than the collective knowledge of all the people. A knowledge management system provides an infrastructure by which that knowledge is harnessed and made available to a community.

As organizations face the need for global knowledge that needs to be easily and quickly used, compounded by shorter time frames for implementing solutions, requirements increase for individuals to share their knowledge and expertise and to reuse what others have learned.

Knowledge management systems provide many benefits, including, but not limited to, the following:

- Increasing organizational effectiveness by creating the ability for individuals to find the information and expertise they need, when they need it, fast–regardless of its location.

- Establishing a common structure that facilitates the easy sharing of experiences and proven practices.

- Facilitating individuals working across organizational and geographical barriers through "global" communities. Because many customers have locations worldwide, there is an increased need for collaboration, sharing of proven practices, and lessons learned.

Adding Readiness Assessments to a Project Schedule

The MSF Readiness Management Process describes how to assess and improve team member readiness in context of the skills needed on a project. What is often less clear is how to use this information in assembling project schedules. One such way is to factor it into each team member's capacity to perform work. Microsoft Project provides a means to cap a team member's contribution to a project by using the "Max. Units" field on the Resource Sheet.

However, because it is expected that a team member's readiness gaps shrink as the project progresses, using this fixed value is not practical. As discussed later in task estimation, a benchmark set of skills should be used to estimate tasks (it is often helpful to have a particular person in mind as the benchmark). Then, all tasks should be estimated as if that benchmark person were to perform them. This simplifies the scheduling process (discussed in Chapter 8, "MSF Plan Track: Planning a Solution").

Once resources are applied to tasks, team members readiness to perform particular tasks can be factored in using the Units field of the assign resource as exemplified in Figure 7-6. In this example, a particular task called Task A has seven resources available to perform the task. With the first resource being the benchmark person (i.e., Cameron), the skills of the other resources are scaled accordingly as exemplified in the "Skill Normalization %." In this example, Kyle is estimated to be able to perform this task in 15 hours, whereas it would take Cameron 12 hours (hence a 75 percent normalization assessment). Many times, if Kyle was the selected resource, the project manager would change the work field to 15 hours upon assigning Kyle to the task. This is fine if resources do not change once assigned, but it makes it challenging when work assignments are fluidly changing. By adjusting the resource unit field (representing capacity), it preserves the benchmark estimate while appropriately stretching the duration. Another way to look at this is it will take Kyle 2 days to perform the same amount of work that it will take Cameron (the benchmark person) a day and a half to perform. The work estimate remains constant while the readiness of the person assigned affects the amount of time needed to perform the work (i.e., task duration).

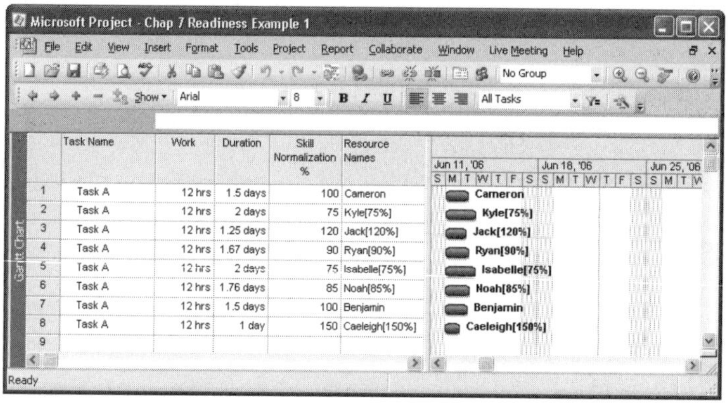

	Task Name	Work	Duration	Skill Normalization %	Resource Names
1	Task A	12 hrs	1.5 days	100	Cameron
2	Task A	12 hrs	2 days	75	Kyle[75%]
3	Task A	12 hrs	1.25 days	120	Jack[120%]
4	Task A	12 hrs	1.67 days	90	Ryan[90%]
5	Task A	12 hrs	2 days	75	Isabelle[75%]
6	Task A	12 hrs	1.76 days	85	Noah[85%]
7	Task A	12 hrs	1.5 days	100	Benjamin
8	Task A	12 hrs	1 day	150	Caeleigh[150%]

Figure 7-6 Example of incorporating readiness into a project schedule

Another common reality is that not everyone on the team is assigned full time to the project. Even if they are assigned full time, they often have some implicit duties that reduce their capacity to perform. As such, availability of each resource can be represented as a percentage of time. For example, if a full-time commitment on a project is 40 hours a week, a resource that is available only 32 hours a week has an 80 percent availability. This too can be represented using "Max. Units," but often a resource's availability changes over the course of a project–especially if it is a project that spans many months. Therefore, a "% availability" factor can be considered as a dynamic attribute of the resource. Combining a resource's percentage availability with that resource's skill normalization percentage gives his or her effective capacity to perform a given task. With both factors represented as a percentage, the resultant effective capacity is a multiplication of both as exemplified in Figure 7-7 (e.g., 75% × 80% = 60%).

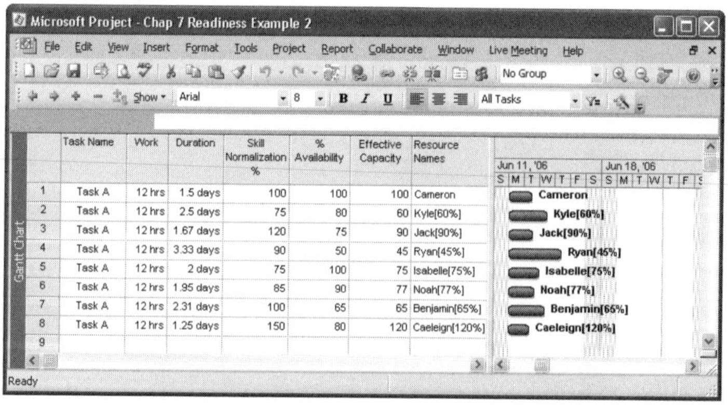

	Task Name	Work	Duration	Skill Normalization %	% Availability	Effective Capacity	Resource Names
1	Task A	12 hrs	1.5 days	100	100	100	Cameron
2	Task A	12 hrs	2.5 days	75	80	60	Kyle[60%]
3	Task A	12 hrs	1.67 days	120	75	90	Jack[90%]
4	Task A	12 hrs	3.33 days	90	50	45	Ryan[45%]
5	Task A	12 hrs	2 days	75	100	75	Isabelle[75%]
6	Task A	12 hrs	1.95 days	85	90	77	Noah[77%]
7	Task A	12 hrs	2.31 days	100	65	65	Benjamin[65%]
8	Task A	12 hrs	1.25 days	150	80	120	Caeleign[120%]

Figure 7-7 Example of incorporating readiness and resource availability into a project schedule

Because this can be cumbersome to track and calculate for each task, it is more practical to assess a skill normalization and an availability percentage for each iteration. This is acceptable because a person's skill does not appreciably change over the course of an iteration—especially if it is a 30-day iteration. Also, most people can reasonably and confidently predict their availability looking forward a month at a time.

If this approach is adopted, team member readiness can easily be incorporated into the scheduling process. It also provides an easy means to adjust schedules based on team members improving their readiness as the project progresses.

Project Structure Document (Deliverable)

Lead Advocacy Group: Program Management

A project structure document is the culmination of many Envision Track activities. It reflects roles with needed skills and abilities as identified by readiness management efforts. It reflects feature and function teams needed to deliver a solution. It reflects stakeholder analysis, making sure the team model advocates for each key stakeholder. Overall, it defines the approach a team will take in organizing and managing a project team.

Defining a Solution

Defining a solution is an evolutionary and coordinated effort between team members and key stakeholders. Typically, a team consists of just a few core members and a few key stakeholders such as sponsors and subject matter experts (often users). They work together to identify, analyze, and define the problem or opportunity. Their wrestling with defining the problem or opportunity usually generates many competing ideas on how to address the problem or opportunity. These ideas are vetted and refined into a shared vision of a solution and a few approaches to deliver the solution. Continuing to refine and define their understanding of what is needed, a team defines high-level requirements for a solution as well as develops an understanding of who and what will use a solution through a set of user scenario–based techniques (e.g., personas, use cases, usage scenarios, user stories). All of this is rolled into a conceptual definition of a solution.

The following sections expand upon these activities.

Defining the Problem or Opportunity

Lead Advocacy Group: Product Management

How does a team quickly get to a workable definition of the problem or opportunity? It might be challenging with a high potential of getting sidetracked discussing noncritical aspects of a solution. This activity is best served if a team establishes some guidelines as to how much and what level of detail to provide while trying to define the problem or opportunity.

Establishing these guidelines is essential because much of the information comes from interviewing existing users and stakeholders, and they do not take too kindly to repeated "clarification" or "oops, we need a little bit more" interviews. When talking with these people about addressing existing problems, it is important to get to the root cause of their pain and not solicit the deficiencies of the features and functions of the current system. Also, try to stay away from technology-based discussions and focus on business-oriented discussions (e.g., strategic capabilities, business processes, customer experience). Before talking with anyone, a team should consider the type of information and how it will be represented, consolidated, and stored for future analysis.

Creating a Shared Vision

Lead Advocacy Group: Product Management

As discussed in Chapter 2, "Understanding Solution Delivery Environments," a *vision* is a concise description, in business terms, of the overall mission. A shared vision orients a team in a common direction, reinforces solution goals, simplifies and ensures consistency in decision making, motivates the team, and maintains focus on solution quality. Not reaching consensus on a shared vision leads to loss of time and effort, as whimsically shown in Figure 7-8.

Alice: "Would you tell me please, which way I ought to go from here?"

Cat: "That depends a good deal on where you want to get to."

Alice: "I don't much care where..."

Cat: "Then it doesn't matter which way you go."

**Alice in Wonderland
by Lewis Carroll**

Figure 7-8   A shared vision gives a team direction

Project vision is best expressed in the form of a vision statement. Although concise—no more than a paragraph—the vision statement describes where the business is going and how the proposed solution will help to achieve business value. A good example of a vision statement is this:

> *I believe this nation should commit itself to achieving the goal...of landing a man on the Moon and returning him safely to the Earth. No single space project...will be more impressive to mankind, or more important for the long-range exploration of space...*

—*President John F. Kennedy, Speech to U.S. Congress, May 25, 1961*

> **Clarity Point**   Instead of calling it a "vision statement," teams sometimes call it a "mission statement." The difference is semantics. A "mission statement" often is more constrained and more focused than a vision statement is. A vision statement seems less bounded and leaves constraining to a project scope.

> **Lesson Learned**   Sometimes it is good to have two vision statements—a brief one (couple of sentences) that people are able to memorize easily and an expanded one that more richly describes the vision.

Defining High-Level Requirements

Lead Advocacy Group: Product Management

High-level requirements are a descriptive way to bound the vision into something deliverable. They are brief statements of *what* a solution needs to do, not *how* a solution needs to do it—those are implementation details left for later. Requirements statements are gathered using techniques such as interviewing, surveys, prototyping, measuring, observing, and examining existing documentation. As discussed later, high-level requirements are decomposed into actionable detailed requirements. But first, high-level requirements need to be defined and reflected in a medium to be shared with the team and stakeholders (e.g., documented in specifications, represented within modeling and design tool(s), explained through user stories, etc.).

"Finding" Requirements

High-level requirements should holistically describe the totality of a solution (i.e., cover every aspect of a solution and its interactions with the outside world) and the environment and constraints under which a solution must operate. They reflect the way users and administrators need to interact with a solution (e.g., a field inspector needs a portable data entry device). As such, high-level requirements can come from many sources. Common sources of high-level requirements are consistent with environmental challenges referenced in Chapter 2, "Understanding Solution Delivery Environments," and sources of risk referenced in Chapter 5, "Managing Project Risks." These include the following:

- **Environmental**   Legal, regulatory, facilities, business governance, site topology, legacy solutions
- **People**   User needs, reflection of skills and abilities of user and administrator, support, training, customer enhancement requests
- **Organizational**   Processes, procedures, roles, structure
- **Schedule**   Time to market
- **Quality features and functions**   Competitive, differentiating
- **Operational**   Qualities of service (discussed in Chapter 8, "MSF Plan Track: Planning a Solution)," high-priority fixes

- **Risk**   Degree(s) of tolerance and avoidance

- **Data**   Sources, targets, structures, rules, retention, auditing

- **Usability**   Performance and usability enhancements

- **Technology**   Hardware, software, networks, communications, infrastructure, security

Writing Requirements

High-level requirements can be expressed in terms of functionality (e.g., new policy data entry form for an insurance solution) as well as rules or parameters that apply to that functionality (e.g., policyholders are limited to one policy per specific property). Like any requirement, high-level requirements need to be "SMART" (i.e., specific, measurable, achievable, results-oriented, and time-bound).[2] Statements like "a solution needs to work as fast as possible" are not requirements. How would a team write the acceptance criteria for that "requirement"? It is not measurable. When writing requirements, it is handy to keep in mind how someone would "test" the requirement. One construct to consider is thinking that all requirements must be evaluated by either *inspection* (observing behavior; e.g., the light blinks as expected), *analysis* (mathematically verified; e.g., mean time between failure), *demonstration* (show that it works; e.g., submitted data is properly formatted in a report), or *test* (measured behavior; e.g., system responds in less than 1.25 seconds).

Creating User Profiles

Lead Advocacy Group: Product Management

Many different approaches and methodologies have their own name for representing a relevant and respectful description of typical users (e.g., user profiles, personas, actors). To avoid confusion, herein, they are referred to as *user profiles* and are defined as descriptions of the eventual users of a solution in terms of geography, organizational and communication structures, user functions, resource availability, knowledge, skills, abilities, goals, motives, concerns, usage patterns, and other relevant information.

To develop user profiles, a team needs to identify categories of users (e.g., remote user) by segmenting and differentiating user activities and interactions with a solution. It might be necessary to segment the categories further by user skill level (e.g., senior account manager). If possible, it is helpful to add user expectations of a solution.

Forming Solution Design Strategies

Lead Advocacy Group: Architecture

Solution design strategies represent notional approaches to implement the conceptual solution. Typically as part of the conceptual solution, a team develops a conceptual architecture and

---

2 There are a few variants of the definition of SMART. The *A* is also referenced as *attainable*; the *R* is also referenced as *realistic*, and the *T* is also is referenced as *time-oriented* and *time-constrained*. Because they all roughly imply the same, which variant you use does not really make a difference as long as the point comes across.

sometimes adds envisioned vendor products and solutions that might be used (i.e., to support "buy" vs. "build" decision approaches).

Architectural Design Strategy

An architectural design strategy describes how the different aspects of a solution will operate together. As exemplified in Figure 7-9, a diagram is an excellent means of illustrating these components and relationships. It enables customers, who often understand more when provided images, to visualize a solution in its environment.

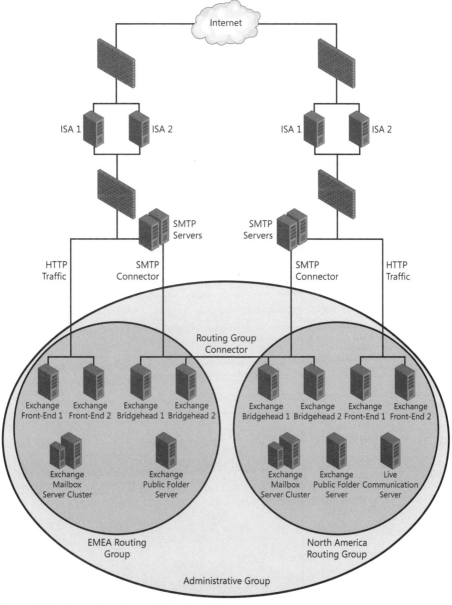

Figure 7-9   Example of a conceptual architecture

Technical Design Strategy

The technical design strategy maps out alternate technologies to implement the architectural design strategy. It is a high-level description of the key products and technologies to be considered for use in building a solution.

Developing a Conceptual Understanding of a Solution

Lead Advocacy Group: Product Management

It is very hard to conjure up a well-structured solution without detailed requirements—usually not sufficiently known until midway through a Plan Track. However, a team can start to form a conceptual understanding of how to solve the problem or realize the opportunity. This involves describing features and requirements in high-level terms. It likely includes a series of high-level "approaches" with matching conceptual architectures.

The conceptual solution should contain as much as is known about a solution, its operations, success criteria, and expectations associated with it, including any assumptions and constraints. A solution should be described in terms of business and design goals with matching objectives that enable achievement of the goals.

The conceptual solution should address all functional areas of the various advocacy groups. Table 7-3 provides a sample of the typical approaches covered in a conceptual solution for each advocacy group.

Table 7-3   Typical Approaches in a Solution Concept by Advocacy Group

Approach	Advocacy Group
Design and architecture approach	Architecture
Communications and marketing approach	Product Management
Project/quality assurance approach	Program Management
Development approach	Development
Deployment and operations approach	Release/Operations
Usability	User Experience
Testing approach	Test

Defining Acceptance Criteria

Acceptance criteria define the terms, conditions, and/or metrics that must be satisfied for the reviewer(s) to sign-off on a solution. They represent that a solution has met the agreed-to requirements and conditions. Within MSF, there are three types of acceptance criteria:

- User acceptance criteria
- Operations acceptance criteria
- Customer acceptance criteria

Although not called *acceptance criteria*, MSF also has the following gating criteria, discussed later, that must be satisfied before proceeding in their respective areas:

- **Success criteria**   What are necessary to declare an event, process, or activity a success
- **Quality criteria**   Define required quality—sometimes collectively defining a *quality bar*
- **Release criteria**   What are necessary to release to a selected environment (e.g., no active issues, satisfy all solution quality criteria, meet stakeholder needs and expectations, satisfy user acceptance criteria, satisfy operations acceptance criteria)
- **Pilot completion criteria**   What are necessary to conclude a pilot successfully

Note that people and priorities can change over the course of a project, so all acceptance criteria should be periodically reviewed and refined accordingly.

User Acceptance Criteria

Lead Advocacy Group: User Experience

Although some users are likely to work with a project team throughout a project, key user champions that are empowered to "accept" a solution on behalf of all users should work with a project team during an Envision Track to define a set of acceptance criteria. Typically, user acceptance criteria focus on usability and capability from an end user's perspective. In a Stabilize Track, a team will present a solution to these user champions for their review and comment. A team will work with these users to refine a solution until it meets user criteria, and then it is expected that they sign off on a solution.

Operations Acceptance Criteria

Lead Advocacy Group: Release/Operations

An operations team establishes operations-specific acceptance criteria with a project team as to the operations team's criteria for deploying a solution into the production environment. Typical operations acceptance criteria focus on operational readiness (e.g., operation and support team training), deployment, and qualities of service. Satisfying these criteria signifies that an operations team is willing to assume responsibility for a solution and proceed with solution deployment.

Customer Acceptance Criteria

Lead Advocacy Group: Product Management

Customer acceptance is part of project closure and sign-off, which happens at the end of a project. Typical customer acceptance criteria establish the terms and conditions for the customer to take receipt of a solution (e.g., upon successful deployment, the customer takes ownership of a solution) and collateral expected at the end of a project (e.g., lessons learned).

Scoping a Solution

Up until this point, the team and stakeholders have brainstormed about what a solution should be. The next step in the life cycle is to start to constrain a solution into something tangible that is able to be delivered within project constraints (i.e., scoping a solution). *Scope* is the sum of deliverables and services to be provided in a project. The scope defines what must be done to support the shared vision. It integrates the shared vision mapped against reality and reflects what the customer deems essential for success of the release. As a part of defining the scope, less urgent functionality is moved to future solution releases.

The benefits of defining the scope are the following:

- Dividing a long-term vision into achievable chunks
- Defining the features that will be in each release
- Allowing flexibility for change
- Providing a baseline for trade-offs

The term "scope" has two aspects: solution scope and project scope. Although these two correlate, they are not the same. Understanding this distinction helps teams manage the schedule and cost of their projects.

Solution scope describes a solution's features and deliverables. A *feature* is a desirable or notable aspect of an application or piece of hardware. For example, the ability to preview before printing is a feature of a word processing application; and the ability to encrypt e-mail messages before sending is a feature of messaging applications. The accompanying user manual, online help files, operations guides, and training are also features of a solution.

Project scope describes the work and services being provided by a project team to deliver each item described in a solution scope. Some organizations define project scope as a statement of work (SOW) to be performed.

Clarifying project scope includes the following benefits:

- Focuses a team on identifying what work must be done
- Facilitates breaking down large, general tasks into smaller, specific ones
- Identifies specific project work that is not clearly associated with any specific feature, such as preparing status reports
- Facilitates subdividing the work among subcontractors or partners on a team
- Clarifies those parts of a solution for which the team is responsible (often referred to as *in-scope*) as well as the ones for which it is not responsible (often referred to as *out-of-scope*)

- Ensures that each aspect of solution delivery clearly has an owner responsible for building or maintaining it, even if the owner is outside of a project team

- Identifies assumptions used to define project scope

Managing Project Trade-offs

Lead Advocacy Group: Program Management

Managing scope is critical for project success. Many projects fail, are completed late, or go dramatically overbudget because of poorly managed scope. Managing scope should not be bureaucratic or complex. Rather, it should be as simple as possible while providing the necessary controls to manage changes in scope. Managing scope prevents unapproved features and services from being added to a solution (i.e., scope creep). The best way to avoid scope creep proactively is to make sure a project team thoroughly understands a solution vision and business goals, and make sure they are able to trace critical features they are building back to the requirements.

There are many ways to implement scope management. One easy means to communicate necessary trade-offs when managing scope is to use a trade-off triangle.

Project Trade-off Triangle

Many trade-off paradigms are used to help teams metaphorically visualize balancing solution delivery parameters (e.g., good, fast, or cheap). MSF offers a trade-off paradigm that balances the relationship between project variables of resources (people and money), schedule (time), and features (scope). These variables are expressed in a triangular relationship as shown in Figure 7-10.

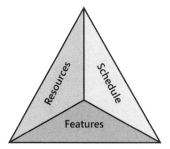

Figure 7-10   MSF project trade-off triangle

The triangle represents an elastic relationship such that a change in one parameter (e.g., resources) has an effect on one or both remaining sides of the triangle to maintain balance. For example, if a project feature set is to be expanded, a compensating change is needed to project resources and/or project schedule to rebalance the triangle. The changes needed to rebalance a project equate to impact realized from the change request.

As stated in Chapter 3, "Foundational Principles, Mindsets, and Proven Practices," different aspects of a solution likely have different quality levels (e.g., a financial component of a solution likely requires higher quality than an employee intranet component). To accommodate this, quality should be viewed as another dimension, which transforms the triangle into a tetrahedron (or three-sided pyramid). The obvious risk to making quality a variable instead of a fixed level that is nonnegotiable is that some teams might choose to lower their quality to enable a reduction in required resources and/or schedule.

A key to deploying a solution that matches the customer's needs is to find the right balance between resources, deployment date, and features. Because customers are sometimes reluctant to cut features, the trade-off triangle helps to explain the impact of that decision (it also supports their adoption of a versioned release strategy if they have not already adopted one).

Project Trade-off Matrix

Another powerful tool to manage trade-offs is a project trade-off matrix. It visually represents an agreement between the team and stakeholders, made early in a project, regarding the default project-wide priorities when making trade-off decisions. For instance, Figure 7-11 shows the typical trade-off matrix used by Microsoft product teams. If the default project priorities do not seem applicable to all parts of a solution delivery effort, use a matrix for each major aspect of a solution (e.g., training). However, there still should be an overarching matrix for a project. Please note that each column must contain only one check mark.

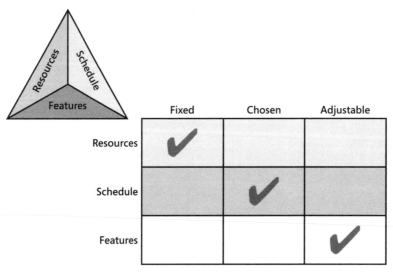

Figure 7-11   MSF project trade-off matrix

Literally interpreting the figure, it reads: *Given **fixed** resources we will **choose** a schedule and **adjust** features as necessary.* In other words, for this example, managing resources is top priority, is essentially unchangeable, and is followed by managing the schedule; taken together, this dictates which features the team is able to deliver.

The main benefit of establishing default priorities is to help make trade-offs less contentious. Note that the real power of using this matrix is the process to reach consensus—the matrix is just a graphical conversation starter.

> **Lesson Learned**   Organizations often begin a project saying that features are top priority, but after assembling rough resource and schedule estimates to deliver those features, they often reprioritize. So make sure the team revisits this matrix a few times with the stakeholders and at each major checkpoint.

Assessing Risk (Deliverable)

Lead Advocacy Group: Program Management

Assessing risk starts from inception of a project. Every decision has direct or implied risk that should be documented. Alternate approaches to implement a solution have inherent risks that should be considered. Making project trade-offs has associated risks, too. Everything has varying degrees of risks. These risks influence all decision making and planning.

All the risks identified during envisioning are documented in an initial risk assessment document. This document forms the basis for ongoing risk management. This is also the time to determine how a team is going to implement the MSF Risk Management Process.

Establishing a Basis for Review and Change

Envisioning activities set the stage and direction for all other activities on delivering a solution. Because envisioning is an iterative process, the deliverables generated from an Envision Track are a basis for review and change. As such, to maintain project integrity, all requirements, designs, plans, and so forth need to be clearly linked back to an Envision Track activity. Therefore, for example, if a design change is warranted, it is understood if the change is in scope or out of scope. These linkages are called *traceability*. Most often, a team traces back to the vision/scope document, discussed next.

Establishing Traceability

Lead Advocacy Group: Product Management

Traceability provides a means to link features to business requirements. This is a two-way benefit. It enables a team to trace their delivery activities back to the initial requirements, goals, and objectives stated during envisioning to validate in-scope decision making quickly. It also facilitates compliance with formal change control and quality management standards (as required by the customer). Figure 7-12 is a graphical depiction of tracing a solution back to business goals.

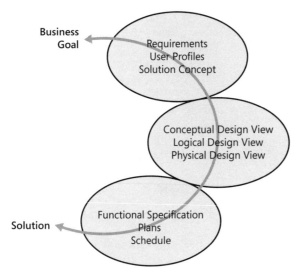

Figure 7-12   Traceability

Drafting a Vision/Scope Document (Deliverable)

Lead Advocacy Group: Product Management

A vision/scope document embodies the results of all envisioning activities. It sets the stage and direction for later tracks. It should be the first document new team members read to get an understanding of a solution, a project, and team member roles and responsibilities.

A typical vision/scope document contains the following information:

- Problem statement
- Vision statement
- Assumptions
- Project constraints
- Objectives
  - ❏ Business objectives
  - ❏ Technical objectives
- High-level requirements
- Key stakeholders
- User profiles
- Project scope

- Solution design strategies
  - ❑ Architectural design strategies
  - ❑ Technical design strategies
- Risks
- Acceptance criteria
- Key deliverables
- Version release strategy

Success Criteria for an Envision Track

With all this envisioning and scoping, how does a team know if they have accomplished their mission of envisioning a solution? Have they done enough? Have they done too much when less would have been sufficient? Well, here are a few commonly observed success indicators:

- Agreement with stakeholders and team has been obtained on the following points:
  - ❑ Project motivation
  - ❑ Solution vision
  - ❑ Solution scope
  - ❑ Conceptual solution
  - ❑ Conceptual architecture
  - ❑ Project team and structure
  - ❑ Technical design strategy
- Constraints and goals have been documented.
- Initial risk assessments have been done.
- Change control and configuration management processes have been established.
- Sponsor(s) and/or key stakeholders have signed off.

Chapter 8

MSF Plan Track: Planning a Solution

In this chapter:

The vision is set. The scope should be deliverable in the agreed-to time frame with the specified resources. The conceptual solution with its various implementation approaches has been mapped out. Now it is time to take what has been envisioned and work through planning details.

The Microsoft Solutions Framework (MSF) Plan Track focuses on what to build, how to build it, when to build the component parts, and what supporting environments are needed to deliver a solution. Specifically, a team evolves envisioning deliverables into requirements that fully describe a solution; documents them in a functional specification; develops detailed designs and architectures; and prepares work plans, cost estimates, and schedules for the various Plan Track deliverables. A team also defines and builds the necessary supporting environments to deliver a solution.

With many areas of parallel activity in this track, efforts to properly establish collaboration, communications, and team structure will be put to a test. If planning is done effectively, it reduces risks, detects gaps in thinking, and improves quality.

Goal

The goal of a Plan Track is to evolve the conceptual solution into tangible designs and plans so it can be built in a Build Track. This involves finding out as much information as possible, as early as possible. It also involves a team knowing when they have enough information to move forward.

Team Focus

Early in a Plan Track, a team identifies, analyzes, and prioritizes requirements that fully describe a solution and its behavior. Typically, these requirements are documented in a functional specification. The functional specification (also referred to as a technical specification) describes in detail how each feature is to look and behave. It establishes a basis for subsequent designing and planning efforts.

A design process gives a team a systematic way to evolve abstract concepts into specific technical details. Results of a design process are used to update a functional specification.

In parallel, detailed planning can begin. Each team lead prepares plan(s) for deliverables that pertain to their role and participates in team planning sessions. As a group, a team reviews and identifies dependencies among plans. All plans are synchronized and presented together as a master project plan.

Team members representing each role define specific activities, generate time estimates, and develop schedules for each deliverable. The various schedules are then synchronized and integrated into a master project schedule.

At the culmination of a Plan Track—project plans approved checkpoint—stakeholders and team members have agreed in detail on what is to be delivered and when. At the project plans approved checkpoint, the team reassesses risk, updates priorities, and finalizes estimates for resources and schedules.

As different deliverables are developed, it is important to maintain traceability among deliverables back to what was specified in envisioning. Maintaining traceability serves as one way to check design correctness and to verify that a design meets the goals and requirements of a solution.

Table 8-1 describes the focus and some of the responsibility areas of each advocacy group during planning.

Table 8-1   Team Focal Areas During Planning

Advocacy Group	Focus
Product Management	Conceptual design, business requirements analysis, communications plan, requirements prioritization
Program Management	Master project plan, master project schedule, budget
Architecture	Conceptual and logical design, technology evaluation, initial build estimates, functional specification content
Development	Logical and physical design, build plan/schedule, build estimates, prototypes
User Experience	Usage scenarios/use cases, user requirements, localization/accessibility requirements, user documentation/training plan/schedule for usability testing, user documentation, training

Table 8-1   **Team Focal Areas During Planning**

Advocacy Group	Focus
Test	Design evaluation, testing requirements, test plan/schedule, test scenarios
Release/Operations	Design evaluation, operations requirements, pilot and deployment plan/schedule, define and build various project environments

Key Deliverables

For a Plan Track, key deliverables are functional specifications, master project plan, and master project schedule. Each of these is discussed in detail in the following sections.

Key Checkpoints

Key checkpoints consist of a major checkpoint for the track and a few interim checkpoints.

Major Checkpoint

The major checkpoint concluding a Plan Track is *project plans approved*.

Project Plans Approved

Lead Advocacy Group: Program Management

This major checkpoint represents that the stakeholders and project team agree that a solution design, implementation plans, and project schedules sufficiently address how to construct a solution within project constraints and with acceptable risks. As part of this, it means that interim checkpoints have been met, due dates are realistic, tasks are detailed enough to be clearly understood, task estimates are reasonable given assigned resources, project roles and responsibilities are well defined, support environments are ready, and mechanisms are in place for addressing areas of project risk.

The approved designs, specifications, plans, and schedules become the project baseline and the basis for making future trade-off decisions. The baseline takes into account the various decisions that are reached by consensus, including trade-off matrix priorities. After the baseline is completed and approved, it is placed under change control. This does not mean that all decisions reached in a Plan Track are final. It means that as work progresses in a Build Track, the stakeholders and team should review and approve any suggested changes to the baseline.

Interim Checkpoints

The interim checkpoints for a Plan Track, as depicted in Figure 8-1, are the following:

- Technology validation completed
- Functional specification baselined

- Master project plan baselined
- Master project schedule baselined
- Supporting environments set up

Figure 8-1   Plan Track checkpoints

Technology Validation Completed

Lead Advocacy Group: Architecture

A solution might involve unproven technology, technology that is new to a team, or a new way to integrate existing technology. For these cases and any others that involve technology risks, a team needs to work with the technology as it will be used in a solution.

This checkpoint is intended to be a quick validation of the technology. Should more involved validation be required, the work done for this interim checkpoint will feed into subsequent prototyping efforts (discussed in the next chapter).

Validating technology often involves three activities. First, a team mitigates risks associated with technology challenges. Second, they compare and contrast alternative technologies for consideration. Third, they assess the feasibility of features and requirements given available technology. Results of this analysis are used as input to a design process and planning; can identify issues and risks that need to be tracked going forward; and can help identify team readiness gaps.

> **Clarity Point**   It is very likely that technology validation, if needed, would begin during an Envision Track and conclude early in a Plan Track. Ideally, it would be an Envision Track activity, but often teams do not know what technology is needed until design details are determined in a Plan Track.

Functional Specification Baselined

Lead Advocacy Group: Program Management

A functional specification is a means to document a detailed description of what a solution will look like and how it will behave. As discussed later, it can be a physical document or a set of documents (e.g., design documents) that collectively represent the functional specification. This interim checkpoint signifies that the detailed description of a solution has been baselined.

Master Project Plan Baselined

Lead Advocacy Group: Program Management

In MSF, a master project plan is a collection (or "roll up") of integrated plans covering all aspects of delivering a solution. It is important to understand that a master project plan is not some voluminous amalgamation; rather, it is a reference document (sometimes called a *project management plan*) showing how the various plans integrate together. This interim checkpoint signifies that the master project plan has been baselined.

Master Project Schedule Baselined

Lead Advocacy Group: Program Management

Like a master project plan that integrates the various plans needed to deliver a solution, a master project schedule integrates the various subteam schedules needed to deliver a solution. It contains schedule summary information, but leaves the details to the respective subteam schedules. It typically calls out significant tasks, deliverables, and checkpoints, providing an overview of a project. This interim checkpoint signifies that the master project schedule has been baselined.

Supporting Environments Set Up

Lead Advocacy Group: Release/Operations

This interim checkpoint signifies that the necessary environments to support preparing and delivering all aspects of a solution (e.g., development, testing, staging, training, research) have been set up and are ready for use. It involves building and administering the infrastructure necessary to perform the various solution delivery activities. These environments need to be isolated from each other and from production to not affect production operations.

Another activity that must be completed at this checkpoint is baselining the portion of the production environment(s) that a solution will be operating. A team performs this by conducting an audit (also known as "discovery") of the "as is" production environment. This includes server configurations, network, desktop software, and all relevant hardware. Organizations using Microsoft Operations Framework (MOF) can take advantage of information contained in the enterprise Configuration Management Database (CMDB) as a kind of bill of materials for understanding what is in the production environment.

Planning What to Build

How do stakeholders and the project team reach a common understanding of what to build? Most often, what to build is embodied in requirements, diagrams, and designs. The means and timing of what to define varies widely. Rapid development approaches (e.g., *eXtreme programming*[1] and *MSF for Agile Software Development*) use a well-structured build process to incrementally identify, build, test, and deploy solution features and function (i.e., define a little, build a little). At the other end of the spectrum, more formal build approaches thoroughly plan and verify what needs to be done before proceeding with solutions development. Both ends of the spectrum and everything in between have merit. Which approach to use is up to the stakeholders and project team in deciding which one best fits their solutions delivery philosophy and project constraints.

For the purposes of this book, the following sections attempt to take an approach-neutral view of planning what to build.

Decomposing and Refining Requirements

Lead Advocacy Group: Architecture

Requirements iteratively gathered during planning further define and refine a solution described by high-level requirements gathered during an Envision Track. They collectively form a detailed description of a solution. As with high-level requirements, detailed requirements address various domains such as business, end users, operations, and systems requirements. They include specifying a solution's behavior, how it interacts with its environment (be it other solutions, users, or administrators), features, functions, and expected operational characteristics (e.g., availability).

How Much Specificity Is Needed?

Requirements are costly to gather and maintain. Especially because they often change before a team acts on them. This is caused in part by changes in the business environment, changes in technology, and changes in project constraints. Compounding that, what are stated as requirements sometimes end up not being what is expected. Therefore, a team should determine what requirements should be collected and when.

Keep in mind that the purpose of requirements is to sufficiently, consistently, and clearly describe and understand a solution. Therefore, a team should gather the fewest requirements necessary to achieve that purpose. This presents a challenge in determining the amount and understanding how the blend of team experience levels and abilities influences that amount.

---

1   K. Beck, *eXtreme Programming Explained: Embrace Change* (Reading, MA: Addison-Wesley, 2000).

Often, more experienced and skilled team members require less specificity. Conversely, team members with less experience and skill often require more specificity. The level of specificity is also influenced by tools and processes used to gather the requirements.

Qualities of Service

As mentioned earlier, a significant source of requirements is defining expected operational characteristics of a solution, commonly called *qualities of service* (QoS). For example, an availability requirement is defined as *a solution shall provide service 99.999 percent of the time* (also referred to as achieving *five 9s*). Another example is a regulatory requirement defined as *a solution shall comply with HIPAA transactions standards.*[2]

QoS are not a new concept. They are sometimes referred to as *nonfunctional* requirements and informally referred to as the "*−ilities*" because so many of them end that way (e.g., maintainability). QoS are commonly found within a *Service Level Agreement* (SLA). Because providing high QoS in all areas is often prohibitively costly, a project team and the stakeholders need to come to an agreement on what is necessary. Often an organization will be able to provide a basic level of QoS through good design principles.

Tables 8-2 through 8-5 provide some common and emerging QoS to consider for a solution and its components.[3] Keep in mind that not all QoS are relevant to all solutions.

Table 8-2   Performance-Oriented Qualities of Service

Performance	
Responsiveness	Allowable amount of delay when responding to an action, call, or event
Concurrency	Ability to perform well when operated concurrently with other aspects of a solution and with its environment
Efficiency	Capability to provide appropriate performance, relative to the resources used, under stated conditions
Fault tolerance	Capability to maintain a specified level of performance irrespective of faults or of infringement of system resources
Scalability	Ability to handle simultaneous operational load
Extensibility	Ability to extend a solution without significant rework

Table 8-3   Trustworthiness-Oriented Qualities of Service

Trustworthiness	
Security	Ability to prevent access and disruption by unauthorized users, viruses, worms, spyware, and other agents
Privacy	Ability to prevent unauthorized access or viewing of data

2 *Health Insurance Portability and Accountability Act of 1996 (HIPAA)*, Public Law 104–191, 104th Congress (August 21, 1996).

3 Sam Guckenheimer, *Software Engineering with Microsoft Visual Studio Team System* (Upper Saddle River, NJ: Addison-Wesley Professional, 2006), 67–71.

Table 8-4   User Experience-Oriented Qualities of Service

User Experience	
Accessibility	Extent to which individuals with disabilities have access to and use of information and data that is comparable to the access to and use by individuals without disabilities
Attractiveness	Measure of visual appeal to users
Compatibility	Conformance to conventions and expectations
Discoverability	Ability of a user to find and learn features of a solution
Ease of use	Cognitive efficiency with which a user can perform desired tasks
Localizability	Ability to be adapted to conform to the linguistic, cultural, and conventional needs and expectations of a specific group of users

Table 8-5   Manageability-Oriented Qualities of Service

Manageability	
Availability	Degree to which it is operational and accessible when required for use. Often expressed as a probability
Reliability	Capability to maintain a specified level of performance when used under specified conditions, commonly stated as mean time between failures (MTBF)
Installability and uninstallability	Capability to be installed in a specific environment and uninstalled without altering the environment's initial state
Maintainability	Ease of modification to correct faults, improve performance or other attributes, or adapt to a changed environment
Monitorability	Extent to which health and operational data are automatically collected while operating
Operability	Extent to which a solution is controlled automatically while operating
Portability	Capability to be transferred from one environment to another
Recoverability	Capability to reestablish a specified level of performance and recover the data directly affected in the case of a failure
Testability	Degree to which the solution facilitates the establishment of test criteria and the performance of tests to determine whether those criteria have been met
Supportability	Extent to which operational problems are corrected
Reusability	Ability to repurpose solution components with little rework
Conformance	Adherence to applicable rules, regulations, policies, and standards
Interoperability	Capability to interact with other solutions in the environment

Prioritizing Requirements

In support of trade-off decision making and forming a versioned release strategy, a team needs a means to prioritize requirements (and features). There are many good approaches to prioritizing requirements.

A commonly used, simple approach is to sort the requirements into three categories: *must have*, *should have*, and *nice to have*. The must-have category contains requirements that are essential to a solution. Stakeholders, customers, and users would be dissatisfied if these requirements were not reflected in the delivered solution. The should-have category contains requirements that, although not critical to the success of a solution, have a compelling motivation to be in a solution. Stakeholders, customers, and users would not be pleased if these requirements were not reflected in the delivered solution. The nice-to-have category contains requirements that, although not necessary, would increase user experience and customer satisfaction. Another similar approach commonly used is referred to as MoSCoW (Must-, Should-, Could-, and Won't-have requirements and features).

Another more systematic approach to prioritizing requirements is to use Kano Analysis.[4] Kano Analysis purports customer satisfaction is related to customer expectations surrounding the performance and functional completeness of a solution. This relationship is usually depicted as shown in Figure 8-2.

Figure 8-2   Kano Analysis diagram

The horizontal axis indicates how much the delivered solution meets customer expectations. The vertical axis indicates customer satisfaction. The three graphed lines convey three requirements categories with different behaviors relating customer satisfaction with customer expectations:

- **Dissatisfiers**   Expected requirements that when absent in a solution generate significant dissatisfaction whereas their presence generates a diminishing dissatisfaction toward a neutral feeling

- **Satisfiers**   Requirements that generate proportional satisfaction with the quality and quantity of what is delivered

---

4 David Walden, "Kano's Methods for Understanding Customer-Defined Quality: Introduction to Kano's Methods," *Center for Quality Management Journal* 2, no. 4 (Fall 1993), 1–28.

- **Delighters**   Unanticipated requirements that when present in a solution generate significant satisfaction whereas their absence is acceptable and therefore does not generate dissatisfaction

Following this method, a team better understands customer satisfaction as related to the presence and absence of requirements and features. As such, when gathering requirements, make sure to ask the respondents about how they feel about degrees of delivering on requirements (i.e., from not delivering on the requirement through moderately delivering up through overdelivering on the requirement). The key is to find where the optimal balance between requirement delivery and customer satisfaction is.

The Kano Analysis diagram can also be used to communicate graphically the expected portions of delighters, satisfiers, and dissatisfiers in each iteration and in each release. As depicted in Figure 8-3, each iteration encompasses the indicated proportions of three require-ments categories. As also depicted, the release is the expected proportion for the releases—identified as the *minimum acceptable level.*

Figure 8-3   Example of managing iterations using the Kano Analysis diagram

Documenting Requirements in a Functional Specification (Deliverable)

Lead Advocacy Group: Product Management

Part of forming a shared vision is presenting the requirements in a form that all team members are able sufficiently, consistently, and clearly to understand for a solution. This often involves a detailed description, as viewed from a user perspective, of what a solution will look like and how it will behave. With increasing usage of tools to retain and present this information, a growing trend is for teams not to capture this information in a physical document called a *functional specification.* Rather, the constructs of a functional specification are contained within a combination of tools and other documents.

A functional specification represents a detailed description of a solution, detailed usage scenarios, and design goals and contains detailed requirements specifying its behavior and how it interacts with its environment (be it other solutions, users, or administrators). Requirements cover all aspects of a solution and often come from various domains such as business, end users, operations, and systems requirements.

Because the principles and underpinnings of a functional specification remain valid, it is up to the team to decide whether a physical document is needed. Beyond describing a solution, a functional specification serves many purposes:

- A contract between the team and stakeholders on what will be delivered
- A basis for estimating work
- A common reference point to synchronize the whole team
- A logical way to break down the problem and modularize a solution
- A path and structure to use for planning, scheduling, and building a solution

A functional specification is the basis for building the master project plan and schedule as well as a solution design. As such, once baselined, a functional specification should be changed only through change control.

Planning How to Build

Planning how to build a solution involves two work streams that build off a solution description contained in the functional specification. One work stream focuses on evolving a solution design from the conceptual solution defined during an Envision Track to detailed designs to enable implementation during a Build Track. The other work stream focuses on assembling various plans that collectively make up the master project plan. These two work streams are discussed next.

Evolving a Solution Design

Lead Advocacy Group: Architecture

As detailed solution requirements are approved, a team starts to incrementally and systematically design a solution and what is needed to support delivery of a solution (e.g., test harnesses). Starting with the conceptual solution defined during envisioning and with requirements and design goals outlined in the functional specification, MSF proposes proceeding with a three-tiered design process: *conceptual design*, *logical design*, and *physical design*; each is discussed in the next few sections and is depicted in Figure 8-4. Each of these designing steps incrementally adds more clarity and design details to the overall solution design and the supporting collateral. This design process is not intended to be used serially where all of conceptual designing needs to be completed before moving on to logical designing and subsequently to physical designing of a solution. Conversely, as soon as a design step for an aspect of a solution is completed, designers proceed to another aspect or take the one they are working with to the next level of detail. The results of a design process are used to update a functional specification and possibly requirements.

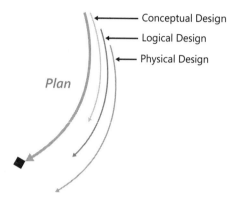

Conceptual Design
Logical Design
Physical Design

Plan

Figure 8-4   Evolving a solution design

A design process is structured so that each design step validates the prior step and sets a foundation for the next step. It is expected that as a team advances through a design process, they might need to revisit prior design steps as errors, inconsistencies, and gaps are uncovered. Revisiting prior steps is not a sign of inadequate designing because usually a team is quickly trying to advance through a design process, and to finish a step to eliminate revisiting is often too costly. In fact, it is the heart of an iterative design process, and therefore revisiting should be encouraged.

Conceptual Design

A conceptual design starts to bring clarity and adds a layer or two of detail to what was described during envisioning. Although the team still works at a conceptual level, a conceptual design incorporates the various aspects of what was covered in the functional specification (e.g., detailed description of a solution, detailed usage scenarios, QoS, test goals, design goals, and detailed requirements). A conceptual design introduces other aspects of designing, including high-level usability analysis, conceptual data modeling, process flows, context models, and initial technology implementation options. Table 8-6 provides an example of a typical use case. Table 8-7 provides an example of a supporting context model. Figure 8-5 provides an example of a matching process flow. Because there are many great books explaining these topics in detail, these examples are provided just for context.

Table 8-6   Example of a Use Case

Name	MM-UC003 Open Model
Type	Summary: ( ) Basic: (X) Extends: ( ) Used by: ( )
Description	
Actor(s) (Person who carries out the business activity)	Primary: User Secondary:
Assumptions	
Preconditions (What conditions exist before business activity can start)	1. Application is open. 2. Application does not contain its maximum number of opened models.

Steps
(Flow of events)
	1. On the File menu, select Open, upon which user is presented with a sorted list of available models either from the file system or from the <u>Library</u>.
	2. User selects desired model and clicks OK.
	3. System loads <u>model metadata (MM-CM001)</u> and <u>metadata of elements contained within model (ME-CM001)</u>.
	4. System reviews element prerequisites (<u>ML-CM001: for model and elements</u>) and notifies user of any required items not currently available in the <u>Library</u>.
	    ❑ For elements in <u>Library</u>:
	        ● Check with Library if there are element updates (MM-UC012).
	        ● If user does not want to update, the process continues.
	        ● If user wants to update, updated element is retrieved from distributor and Library is updated (ML-UC013).
	    ❑ For elements not in <u>Library</u>, Library checks to see whether elements can be subscribed from a third-party distributor.
	        ● For those items that are available, user is prompted to subscribe.
	5. System notifies user of any elements not in <u>Library</u> and provides availability status (<u>ML-CM002 Item Availability Status</u>).
	6. Model is displayed and elements in the model that are available are visually identified as such.

Table 8-6   Example of a Use Case

Postconditions (What conditions will exist after business activity occurs)	Model is ready for editing.
Exceptions	
Extension Points (Conditionally add behavior to this use case)	Either provide way to immediately import/subscribe/add to the Library the missing data sources and elements—or, when model is displayed, differentiate those elements that need to be acquired.
Unresolved Issues	Can a user open files directly or does user always need to import into Library and then open from there?
	Is there a model type? Alternatively, is there just one type of model?
Requirements Traceability (Original business requirements)	
Context Model References (Supporting exhibits)	MM-CM005 Saved Model Information
Other References	MM-PF001 Open Model

A conceptual design also maps out other aspects of a solution (e.g., usability evaluations). Each role contributes to the overall solution delivery effort and designs their deliverables (e.g., deployment strategies). For instance, a test group uses a functional specification and Envision Track outputs to form test strategies. Proceeding through a design process, a test team designs test cases and test harnesses, among other things.

Table 8-7   Example of a Context Model

MM-CM005 Saved Model Information	
Model Metadata	MM-CM001 Model metadata
Model ID	Model identifier
Model Name	Name of model
Item Collection	Items used in model

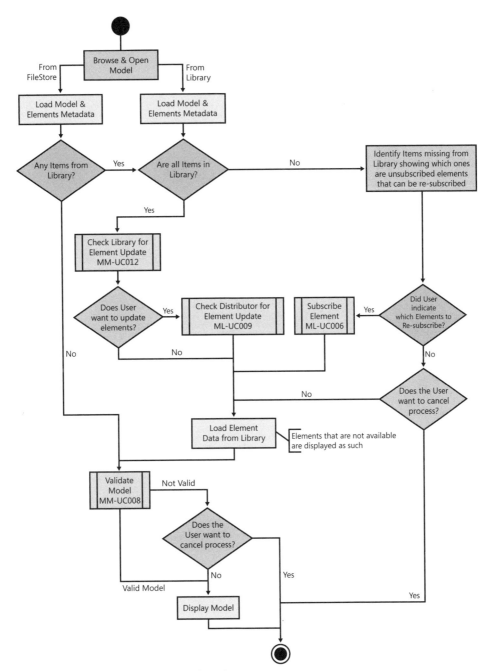

Figure 8-5   Example of a process flow diagram

Many approaches and techniques can be used to gather the necessary information, data, and knowledge needed to develop the conceptual design. A few examples are as follows:

- Interviewing
- Shadowing users on the job
- Reviewing existing documentation
- Examining infrastructure "as built" diagrams
- Prototyping
- Focus groups
- User surveys
- Talking with help desk personnel and reviewing trouble tickets
- Having users teach the team their roles and responsibilities

Logical Design

A logical design describes a solution in terms of organization, structure, and interaction of its parts. It achieves this by clustering like capabilities, functions, and needs and collectively sorts them in a logical manner. For instance, data storage, data reporting, and data retrieval activities might be clustered and represented in the logical design as a generic database management system or, if enough is known, labeled as Microsoft SQL Server. Another way to look at the logical designing activities is to consider assembling a complex puzzle. Often, the first thing you do is find the edge pieces to understand what the extremities of the puzzle look like. Then, you separately group sky pieces, grass pieces, and so forth—effectively decomposing the problem into smaller, more manageable problems.

A common practice is to start not only to group like items but also to sort them based on where they will likely end up in a solution architecture. For example, if a *service-oriented architecture* (SOA) is an appropriate choice, Figure 8-6 provides an example of typical grouping categories. Please note that a team should be knowledgeable of relevant architectures and technologies and thoroughly understand the impacts of architecture and technology choices before selecting them during the logical design step.

A logical design adds more detail and introduces more models and diagrams (e.g., interaction models, logical object models, logical business services, logical data model, and sequence diagrams). For context, Figure 8-7 provides an example of a sequence diagram.

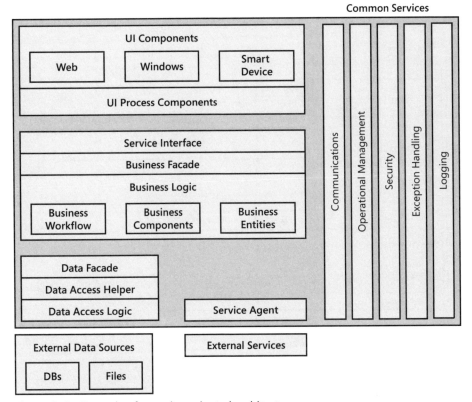

Figure 8-6   Example of a service-oriented architecture

Physical Design

A physical design works through all design details so each subteam is ready to implement a solution and their supporting collateral. The level of details necessary often is based on team member abilities and project constraints. A physical design creates a set of physical solution design models, including components design, user interface design, and physical database design. A physical design addresses other supporting aspects of delivering a solution (e.g., performance testing environment). It explains how a solution integrates and behaves in its target environment.

With all design details mapped out, a team should revisit their task and resource estimates. They also should revisit the implementation options outlined previously and select the one that best matches project constraints and how a team wants to implement a solution.

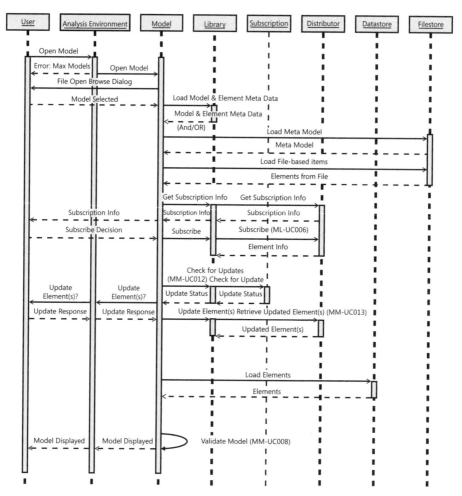

Figure 8-7   Example of a sequence diagram

Creating a Master Project Plan (Deliverable)

Lead Advocacy Group: Program Management

> **Clarity Point**   People often refer to what is contained in a Microsoft Project .mpp file as a "project plan"—actually, it is a project schedule. Project schedules are discussed later.

A *project plan* is a description of how to deliver an aspect of a solution or supporting activity. The various project plans evolve out of strategies and approaches outlined during envisioning. Although some plans are reliant on a solution design, most are not, so planning in parallel with solution designing is recommended.

A master project plan, driven by program management, is a reference document that shows how the various project plans synchronize and integrate together. The benefits of presenting these plans as one are that they facilitate synchronization into a single schedule, ensure proper sequencing of activities, facilitate reviews and approvals, and help to identify gaps and inconsistencies. Conversely, the benefits of having a plan made up of smaller plans are that these facilitate concurrent planning by various team advocacy groups and provide for clear accountability because specific advocacy groups are responsible for specific plans. Although a single accountable advocacy group is designated for each plan, planning is a shared responsibility, and every advocacy group is accountable to provide planning input.

Plans to be included in a master project plan depend on project characteristics (e.g., type and size). The next few sections identify plans to consider for every project. Obviously, not all are needed for every project. However, their inclusion or exclusion should be considered carefully. Their complexity and depth vary in accordance with delivery challenges. Typical plans included in a master project plan are shown in Figure 8-8.

Figure 8-8   Typical plans incorporated into the master project plan

Communications Plan

Lead Advocacy Group: Product Management

A Communications Plan maps out how, when, and what information to share with the various stakeholders and with the team. This information can be shared through project deliverables (e.g., end-user e-mail message announcing a solution rollout developed by a user experience team), project events (e.g., training and launch events), project meetings (e.g., monthly project status reports), and approval processes (e.g., business sponsor sign-off of functional specification). Table 8-8 provides a few more examples of external communications.

Table 8-8   Examples of External Communications

Potential Audiences	Potential Vehicles	Potential Messages
All users	Newsletters	What's happening and why
All affected users	Memos	When it will happen
Management	Face-to-face meetings	Who it will affect
All IT personnel	Intranet	How users will be affected
IT administrators	E-mail	How users should prepare
Help desk	Voice mail	How users get more information

Roles and Responsibilities

Lead Advocacy Group: Program Management

A Roles And Responsibilities document, sometimes called an organizational plan, details the roles needed on a project; their focus; how they fit into the team structure; and what their responsibilities, competencies, activities, and major deliverables are throughout a solution life cycle.

Staffing Plan

Lead Advocacy Group: Program Management

A Staffing Plan describes when and what skills and abilities need to be added to a team to deliver a solution, how to acquire those skills and abilities if they are not readily available, and when and how those resources are rolled off a project team. It identifies how to approach and conduct project orientation for new team members. It details the numbers and types of personnel needed throughout a solution delivery life cycle, as exemplified in Table 8-9.

Table 8-9   Example of Planned Staffing Levels

Full-Time Equivalent Staffing Levels	Envision	Plan	Build	Stabilize	Deploy
Product Management	2.0	1.5	1.0	1.0	1.0
Project Management	1.0	1.0	1.0	1.0	1.0
Solutions Architect	1.0	1.0	1.0	1.0	1.0
Dev Architect	1.0	1.0	1.0	1.0	1.0
Developers		3.0	8.0	6.0	2.0
Test Lead	1.0	1.0	1.0	1.0	1.0
Testers		4.0	5.0	5.0	1.0
User Experience Lead	1.0	1.0	1.0	1.0	1.0
Trainers		1.0	1.0	2.0	2.0
Technical Writers		1.0	1.0	1.0	1.0
Infrastructure Architect	0.5	0.5	0.5	0.2	0.2

Table 8-9 Example of Planned Staffing Levels

Full-Time Equivalent Staffing Levels	Envision	Plan	Build	Stabilize	Deploy
Infrastructure Engineers			2.0	1.0	1.0
Deployment	1.0	1.5	2.0	2.0	3.0
Staffing Total	**8.5**	**17.5**	**25.5**	**23.2**	**16.2**

Readiness Plans

Lead Advocacy Group: Program Management

A Readiness Plan outlines how to approach team readiness and how to implement and manage the MSF Readiness Management Process (discussed in Chapter 7, "MSF Envision Track: Defining a Solution").

Risk and Issue Management Plan

Lead Advocacy Group: Program Management

A Risk And Issue Management Plan outlines how to manage the identification and mitigation of risks and issues. Although risks and issues are managed somewhat differently, the overall approach is consistent with what was discussed in Chapter 5, "Managing Project Risks" (i.e., MSF Risk Management Process).

Configuration Management Plan

Lead Advocacy Group: Program Management

As a solution is incrementally built and deployed to the various supporting environments, a Configuration Management Plan details how and which of the various project elements (e.g., deliverables, documents, configurations, and settings) to track. As expressed in Chapter 6, "Establishing a Solution Delivery Life Cycle," configuration management provides controlled deployment and facilitates "rollback" to an earlier configuration of some or all of a solution if needed.

Change Management Plan

Lead Advocacy Group: Program Management

A Change Management Plan identifies the goals and approaches of how to handle changes to the agreed-to project scope, cost, time lines, and assigned resources. It delineates the process used to request, review, approve, document, and distribute changes.

As with other plans, a team or organization needs to agree and document within this plan how formal the change management process should be. Rigor and formality might be enablers, especially for large teams; however, they come at a cost. Effectively, this plan dictates how a team must behave when looking to alter any feature and functionality of a solution once the solution is placed under change control. This means that features and functions cannot be added or changed without review and approval by both the team and stakeholders.

Quality Management Plan

Lead Advocacy Group: Test

A Quality Management Plan details how the quality goals for each advocacy group (discussed in Chapter 4, "Building an MSF Team") will be implemented and measured throughout a solution delivery life cycle. It determines what quality metrics will be used and how they will be measured.

Test Plan

Lead Advocacy Group: Test

The basic goals of testing are to find where gaps are between what was built and what was specified (Build Track) and later what was expected (Stabilize Track), and to manage gap remediation. Depending on the selected build methodology and solution delivery technologies (e.g., infrastructure, software development), testing either precedes a build effort (e.g., test-driven development) or follows a build effort.

To assemble a testing plan, a team needs to decide how best to approach and implement testing for this project. After all, testing that might be sufficient for one project might not be for another. This involves forming testing strategies and approaches as to how to make sure a solution not only adheres to the requirements (i.e., verification) but also that the requirements delineate what is needed and expected (i.e., validation). Quality bars (i.e., levels of quality) and success criteria need to be set for the various aspects of a solution. Which quality metrics will be used and how they will be measured need to be determined. Specific goals for testing need to be established. The types of tests to be performed need to be identified. Test coverage decisions need to be made. Usage testing needs to be defined. Test collateral (e.g., test cases, test scripts, test harnesses, and test data) needs to be identified and developed prior to a solution being developed. Problem triage strategies and processes need to be defined.

Pilot Plan

Lead Advocacy Group: Product Management

A pilot deployment is an opportunity to validate with "real" users that a solution works as expected in a controlled, production-like environment under live conditions. A Pilot Plan defines the strategies, goals, objectives, success criteria, and scope for conducting and assessing the pilot; plans out deployment logistics; and identifies target user populations to participate in the pilot. The plan details how the entire solution will be reviewed and evaluated by the pilot group. Table 8-10 provides some implementation options to consider.

Table 8-10   Pilot Plan Focal Areas

Key Areas to Address	Techniques
Pilot participant selection	Urgent business needs, visibility or influence of user group, or risk of failure
Pilot scope	Partial test of solution functionality and deployment processes, or full solution and deployment process test
Number of pilot participants	Small number of participants, entire department, or entire site
Number of pilots	One or a few
Pilot feedback mechanisms	All at once or phased

Because the pilot has real users using a solution in real conditions, many production support processes and resources need to be completed in time and be put in place to support these pilot users. For instance, the help desk, user administration, and training need to be ready to support users prior to the start of pilot. Although the pilot can be conducted in a staging environment (i.e., one that mirrors production), it can be hosted in production where resources need to be procured and deployed ahead of the full deployment. All of this can be quite challenging because pilot is usually conducted during a Stabilize Track when most of the team is busy finalizing a solution and getting ready for deployment.

Training Plan

Lead Advocacy Group: User Experience

Training has a simple mission: bring user readiness up to the necessary levels. Like the readiness management discipline discussed in Chapter 7, "MSF Envision Track: Defining a Solution," where great planning and effort are expended to ready the team, a Training Plan has the same challenge, but this time it is users that need to be ready. It might even be more challenging because users likely have a broader skills variance. They might also have more varied learning styles. All of this needs to be factored into a Training Plan.

A Training Plan also needs to consider training vehicles (e.g., hands-on workshops), availability of users for training (e.g., usually the time needed to properly train far exceeds user availability), and development of training materials. Training logistics need to be planned out (e.g., trainer availability and training facility availability). Table 8-11 provides some implementation options to consider.

Table 8-11   Training Plan Focal Areas

Key Areas to Address	Techniques
Training audiences	All affected users, IT administrators, and help desk
Training vehicles	Hands-on training, presentation-style training, computer-based or Web-based training, one-on-one training, job aids, and handouts
Training materials development	Buy versus build

Table 8-11   Training Plan Focal Areas

Key Areas to Address	Techniques
Training duration	All day, half day, two hours, or ad hoc
Training delivery timing	Just prior to deployment, at deployment, just after deployment, and at user's request
Training resources	Internal or contract trainers, central or field training facilities

> **Lesson Learned**   Keep in mind that business unit managers likely will not let their folks go off for week(s) of training. Make sure the team finds out early what managers are willing to support. Most likely, training will need to be pared down to no more than a few days supplemented by self-study materials.

Deployment Plan

Lead Advocacy Group: Release/Operations

A team must work through many deployment strategies, approaches, and considerations to have a successful deployment, as exemplified in Table 8-12. A deployment plan documents these, and then identifies how to best deploy all the different aspects of a solution (i.e., different aspects might take different deployment strategies and approaches). It maps out which resources are needed, including people, tools, and scripts. It identifies which solution components are located at a central or key location to enable interoperability of the overall solution (i.e., core components) and which components are located at individual locations (i.e., sites) to enable users to access and use a solution. These components should be grouped for efficient deployment.

Table 8-12   Deployment Plan Focal Areas

Key Areas to Address	Techniques
Installation strategy	Phased, all at once, by geographical site, by business unit, user pull
Contingency (business continuation) planning	Parallel systems, full backup with restore capability, or no contingency
Feedback approach	*Proactive:* Phased, all at once, by geographical site, by business unit, random survey
	Reactive: Trouble tickets
Deployment mechanisms	Fully automated network installation, partially scripted installation, or manual
Deployment resources	Internal staff or contractors
Systems support approach	Tiered support or pilot and rollout support

Added to this planning is how to promote a solution through the various supporting environments before deploying to production. It also covers how to document the deployed solution (commonly called "as built" documents) to be handed over to operations.

Lesson Learned   Find out early when deployments to Production are allowed. Usually, deployments must be performed during limited production maintenance windows (often over weekends). A growing challenge is that these windows are becoming shorter and less frequent because increasingly most organizations have global operations.

Change Enablement Plan

Lead Advocacy Group: Product Management

The full value of a solution is not often realized without complementary changes to business processes. A Change Enablement Plan addresses how to engage the stakeholders to help make this happen.

Knowledge Management Plan

Lead Advocacy Group: Program Management

In support of the MSF foundational principle of learning from all experiences, a Knowledge Management Plan expounds on how to capture and harvest lessons learned while delivering a solution. It details the approaches and processes used. It outlines how to categorize and tag knowledge. It architects the tools and means to manage knowledge. In addition, it discusses how others in an organization will retrieve relevant knowledge.

Disaster Recovery Plan

Lead Advocacy Group: Architecture

A Disaster Recovery Plan defines the strategies and important aspects of a solution that warrant disaster recovery for both a delivery effort and for a deployed solution. This plan can be as simple as clustering servers or as elaborate as full alternate sites with near-real-time synchronization. It identifies threats and worst-case scenarios that might significantly affect solution delivery. It provides trade-off analysis to help justify the potentially huge costs of implementing these measures.

Purchasing and Facilities Plan

Lead Advocacy Group: Release/Operations

A Purchasing and Facilities Plan, sometimes called a procurement plan, maps out how to acquire the necessary resources to deliver a solution. This includes ordering the hardware, software, and networking equipment for the supporting environments as well as what is required to deploy a solution in production. It sometimes involves securing warehouse space to build and store a solution incrementally as it is deployed globally. It might involve physical plant logistics (e.g., running cables and installing air conditioning), construction logistics (e.g., securing building permits), and disposal of decommissioned equipment.

Security Plan

Lead Advocacy Group: Architecture

A Security Plan describes how to identify security requirements, how to adhere to established security guidelines and policies, what actions will be taken to mitigate any risk in the absence of established security guidelines, and what interim security measures will be taken if established security measures conflict with the successful completion of a project.

Integration Management Plan

Lead Advocacy Group: Architecture

When there are many disparate aspects of the deployed solution as well as many existing systems to integrate with, effort to draft an Integration Management Plan is often justified. It describes how to integrate the parts of a solution and how to integrate a solution into its destination environment.

Benefit Analysis Plan

Lead Advocacy Group: Product Management

Like technical measurement of solution operations, the business value being realized through solution operations can also be measured. The ways and means of approaching and implementing this are detailed in a performance management plan. This plan typically maps out how to track what was presented in the cost/benefit analysis used to justify a project. It can involve tracking cost performance, earned value analysis (EVA), and other less tangible measures of business value.

Capacity Plan

Lead Advocacy Group: Architecture

When solution growth is critical, it is best to draft a Capacity Plan. It goes into more detail than what is normally covered within design documents. It forecasts future solution loads, details potential user experience impacts through that growth, and specifies what needs to be incrementally done to a solution and environment (e.g., networks) to handle that planned growth.

Budget Plan

Lead Advocacy Group: Program Management

A Budget Plan maps out how to deliver a solution within financial constraints. It instruments how to identify expected costs and cost constraints. It often uses information from the other plans to forecast financial impacts related to their various options and approaches. It paints an overall financial picture.

Planning When to Build

Lead Advocacy Group: Program Management

Solution requirements specify what needs to be built. Solution designs and project plans specify how to build a solution. The next step is defining actionable tasks from this information and sequencing them to start to form a project schedule. To complete the effort, a schedule needs additional data such as how long will it take to complete the tasks, how the tasks relate, and who will be performing them.

Depending on the size of the effort, each subteam forms their own schedule and integrates them together in a master project schedule. Having a master project schedule provides the same benefits as discussed for having a master project plan (e.g., facilitates concurrent scheduling by various subteams). In addition to subteam schedules, it might be warranted to have cross-team schedules that correspond with projects plans (e.g., training plan). Table 8-13 provides a few examples of these plans and identifies which advocacy group leads the scheduling effort.

Table 8-13   Examples of Typical Cross-Team Schedules

Typical Schedules	Lead Advocacy Group
Communications schedule	Product Management
Build schedule	Development
Training schedule	User Experience
Test schedule	Test
Budget schedule	Program Management
Deployment schedule	Release/Operations
Purchasing and facilities schedule	Release/Operations
Pilot schedule	Release/Operations

Assembling schedules involves a few steps that should be followed in order, as depicted in Figure 8-9. The first step is to figure out *what* needs to be done (i.e., tasks). The second step is to estimate the work necessary to complete each task. The third step is to identify task dependencies (i.e., predecessors). The fourth step is to figure out *who* is to perform each task. The final step is to identify *when* to perform each task. This iterative process takes a few passes to get all schedule elements balanced and optimally adhering to project constraints and personnel commitments (e.g., vacation, holidays, and training). Each of these steps is discussed in the next few sections.

Step 1: Identify Tasks

Guided by project plans, teams must convert requirements and design elements into actionable tasks. It is expected that these tasks will be at different levels of granularity. The goal is to get a consolidated list of tasks that represents all work necessary to deliver a solution. Within the list, the tasks are then sorted by a number of means (e.g., by feature team and then by role). This sorted list is often referred to as a work-breakdown structure (WBS).

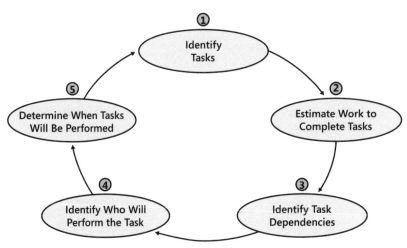

Figure 8-9   MSF scheduling process

While assembling the WBS, it is helpful for later trade-off analysis to assign an overall priority to each task and potentially identify alternate tasks that represent alternate approaches. Later iterations of the scheduling process will eliminate the less favorable alternatives.

Step 2: Estimate Work to Complete Tasks

With the body of work identified as actionable tasks, the focus changes to estimating how much work is required to complete the tasks. Not to be confused with *duration estimating*, which is the period of time in which to perform the work (discussed in step 5), the estimated work is a measure of how long it would take one person with the benchmarked skills to complete the task. It is important to understand why the estimates need to be calibrated to some benchmark. If one person estimates the task given his or her own skills but another person with different skills is assigned the task, it is highly unlikely that the estimate is valid. Typically, a team agrees to a benchmarked set of skills when developing the estimates.

Many good approaches can be used to derive estimates—too many to cover here. Here is a quick summary of some commonly used approaches:

- **Program, Evaluation, and Review Technique (PERT)**   A mathematically derived estimate based on an optimistic, expected, and pessimistic estimate

- **Delphi**   An estimate based on expert opinion

- **Parametric**   An estimate based on actuals from other projects doing similar activities

- **Prototyping**   An estimate derived from performing a limited portion of the scope to get a sense of how to estimate the remainder of the tasks

These approaches are used in top-down or bottom-up estimating. Commonly, the Product Management and Program Management teams drive a top-down view of the estimates to reflect the various project constraints, whereas team members drive a bottom-up approach. It is healthy to compare and contrast these two opposing approaches because the process often uncovers requirements gaps, readiness gaps, mismatched stakeholder expectations, and unrealistic project constraints.

Having team members estimate their own tasks is an important aspect of team empowerment. That way, the people doing the work make commitments as to when it will be done. The result is a schedule that the team supports because they believe in it. MSF team members are confident that any delays will be reported as soon as they are known, thereby freeing team leads to play a more facilitative role, offering guidance and assistance when it is most critical. The monitoring of progress is distributed across the team and becomes a supportive rather than a policing activity.

> **Lesson Learned**   As a rule of thumb, tasks should be decomposed such that their estimates are greater than four hours, but less than one week. Tasks with estimates of less than four hours are too granular. Tasks with estimates longer than a week should be decomposed into smaller tasks—even if it is just splitting a task by adding a review checkpoint or publishing a draft of a deliverable. Ideally, tasks should be a day or two in duration.

> **Lesson Learned**   Rather than confusing a team with project manager jargon such as asking for PERT estimates, just communicate that each team member needs to provide three estimates for every task: *reasonable best case* (i.e., optimistic), *expected*, and *reasonable worst case* (i.e., pessimistic). In addition to being necessary estimates for scheduling, these estimates show the estimator's level of confidence in performing the tasks. Specifically, a small estimate variance between the best-case and worst-case estimates shows the estimator is confident (i.e., minimal uncertainty); a large variance signals low confidence that translates into risk. Low confidence might be a result of many factors (e.g., technical challenges, lack of skills, and clarity of requirements) that should be investigated.

Buffer Time

Classically, on every project, the question comes up about how buffer time should be factored into a project schedule. This is typically an awkward conversation with sponsors because project teams seldom provide adequate justification surrounding the need and application of buffer time. As such, sponsors typically balk at buffering estimates because they view it as unnecessary padding.

To break this pattern, there should be an open and frank discussion surrounding buffer time. Experience shows that no matter how seasoned a team is, unplanned events, risks, and issues that result in nominal impact on a project—too incidental to submit for change management consideration but significant enough that a team must plan to absorb them into the schedule—are realized. Buffering adds time into a project to enable a project team to absorb these unexpected issues. Buffer time should not be used to compensate

> for the time needed to add a feature or change a resource. These changes should continue to be processed through change management.
>
> A project team and sponsors need to reach agreement at how buffer time should be incorporated into a project schedule. Buffer time should not be associated with individual tasks because, inevitably, it will be absorbed as part of the task estimate and, accordingly, the planned work will expand to fill the allotted time (Parkinson's Law)[5] as opposed to being used for unplanned events—the intended reason for buffer time. Instead, buffer time should be associated with higher-level task aggregations such as work streams.
>
> Rather than building in the classic 20 percent buffer time around major deliverables and checkpoints, a recommended approach at figuring how much buffer time is needed for a given project is to use the results from the PERT analysis (i.e., difference between the expected and pessimistic estimates). This approach is much more defensible because it is supported with data down to the task level.

Step 3: Identify Task Dependencies

A *task dependency* exists when other tasks must be started or completed before the task in question can start or be completed. For example, the *install Microsoft Windows operating system* task needs to come before the *install Microsoft Exchange Server* task. It is important for team members to define their tasks in consideration of what else is needed to perform the tasks (i.e., task dependencies). This is especially important when dependencies cross team boundaries— the other team might not know of the dependency and might overlook it.

Adding dependencies is not as simple as sequencing tasks. It also includes identifying situations where it is prudent to delay tasks (i.e., waiting with no planned activity before starting a task). For instance, after a server build, it is prudent to wait a short time to make sure the server is operating as expected before performing other tasks with that server— often called a "burn-in" period. These quiet periods do not show up as tasks. Rather, the time is built into the dependencies. For instance, a task of hanging a picture (task 2) on a newly painted wall can start no earlier than two days after completing the painting task (task 1). Needing to wait while the paint dries is not a task. It is a condition placed on the association of the two tasks (i.e., task 2 is dependent on the successful completion of task 1, plus a minimum of an additional 2 days).

Step 4: Identify Who Will Perform the Task

At this point, the team has identified and estimated tasks and has identified cross-task dependencies. The focus changes to evenly distributing the work among the available resources.

---

5 C. Northcote Parkinson, *Parkinson's Law: The Pursuit of Progress* (London: John Murray, 1958).

A few approaches can be used to assign resources. One approach for the first pass is to assign a role title for each task (e.g., Senior Exchange Engineer 1). Later on, these role placeholders are replaced with team member names. This is helpful if team members are playing multiple roles. Putting role placeholders first enables a team to think about what is needed and helps them avoid getting caught up with specific team member skills and constraints (e.g., availability). Cost might also be a consideration. Putting role titles first is often much easier to change later than is assigning specific team member names (e.g., when project cost constraints necessitate using a less senior resource).

Another approach is to make resource assignments based on small subteams (e.g., commonly called work streams). With this approach, work is assigned to a work stream team, and the work stream lead is empowered to manage the assignments among the subteam handling the work stream—providing team cohesion. This approach of balancing work among work stream teams is much easier than balancing among individual team members.

Lesson Learned   When using tools such as Microsoft Project to help balance work among resources, adjust the time interval in the resource usage report from the daily view to something more practical. A commonly used period to balance is a work week (e.g., 40 hours), as shown in the following figure. Balancing work to a shorter interval than a week does not add more value and is much more work.

Resource Name	Work	October			November	
		16-Oct	23-Oct	30-Oct	6-Nov	13-Nov
Denise Smith	191 hrs	40h	35h	38h	40h	38h
Joe Healy	190 hrs	38h	39h	34h	40h	39h

Step 5: Determine When Tasks Will Be Performed

Up until now, the scheduling process has not been influenced by project trade-off matrix decisions. As such, task start and finish dates have floated to be what was dictated by the sequencing effort. If the lowest trade-off priority from the *Project Trade-off Matrix* (discussed in Chapter 7, "MSF Envision Track: Defining a Solution") is *schedule*, the schedule is what it is, and therefore scheduling is done. However, this is rarely the case. This step focuses on adjusting these dates to fit date-oriented project constraints.

Many approaches to compressing a schedule can be used to make the schedule fit within date-oriented project constraints (commonly called "crashing the schedule"). The best guidance on how to proceed is to reference the priorities specified in the trade-off matrix. If features are a higher priority than resources are, adding resources is the best course of action. Otherwise, removing features is the best course of action.

Another aspect of determining when tasks will be performed is to look at the environmental constraints. For example, organizations often have "black-out" or "freeze" periods where no production changes happen (e.g., accountant organizations often declare a few months prior to tax day a period where no production changes are tolerated).

Lesson Learned   Microsoft Project is a helpful tool in agile-oriented iteration planning. If the project governance approach is to have little up-front planning, here is a resourceless way to approach it. Add work tasks to Project as usual. It is OK to use the Duration field for work estimates, but it is much better to use the Work field to reflect your estimates. Create a set of parent tasks (e.g., Iteration 1). Use milestones to indicate iteration end dates (an iteration start date is the end date of the prior iteration). Calculate your team's work capacity (i.e., amount of work your team can handle during an iteration, such as 6 people * 6.5 hours/ day of work * 20 work days/month * 1 month iteration duration = 780 staff hours). As you add tasks to an iteration, the work associated with that iteration parent task starts to increase. It is good to leave a buffer, so maybe add only 600 hours of work per iteration. Rather than using a buffer, I like to use the PERT fields (i.e., high, low, and expected as discussed earlier). Use a planning number between the expected and high estimates for the number of staff hours per iteration (closer to the high). If unplanned tasks need to be added into an iteration, bump lower-priority items to the next iteration.

If you need to assign resources, use the preceding approach, but instead of calculating the team's capacity, calculate each team member's capacity. Fill up team members' buckets of work per iteration just as described here.

Creating a Master Project Schedule (Deliverable)

Lead Advocacy Group: Program Management

In addition to balancing schedule elements on each subteam, the elements need to be integrated and balanced across a project. The cross-project elements and activities are consolidated, integrated, and balanced within a master project schedule.

The master project schedule integrates the various subteam schedules needed to deliver a solution. It typically calls out significant tasks, deliverables, and checkpoints, providing an overview of a project. Figure 8-10 is an example of a project schedule summary with three work streams.

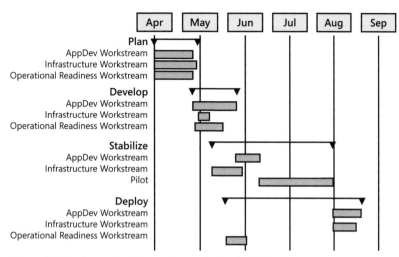

Figure 8-10   Example of a master project schedule summary

Preparing Supporting Environments

Lead Advocacy Group: Release/Operations

With design details being mapped out and plans and schedules being drafted, a team needs to finalize the necessary supporting environments (e.g., development, test, training, staging, training, research). As part of this, they need to identify what is needed, submit requests to acquire the necessary resources (e.g., servers, sample data, data center rack space, networks, power, and air conditioning), and build and administer the environments before the start of a Build Track.

As part of preparing these environments, configuration management and change control need to be established. Often, many different teams use and contribute to these environments, so tight controls are essential. In addition, these environments need to be synchronized (e.g., a network device change needs to be applied to all environments). Other preparation activities include these:

- Develop solution configurations

- Build deployment scripts and processes

- Employ automated deployment tools and deployment checklists

- Develop troubleshooting and problem-resolution guidelines

- Develop backup and recovery or fallback procedures, as specified in planning documents

These environments need to be as similar to production as necessary. This typically means that the environment most removed from production (e.g., development) is the least similar, whereas preproduction environments (e.g., staging) need to be the most like production.

> **Lesson Learned**   After a seemingly successful test session, a team deployed a solution to production, where it summarily failed. After triaging the issues, the team found that test users had administrator rights so they could perform various activities beyond their defined role, whereas in the production system, those users had restricted rights, resulting in their inability to use functionality in production.

> **Lesson Learned**   A team thought it planned sufficiently for getting lab hardware in place. They planned for the usual ordering of the hardware and having it "racked and stacked." What they failed to plan for properly was that the facilities electrician needed much more advanced notice than planned. The team mistakenly placed a "regular" work order instead of a "special" 4-week lead-time work order to run power to a rack. The team still does not understand the difference, but this misstep cost the project a few extra weeks.

The following briefly discusses the potential environments needed to deliver a solution.

Development Environment

There needs to be an environment in which builders of a solution are able to construct a solution incrementally. This includes all aspects of a solution. For example, it is where developers push their code to compile, where the trainers assemble their training collateral and potentially their online help material, where deployment engineers build their deployment solutions, where the infrastructure builders build and configure their servers, and so forth. Team members should first validate that their components work in their private environment and push to development once they have incrementally completed their components for integration to the other solution components.

This environment often has a representative set of servers and services found in production. However, those services are often combined onto the same server to save costs. For example, it is good practice to separate Web gateway and authentication servers. Because a development environment is not usually exposed to the outside, combining these services onto one server, each on its own virtual server image, is commonly done.

With this environment being the initial environment to integrate components and validate features, its stability is inherently unpredictable. As such, this environment is inhospitable for user demos and feature reviews. It also needs to be administered so that should the environment be "polluted," it is easy to rebuild and restore.

Test Environment

A test environment is a more controlled and more production-like environment. It is used to test and evaluate completed aspects of a solution as the solution is promoted from a development environment.

Like a development environment, a test environment needs an easy way to be restored. It will have test data, test scripts, and test user accounts that need to be restored. Successfully restoring the test in a timely fashion involves having a good Configuration Management Plan.

Ideally, the promotion from the development environment to the test environment should be accomplished using deployment automation tools. Although it might seem like overkill for a simple deployment, the benefits are that it gives a deployment team means to refine their deliverables (i.e., deployment process and scripts), and it helps to minimize human error in configuring a solution.

Staging Environment

A staging environment is a limited mirror of the production environment. It is limited in that it replicates a representative set of those services offered in production and is configured and managed like production (e.g., hardware, configurations, user accounts).

Another useful benefit of having a staging environment is that it can be used as a configuration management test bed (e.g., test and evaluate patches). Because staging should be a stable environment, it should be used for demos and pilot evaluations. Sometimes, organizations use staging as a disaster recovery site.

Training Environment

Given that a staging environment is part of stabilizing a solution, it likely needs to be refreshed frequently during the later part of a delivery life cycle. Therefore, dual use of a staging environment for training is not conducive. As such, if online training is part of an operational readiness strategy, it might be necessary to have a training environment.

This environment also needs an easy means to refresh servers and client machines to reset them to defined training scenarios, user accounts, and training data.

> **Lesson Learned**   When sizing a training environment, keep in mind that the number of concurrent users might be more than the number in production. For instance, a team builds a Web-based solution sized to support 50 concurrent user sessions. If training requirements necessitate training classes of 100 users, the solution likely is not able to handle the increased load because 100 users are hitting the same part of the solution at the same time.

Research Environment

Organizations that frequently test and evaluate new technology often find it necessary to have a research environment. Because this is a test bed, it should be isolated from production. Often, research environments are used to develop and demonstrate portions of next-generation solutions.

Success Criteria for a Plan Track

The team has expended great energy planning and designing a solution. They have worked with users and stakeholders to validate designs, identify requirements, and form plans that meet the needs and expectations of everyone. Here are a few commonly observed success indicators:

- Agreement with stakeholders and the team has been obtained on the following points:
  - Solution components to be delivered
  - Key project checkpoint dates
  - How a solution will be built
- Supporting environments have been constructed.
- Change control and configuration management processes are working smoothly.
- Risk assessments have been updated.
- All designs, plans, and schedules are traced back to their origins in the functional specifications, and the functional specification are traced back to envisioning deliverables.
- Sponsor(s) and/or key stakeholders have signed off.

Chapter 9
MSF Build Track: Building a Solution

All the plans have been formed. All detailed designs have been drafted. The environments used to incrementally develop, test, and evaluate a solution have been built. Now it is time to build the various aspects of a solution incrementally. How to approach this construction is highly dependent on the selected build methodology (e.g., *MSF for Agile Software Development*). As such, this chapter discusses common elements found in most methodologies.

Goal

The goal for a Build Track is to build the various aspects of a solution in accordance with Plan Track deliverables (e.g., designs, plans, schedules, requirements). This involves developing solution features and components as well as completing the deliverables and other elements of a solution. Testing performed during this track either drives or supports construction to verify that what is built is in accordance with what was specified. Other testing objectives during a Build Track include exposing issues, uncovering design flaws, and identifying unexpected behaviors. Making sure a solution meets stakeholder expectations, usability assessments, and other types of testing are covered as part of a Stabilize Track.

Team Focus

Based on plans and designs assembled in a Plan Track, each team and subsequently each team member are focused on their respective work items, including building their portion of a solution, resolving issues, helping verify that a solution works as specified, or addressing project risk. Table 9-1 outlines these focal areas in a bit more depth for each advocacy group.

Table 9-1 Team Focal Areas During Building

Advocacy Group	Focus
Product Management	Clarifying scope, requirements, and stakeholder expectations; market channels and sales aids
Program Management	Functional specification management, project tracking, plan updating
Architecture	Architectural validation, functional specification validation, clarifying design details
Development	Solution construction, infrastructure development, configuration documentation
User Experience	Training, usability testing, graphic design, support tools and manuals
Test	Technology/unit and limited functional testing, issues identification, documentation testing, test plan updates
Release/Operations	Rollout checklists, rollout and pilot plans updates, site preparation checklists

Key Deliverables

Key deliverables for a Build Track are the many developed aspects of a solution as well as the supporting deliverables (e.g., training materials and deployment scripts). Examples of these deliverables for each advocacy group are listed in Table 9-2.

Table 9-2 Example of Key Build Track Deliverables for Each Advocacy Group

Advocacy Group	Deliverables
Product Management	■ Marketing materials ■ End-user communications
Program Management	■ Updated master plan, schedule, and risk document ■ Frozen functional specification
Architecture	■ Finalized designs
Development	■ Source code and executables ■ Build images and documents ■ Performance support elements
User Experience	■ User reference materials (manuals and help files) ■ User interface graphic elements ■ End-user training ■ Usability test scenarios
Test	■ Test specifications, test cases with expected results, test metrics, test scripts, test data, test harnesses

Table 9-2   Example of Key Build Track Deliverables for Each Advocacy Group

Advocacy Group	Deliverables
Release/Operations	■ Deployment processes and procedures ■ Installation scripts and configuration settings for deployment ■ Operations guides, standard operating procedures ■ Help desk and support procedures ■ Knowledge base ■ Support staff training ■ Support and troubleshooting documentation

Key Checkpoints

Key checkpoints consist of a major checkpoint for the track and a few interim checkpoints.

Major Checkpoint

The major checkpoint concluding a Build Track is *scope complete*.

Scope Complete

Lead Advocacy Group: Development

Why is *scope complete* the major checkpoint for a Build Track? Wasn't scoping a solution completed back in the Plan Track? The answer is, sort of. A solution was scoped back in the Plan Track but will be adjusted as issues turn up during solution construction. Therefore, the scope is not final (i.e., complete) until the team finishes building a solution. Note that scope is not frozen until the end of the Stabilize Track.

At this checkpoint, team members believe they have finished building their respective aspects of a solution, including deliverables. Although it is likely that some components of a solution are already being stabilized at this point, this checkpoint signifies all solution construction and supporting deliverables have been completed in accordance to the plans and specifications.

Interim Checkpoints

The interim checkpoints for a Build Track are *prototyping completed* and as many *internal solution releases* as needed, as depicted in Figure 9-1.

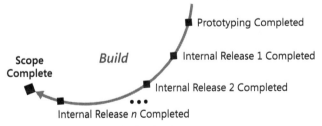

Figure 9-1   Build Track checkpoints

Prototyping Completed

Lead Advocacy Group: Architecture

Building off the technology validation effort, it might be necessary for a team to prototype aspects of a solution to gain more in-depth validation of high-risk and/or high-complexity aspects of a solution; to compare and contrast alternative technologies and approaches; and to assess feasibility of features and requirements before the full build effort starts. This interim checkpoint signifies the conclusion of planned prototyping. Note that it might be necessary to perform additional prototyping should unplanned technology issues arise.

A prototyping effort, also called a *proof of concept* (POC), helps define and validate requirements, estimates, design decisions, and constraints throughout solution planning and design. It allows predevelopment testing from many perspectives, especially usability, and helps create a better understanding of user interaction. Each prototyping effort needs specific goals and release criteria defining the effort. The goals and criteria should be documented and used throughout the effort to make sure the effort is successful.

On smaller projects, prototyping can be combined with technology validation efforts. On larger projects, prototyping can be more prevalent because often more technology questions and uncertainties exist.

Because the team is busy assembling the physical design in a Plan Track, prototyping efforts sometimes wrap up early in the Build Track—hence why it is shown here as an interim checkpoint of a Build Track. However, planning-oriented approaches might require designs be validated during a Plan Track, and so this checkpoint should be within a Plan Track. Another perspective is with agile-oriented approaches where designing and prototyping occur throughout solution construction. Hence, with these approaches, this checkpoint might be at the end of a Build Track.

Internal Solution Release 1 Through *n* Completed

Lead Advocacy Group: Development

As mentioned in Chapter 6, "Establishing a Solution Delivery Life Cycle," a release is an incremental version of a solution assembled through multiple, progressive iterations. It is an achievement of predetermined criteria, features, and capabilities. Releases are deployed internally to help synchronize the team, make planning changes, measure progress, and solicit stakeholder feedback. Although it is acknowledged that a solution is still being assembled and might be in various states of completion, these interim checkpoints typically signify that stabilization can begin on those portions of the release that are complete.

It is expected that multiple internal solution releases will be necessary. How often these interim checkpoints occur depends on the build methodology as well as the size and duration of a project.

> **Lesson Learned** Often, it makes sense to have an internal solution release corresponding with the visual design freeze and database design freeze. This is because typically so many other aspects of a solution are affected by these. For example, user interfaces often are used to create documentation, and the database schema drives many aspects of a solution implementation.

Executing Project Plans

Even though how to proceed with building a solution is dependent on which build methodology is used, it should be clear to everyone as to when and what each subteam should be doing throughout this track. This is because this knowledge should already be embodied within the various project plans, schedules, and designs; and taken together provide an understanding of *what*, *how*, and *when* the different aspects of a solution, broken down into work items, need to be completed.

Because a project team is typically augmented with additional personnel to help build a solution, each build team should review and validate the plans, designs, and schedules developed in the Plan Track that affect them before starting construction to make sure they completely understand the scope of their work, including tasks and deliverables. As part of the review, each build team needs to work with the architect team to flesh out details should any plans or designs not be sufficiently detailed enough as per the build team. An important aspect of this review is to make sure each build team understands the release criteria for their work items (i.e., what does it mean to be "done"). Not understanding the release criteria likely leads to over or under delivery on work items. An example of a common release criterion is that a solution meets a defined minimum acceptance level of functionality and capability within the three requirements categories (i.e., delighters, satisfiers, and dissatisfiers) as discussed in Chapter 8, "MSF Plan Track: Planning a Solution."

With build teams working concurrently, it is important to leave enough time to work out cross-team issues and inconsistencies. This plays out especially as the team starts to integrate and test their component parts.

Testing a Solution

> **Clarity Point** Testing during a Build Track involves assessing the state of quality of a solution from a specification compliance perspective (referred to as *verification*). Making sure a solution works as expected from a user perspective is performed during a Stabilize Track (referred to as *validation*).

As mapped out in a test plan, testing either precedes a build effort (e.g., test-driven development) or follows a build effort. Leading with testing is a form of further specifying a solution and validating a design. It also helps with establishing a shared vision because a solution is wholly described by a set of test cases. Many methodologies (e.g., eXtreme programming) exist and even more books describe them, so I do not explain them herein.

The other mode of testing trails a build effort. Depending on selected build methodology, testing could be performed in conjunction with building and designing as part of very small iterations (e.g., design a little, build a little, test a little) or longer iterations with more solution development between testing. As such, it is hard to provide guidance and best practices other than that commonly found across methodologies. Because most methodologies have the concept of a "test team," the following likewise references a test team, but keep in mind that it could also be a virtual team.

Either way, it is important to understand that testing is not just for testers. Testing can be performed by anyone helping a team member improve the completeness and/or quality of his or her work item deliverable. This includes a wide spectrum of testing options from informal testing such as peers checking each other's work (i.e., buddy testing) to formal testing where an independent team runs through a rigorous battery of tests. The goal of having everyone testing is to help expose issues, uncover design flaws, and identify unexpected behavior.

In the beginning of a Build Track, a test team starts to refine test scenarios drafted during planning and, in accordance with a Test Plan, develops the necessary elements needed for testing. This includes test cases with expected outcomes, test harnesses to drive testing, automated and manual test scripts, and test data for both positive and negative testing.[1] It means making test goals real and measurable for the various aspects of a solution. It means mapping out the details of how to implement the various types of testing to be performed in a Build Track as well as in the Stabilize and Deploy Tracks.

Testing basically involves two areas of activity: finding where gaps are between what was built and what was specified (later in a Stabilize Track, what was expected is also included); and managing gap remediation. Typically, gaps are identified by different types of testing (e.g., regression testing) and resolved through a structured process (e.g., issue tracking cycle). Each of these areas is discussed next.

Types of Tests

Gaps in what was built versus what was specified are identified throughout a build process by using different types of tests. Although so many testing philosophies, approaches, and ways to instrument testing exist, what needs to be accomplished through the different types of tests— sometimes called by different names—is basically the same. The types of tests typically involve team members testing their own work item deliverables (e.g., unit testing for software developers); integrating their work item deliverables into a larger collection of deliverables built by other team members (e.g., integration testing); and verifying that what was previously built is still functional with the addition of new solution elements (e.g., regression testing).

---

1 Positive testing is testing within specified parameters (e.g., entering a realistic numerical age within an age field). Negative testing is testing outside of the specified parameters (e.g., entering letters or a negative number within an age field).

Although what is tested and how it is tested should be spelled out in a test plan, the concept of *coverage testing* is commonly used during a Build Track. Coverage testing indicates the collective volume of testing from a whole solution perspective (e.g., test cases encompass testing 83 percent of a solution). Coverage is achieved by collectively testing the various features and capabilities contained within a solution. The level of testing completeness can vary depending on what is called for in a test plan. Typically, critical areas of a solution are thoroughly tested while the less critical areas might call for only spot testing (i.e., sampling).

Lesson Learned   Teams typically find it relatively easy to assemble tests that cover up to 60 percent of a solution's features and capabilities. They often need to get increasingly creative to come up with test cases to raise the coverage to 95 percent. These test cases typically are situations that infrequently happen in production. To raise the coverage to 100 percent typically involves test cases that are not representative of normal production activities. These test cases often involve contrived situations.

Issue Tracking and Remediation

Testing identifies gaps between current solution behavior and specified behavior. These gaps are referred to by a variety of names (e.g., bugs, defects, issues, problems). For the purposes of this discussion, these gaps are referred to herein as *solution issues*. Issues also arise from project governance and are referred to as *project issues*, as depicted in Figure 9-2. All issues need to be tracked, and those deemed necessary to address and mitigate for a given release must be worked into a project work queue (e.g., referred to in software development as *defects* or *bugs* that must be addressed before solution release). This is to say that some issues are acknowledged but not addressed for a given solution release—if at all.

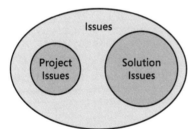

Figure 9-2   Two sources of issues

As should be outlined in the Risk and Issue Management Plan, an *issue-tracking process* is needed to handle issues systematically, efficiently, and expediently. As with much within MSF, the process can be formal or informal. At its core, it needs to address the intent of the process steps shown in Figure 9-3.

Step 1: Report

Issues can be identified and logged into the issue-tracking tool by anyone. As expected, the issue should be described in as complete terms as possible to help the team understand the issue and the source or stimulus of the issue, and know its perceived impact. It sometimes helps if the originator assigns a perceived rating for the issue in terms of *severity* (i.e., the degree of perceived impact) and *priority* (i.e., the degree of perceived urgency).

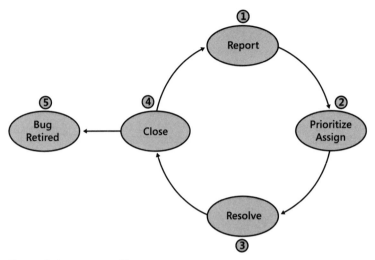

Figure 9-3 Issue tracking process

Step 2: Prioritize and Assign

Once the issue has been submitted, it is reviewed and its ratings are revisited and adjusted, if necessary, to make sure they are consistent with established project ratings (i.e., the originator might perceive ratings differently than a project issue rating scale would). Like with risk impact ratings discussed in Chapter 5, "Managing Project Risks," issues are prioritized based on a combination of their severity and priority.

Issues are then assigned to an appropriate team member for resolution. As part of the assignment step, work queues for potential assignees are considered. Once an assignment is made, issue resolution is added to that person's work queue. Note that sometimes an issue is assigned to the appropriate team lead so that person can decide who on the team should resolve the issue.

Step 3: Resolve

It might be hard to believe, but sometimes the best course of action to resolve an issue is not to take any action. As such, an issue is first reviewed and a determination is made as to how to resolve it. The following are typical issue resolution recommendations:

- **Fix** Resolve for this solution release
- **Duplicate** Has already been identified
- **Postpone** Defer to a later release
- **Can't reproduce** Could not be reproduced in a controlled environment
- **By design** Not an issue because solution performs as specified

- **Decide not to fix**   Known issue that will not be addressed (i.e., willing to live with issue)

- **Feature request**   Not an issue because it ends up being a new feature not currently supported by a solution

Step 4: Close

Once the recommended resolution is considered and approved, the assignee takes the appropriate action to close the issue for the current release. Those recommendations that defer action keep the issue active for consideration in the next release.

Step 5: Retire

Issues that are closed out (i.e., are resolved or no longer tracked for later consideration) are retired. If possible, lessons learned are extracted and shared with the team.

> **Lesson Learned**   Use a project's issue database as a starting point for a help desk knowledge base.

Success Criteria for Build Track

A Build Track has been successfully completed when all solution elements are built and complete, where *complete* means a solution operates as specified and requires no additional development of features or capabilities other than to stabilize what has been built. Depending on the build methodology used, testing plays a role in either leading or supporting solution construction. Either way, the team and the stakeholders have a high degree of confidence that a solution operates as specified.

Chapter 10

MSF Stabilize Track: Stabilizing a Solution

Stabilizing a solution is a holistic look beyond specified behavior. As solution elements are built according to what was specified, stabilization provides another level of assessment and refinement needed not only to ensure the integrated solution meets release criteria and will deploy and operate successfully in its target environment(s), but also to ensure a solution is highly usable according to users and meets the needs and expectations of the stakeholders. As such, it is the beginning of soliciting solution feedback beyond the extended project team. A Stabilize Track culminates with broad concurrence that a solution is ready for full deployment to the live production environment(s).

With such a diverse set of goals, many unique challenges are associated with a Stabilize Track. These challenges are around a team needing to perform structured testing (e.g., system testing) and subjective testing (e.g., usability testing) while continually assessing whether a solution meets release criteria. Compounding these challenges is the need to be able to predict accurately at every step when a solution will satisfy the various quality criteria.

As with a Build Track, a team can approach stabilization in numerous ways. Accordingly, this chapter discusses common activities and checkpoints associated with stabilizing a solution and its supporting collateral and services.

Goal

The goals for a Stabilize Track are as follows:

- Improve solution quality to meet release criteria for deployment to production

■   Validate that solution meets stakeholder needs and expectations

■   Validate solution usability from a user perspective

■   Maximize success and minimize risks associated with solution deployment and operations in the solution's target environment(s)

Team Focus

With all new construction completed, the focus completely shifts to polishing and readying what was built in preparation for releasing a solution to its target environment(s) (sometimes called focusing on *quality, fit,* and *finish*). Because Build Track testing verified that the built solution is in accordance with what was specified, now it is time to stabilize a solution by incrementally improving solution quality until all quality criteria have been satisfied.

Although the team continues to expose, triage, and resolve issues; manage risks; uncover design flaws; and identify unexpected behaviors, what is different is that these activities are done with an eye for wrapping up a solution in preparation for solution deployment. This means that lots of trade-off discussions will occur in which some features and capabilities will be deferred to the next release should a significant issue or delay be discovered. It also means that a project trade-off priority is switched to *schedule* over *features* (if it was not already). When a solution is polished enough to solicit user feedback through a pilot, the team focuses on transitioning control of solution deployment to operations.

Table 10-1 describes the focal areas of each advocacy group during a Stabilize Track.

Table 10-1   Team Focal Areas During Stabilization

Advocacy Group	Focus
Product Management	Communications plan execution, launch planning, scope trade-off prioritization
Program Management	Project tracking, constraint and scope trade-offs
Architecture	Issue triage
Development	Issue resolution, solution optimization
User Experience	User documentation stabilization, training materials, user acceptance, usability assessments, training pilot users as well as operations and support teams
Test	Functional, system, and regression testing; issue reporting and status; configuration testing
Release/Operations	Pilot setup and support, deployments, operations and support readiness

Key Deliverables

The key deliverables for a Stabilize Track are release-ready versions of the following:

■   Integrated solution components

■   Scripts and installation documentation

- End-user help and training materials
- End-user communications
- Operations documentation
- Testing and issue reports
- Quality metrics reports
- Release notes

Key Checkpoints

Key checkpoints consist of a major checkpoint for the track and a few interim checkpoints.

Major Checkpoint

The major checkpoint concluding a Stabilize Track is *release readiness approved.*

Release Readiness Approved

Lead Advocacy Group: Test

A release readiness approved checkpoint signifies that the stakeholders concur a solution is ready to be deployed. Before seeking stakeholder approval, the team addresses all outstanding issues, satisfies all solution release criteria, prepares Operations to take receipt of a solution, and validates that a solution satisfies the needs and expectations of the stakeholders. At this checkpoint, responsibility for ongoing management and support of a solution officially transfers from a project team to operations and support teams. It also signifies that a solution design and scope are frozen for this release.

Interim Checkpoints

The interim checkpoints for a Stabilize Track, as depicted in Figure 10-1, in roughly the order expected are as follows:

- 1st through nth functional testing pass completed
- Issue convergence
- User interfaces stabilized
- Issue log cleared
- System testing completed
- Pre-production testing completed
- Release candidate 1 through n completed

- User acceptance testing completed

- Pilot completed

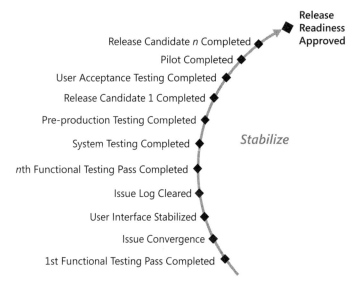

Figure 10-1   Stabilize Track checkpoints

Microsoft Solutions Framework (MSF) avoids *alpha* and *beta* checkpoints to describe the state of solution readiness. These terms are widely used, but are interpreted in too many different ways to be meaningful. Teams can use these terms if desired, as long as the terms are defined clearly and the definitions are understood among the team and stakeholders.

1st through *n*th Functional Testing Pass Completed

Lead Advocacy Group: Test

Unlike verification testing performed in a Build Track, functional testing assesses capability from a user-based activity perspective—often spanning across multiple solution components. For instance, a "create new user" test case looks at a solution from a user's perspective regardless of which solution components are involved. Functionality testing often starts as soon as enough completed solution components enable scenario or activity testing. A functional testing pass is one complete run through test cases that functionally test a solution. Often a few test passes (also called *cycles*) are needed to make sure there are no active issues related to solution functionality.

Getting a sense of solution quality from a functional perspective is important because it drives subsequent testing such as usability testing. Typically, a solution is not presented for end-user testing (e.g., usability testing and pilot) before a solution works reasonably well in those areas being considered. Otherwise, users can get hung up on technical glitches rather than assessing a solution from a usability perspective.

Issue Convergence

Lead Advocacy Group: Test

Experience shows, on average, that a team has the capacity to resolve issues at a consistent rate. *Issue convergence* is the point at which the rate of issues identified falls below the rate of issues resolved, as exemplified in Figure 10-2. This is a stabilizing indicator that helps forecast when a solution will be ready for release (i.e., all active issues resolved) and provides an objective indicator of team progress.

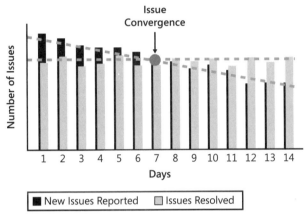

Figure 10-2   Illustration of issue convergence

Because the issue identification rate will still go up and down—even after it starts its overall decline—issue convergence usually manifests itself as a trend rather than a fixed point in time. After issue convergence, the number of issues should continue to trend lower. Issue convergence checkpoint is often a morale booster because it signals to the team that the end is actually within reach. Should ongoing analysis of issue convergence show that the trend flattens, or worst yet reverses, it is a clear warning sign that should be investigated.

User Interfaces Stabilized

Lead Advocacy Group: User Experience

A *user interface* is any interaction point between a solution and users or administrators. Whether it is an infrastructure or software development effort, these interaction points need to be planned, built, and stabilized because they are referenced and used within so many project and solution deliverables. For instance, the Training team typically uses screen shots as part of the training material; the Deployment team uses screen shots (e.g., administrator consoles) as part of deployment guides; the User Experience team uses screen shots as part of user manuals; and the Test team uses screen shots as part of test case instructions. As such, it is important to understand when in a schedule that respective team members should plan on incorporating final versions.

Issue Log Cleared

Lead Advocacy Group: Test

An *issue log cleared* checkpoint is the point in a release when the Build team initially, and unfortunately temporarily, clears the issue log of all active issues. Figure 10-3 illustrates this. After the issue log is initially cleared, the subsequent peaks should become noticeably smaller and should continue to decrease until a solution is stable enough for the team to build the first release candidate.

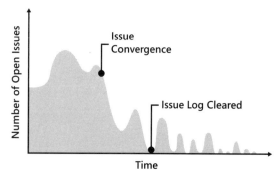

Figure 10-3   Illustration of issue log cleared checkpoint

Careful issue triaging is vital because every issue that is resolved risks the creation of a new issue. Achieving the issue log cleared checkpoint is a clear sign that the team is in the endgame as it drives to a stable release candidate.

Note that new issues certainly will be found after this checkpoint is reached. However, this checkpoint marks the first time when there are no active issues—even if it is only for the moment—and it focuses the team on working to stay in that state.

Preproduction Testing Completed

Lead Advocacy Group: Test

Once a solution has been deployed to live production environment(s) (or at least a staging environment that mimics production), preproduction testing is the final battery of tests conducted before making a solution available in production, albeit as a release candidate. This testing ensures a solution still functions properly, is integrated correctly, and its supporting elements are in place and ready for operations (e.g., help desk knowledge base, support systems, online training). Preproduction testing also includes completing and testing rollback plans. This interim checkpoint signifies that everything has been verified and ready for limited production operations (e.g., conduct a pilot, as discussed shortly).

Release Candidate 1 Through *n* Completed

Lead Advocacy Group: Test

As mentioned in Chapter 6, "Establishing a Solution Delivery Life Cycle," a release is an interim, incremental version of a solution assembled through multiple, progressive iterations. It is an achievement of predetermined criteria, features, and capabilities. A *release candidate* is a release that has been deemed a possible final release of a solution because the team thinks it satisfies all release criteria. Until a release candidate is proved to satisfy the release criteria, the team continues to refine a solution and produce release candidates. The successful deployment of each release candidate is considered an interim checkpoint.

The first release candidate checkpoint typically marks the completion of testing by a project team and select stakeholders and users, and marks the start of testing by a much broader audience. This first release candidate is typically a solution build that passed the preproduction testing. Typically, a release candidate is stable and complete enough to use for the pilot effort and user acceptance tests (both discussed shortly).

System Testing Completed

Lead Advocacy Group: Test

System testing assesses a solution from a black-box perspective—when a solution is assessed by its external behaviors and characteristics; the inner workings are not considered. Typically, this type of testing includes the following (each discussed in more detail later):

- **Deployment testing**   Provisioning to operations
- **Disaster recovery testing**   Failover capabilities
- **Integration testing**   Assimilation into operations
- **Performance testing**   Throughput capabilities
- **Capacity testing**   Load capabilities

This interim checkpoint signifies that all system testing has been satisfactorily completed.

User Acceptance Testing Completed

Lead Advocacy Group: User Experience

User acceptance testing secures user agreement that a solution meets user and business needs, as defined previously as user acceptance criteria. These tests measure and confirm usability and capability from an end user's perspective. Testing typically commences during a Build Track when users assess solution components and continues throughout stabilization. As a solution is more complete, the scope of this testing broadens.

This interim checkpoint signifies that user acceptance testing has concluded. It is achieved when a representative population of users (sometimes called *user champions*) has assessed a solution and concurs that the solution meets their needs and is sufficiently usable.

User acceptance testing also gives support personnel and users the opportunity to understand and practice using a solution through limited hands-on training. The benefit for the team is that it gives them an early understanding of where users have trouble understanding, learning, and using a solution.

Pilot Completed

Lead Advocacy Group: Product Management

As mentioned in Chapter 8, "MSF Plan Track: Planning a Solution," a pilot is an opportunity to validate with real users the degree of solution usability, as well as that a solution works as expected in a controlled, production-like environment under live conditions. Successful completion of the pilot, or set of pilots as detailed in the pilot plan, typically signifies that a solution is ready to be deployed for general availability. A pilot is not complete until the team ensures that a solution meets all defined release criteria, is viable in the production environment(s), and the prospective users are ready to use a solution effectively (e.g., right level of usability, planned training is sufficient, sufficient support options are effective).

Sometimes a pilot does not go as planned, and therefore pressing forward with the pilot might not make sense (e.g., a critical issue is discovered). As with any issue triage, a team needs to assess the situation to determine how to proceed:

- **Restart**   Resolve and deploy a new release to the pilot group
- **Suspend**   Suspend the pilot (typically considered only for critical issues that are not easily resolved)
- **Patch**   Continue with the pilot after a solution is patched

Getting to "Done"

Unlike during a Build Track where testing focuses on assessing a solution against what was specified, a Stabilize Track readies a solution from a more subjective perspective (e.g., usability, end-user acceptance, and stakeholder expectations) as well as from more classic, measured approaches such as functional testing and system testing. Unlike classic testing, which usually has defined test cases, subjective testing presents a challenge to know when the team has sufficiently stabilized a solution (i.e., when they are done). For example, how does a team quantify usability to know when a solution is sufficiently usable? Especially with subjective testing, everyone having a fixed ship date mindset clearly helps getting to done.

What Is *Done*?

Lead Advocacy Group: Product Management

Being done means a solution and all of its supporting elements satisfy their respective release criteria and have been signed off by users and stakeholders. It is critical that release criteria are clear and quantifiable so as to not under- or overdeliver. These criteria should be defined within their respective project plans for each aspect of solution delivery. A team needs to be able to track and report on all criteria throughout a Stabilize Track (and hopefully as early as Build Track testing).

Often overshadowed by completing a solution, being done includes completing the various supporting elements, such as finalizing training; hosting launch events; finalizing end-user communications announcing what, why, and when it is happening; training operations and support teams; and finalizing user and operations documentation.

Predicting Done

Lead Advocacy Group: Test

Early during this track, it is common for testing to report issues at a rate faster than the team is able to resolve them. There is no way to tell how many issues there will be or how long it will take to resolve them. There are, however, statistical indicators such as *issue convergence* and *issue log cleared* that help the team estimate when a solution will achieve defined release criteria.

With the end-state criteria clearly understood, a team needs effective techniques to make accurate predictions confidently as to the current stability status of a solution and when a solution is likely to satisfy its release criteria. This is accomplished using various techniques such as trend analysis supported by a set of trusted metrics and indicators. Many books are written on this topic; here is just a sample of useful quality indicators commonly tracked:

- Rate of issues identified vs. rate of issues resolved

- Percentage of solution revisited

- Percentage of test cases passed

- Percentage of scenarios tested

- Percent coverage

- Number of issues found per solution component

Assessing Solution Stability

Lead Advocacy Group: Test

Various forms of testing are used to assess stability. As discussed next, common test types include these:

- Regression testing
- Functional testing
- Usability testing
- System testing

Although the names might differ a bit in various industries, the intent and purpose of each are the same—assess solution stability from various perspectives. Taken together, the output of these tests forms a holistic view of a solution's stability and therefore its readiness.

Regression Testing

When an iterative approach is used, it is possible that new builds disrupt previously completed solution components. As such, regression testing is used to retest what was previously built and successfully tested to make sure it still works. Depending on what is called for in a test plan, regression testing falls somewhere on the scale from complete retesting of all previously completed components to just exploratory testing that spot-checks selected functionality and capabilities.

Functional Testing

As mentioned previously, functional testing assesses a solution to see if it behaves as desired and as expected as well as functions according to documented requirements. This includes evaluating the overall flow of a solution, how easy it is to navigate through a solution, how intuitive it is to enter data, how easy it is to retrieve data, and how nicely a solution presents data. As such, functional testing closely aligns with previously defined user scenarios and activities and is not typically performed until enough solution components have been developed and integrated to facilitate this type of testing.

Usability Testing

A solution might be technically compliant with its requirements, but is it usable? Usability testing answers this question. It is a user-perspective set of tests that is similar to functional testing, but instead of assessing how a solution behaves, usability testing concentrates on how users and administrators interact with a solution. Sometimes it measures how intuitive a solution is.

Keep in mind that usability extends to all aspects of a solution and its supporting materials such as configuration guides. That is, in addition to assessing the flow of a solution, the other aspects of a solution such as administrator manuals, online help, and other aspects of a solution need to be considered, too.

System Testing

Unlike the other types of testing just discussed, system testing is really a category of tests used to assess a solution as a whole and to evaluate how a solution integrates with other solutions already in production and operates within its target environment(s). As such, system testing needs to be performed in production or in a production-like environment. System testing commonly includes the following types of tests:

- Deployment testing
- Disaster recovery testing
- Integration testing
- Performance testing
- Capacity testing

Deployment Testing

Deployment testing (sometimes called *release testing*) evaluates the procedures to roll out a solution to its final destination (e.g., production environment). It considers deployment of all of the different solution aspects, such as deployment tools and scripts. It verifies that deployment documentation is not only accurate but also sufficiently detailed for operations personnel. As part of this testing, it gives an operations team an opportunity to identify issues that could prevent successful implementation.

Disaster Recovery Testing

Systems-level disaster recovery (DR) testing of a solution in production is typically very hard to perform because not too many organizations allow a team to "break" production just to test DR. Conversely, neither do many organizations have the funding to build out a full mirror of the production environment just to test DR. This is one of those areas of testing that an organization tests as much as financially capable. Likely, DR testing will be limited to subsystem testing such as downing a clustered server to make sure it properly fails over. It might also include smaller tests such as pulling a drive from a redundant array of independent disks (RAID) array to make sure operations continue.

Integration Testing

Integration testing validates successful assimilation of a solution into its target environment(s). In involves looking at the solution from the environment's perspective in ensuring the introduction of a solution does not impede or degrade existing operations and looking at it from a solution's perspective in making sure a solution is able to coexist and function within each target environment. This could be very challenging because each environment can have a range of legacy solutions built from vast collections of new and old technologies. Each interaction with each previously deployed solution should be another integration test case.

A big challenge with integration testing is getting legacy solutions to participate in testing. Often, older legacy solutions are harder to integrate with and often are closed systems. For example, a critical mainframe-based solution might generate only analysis data on a monthly cycle. Testing with this system will need to work around this cycle, leaving small windows of opportunity for testing.

Performance Testing

Often, a solution has time-based performance requirements. Performance testing measures solution performance in production or a production-like environment (e.g., staging environment). Depending on what is called for in a test plan, performance testing can involve testing individual subsystems (e.g., order processing) up through testing whether all solution components work together in their target environment(s). An example of a performance requirement to test is: a solution must process a "create new account" transaction within 3 seconds under a load of 100 concurrent users and within 5 seconds under a load of 500 concurrent users. Testing this requirement involves testing a solution as a whole but also might involve testing each component part involved in handling the request (e.g., 0.1 seconds allocated to the Web server).

Capacity Testing

Capacity testing validates capacity and growth planning and enables a team to understand usability and operational behaviors and characteristics as users and data loads are incrementally increased beyond what is expected in production. Testing involves not only assessing a solution but also the environment(s) in which the solution operates (e.g., assess network impacts).

Testing usability under load in addition to operational performance is important because sometimes a service might appear as if it is available and servicing users, but from a usability perspective, the service has degraded so much that it is unacceptable to users. Another example is when network capacity is added as part of deploying a solution, but because of network latency, a solution does not provide adequate perceived performance.

Testing Under Live Conditions

Lead Advocacy Group: Test

It is amazing that no matter how good the requirements are and how much user feedback is solicited, some users will always surprise the team with how they approach and use a solution. As such, there is no substitute for putting a solution out in front of a broad array of users to observe and measure their experience. Commonly called piloting a solution, this process involves deploying a limited release to production or to a production-like environment (e.g., staging environment) to validate that a solution works as expected under live conditions with "real" users.

As outlined in the Pilot Plan, successive pilots might be needed. Typically, each successive pilot broadens user involvement (e.g., pilot first to a team, then to a department, and then to a division). As per the Pilot Plan, the pilot is concluded after a fixed period or after specific goals and objectives have been satisfied.

In many ways, a pilot is a project within a project. It needs a plan that details what, when, why, who, and how the pilot is to be conducted. It needs to be well planned, executed, and concluded. It involves piloting other solution elements to assess such as support and training of pilot users as well as end-user communications (e.g., launch preparedness announcements). The next few sections discuss these topics.

Goal

The goals of a pilot are to stabilize a solution further using feedback from a broad representation of users and to reach consensus with the stakeholders and users that a solution satisfies their needs and meets their expectations.

Focus

A pilot should be a well-orchestrated review of a solution to accomplish specific goals and objectives—not a random walk by users through a solution. Conversely, it should not be a tightly controlled guided tour through a solution either. A team should make the purpose of the pilot and the measurement of feedback clear but let users go where they may within the context of what needs to be reviewed—this is necessary to surface any unexpected behaviors. Otherwise, if a team makes pilot users go down the exact same paths that testers did, users are unlikely to turn up anything new.

As part of the goal of using a pilot to stabilize a solution further, a pilot is a great opportunity to stabilize the support and training aspects of a solution as well as solution deployment. As mentioned previously, pilot users are real users that typically have not been involved with a solution, and as such, they will need more support and assistance. This necessitates that the help desk and training aspects of a solution be up and operational. It is also a good opportunity for a team to engage more with Operations to have them attempt a solution deployment and to support Operations as needed.

Preparing for a Pilot

To do it right, many things need to be accomplished and prepared before a pilot commences. Preparing for a pilot basically involves three areas: user involvement, solution evaluation, and solution deployment. User involvement focuses on identifying, soliciting, engaging, supporting, and maybe training users. Solution evaluation focuses on identifying what needs to be reviewed and gathering user feedback, including putting processes and tools in place to gather feedback. Solution deployment focuses on getting a solution deployed to the environment(s) used for pilot, including support aspects of a solution (e.g., online training).

As if it were a production deployment, a project team and operations team need to verify readiness of all aspects of a solution. It should be used as a rehearsal to work out any last-minute issues and to hone everyone's skills.

Conducting the Pilot

The trick to conducting a successful pilot is to engage with the pilot users just enough to keep them productive and providing feedback while not being bothersome. As part of engaging with pilot users, the team follows up with them on suspected issues and handles the issues accordingly.

During the pilot, the team is continually collecting, compiling, and evaluating pilot feedback and operations data.

Concluding the Pilot

Once the pilot completion criteria have been satisfied, the team concludes the pilot and regroups to address all outstanding issues and to refine a solution and supporting material based on the results of the pilot. If the schedule allows, a team might choose to address frequently experienced user errors through changes in a solution or through improved support and training.

Success Criteria for a Stabilize Track

A Stabilize Track has been successfully completed when the *release readiness approved checkpoint* is achieved, signifying that the solution meets the release criteria for deployment to production, the stakeholders concur the solution meets their needs and expectations, and Operations is ready to assume responsibility for deployment of the solution as well as its ongoing management and support. A successful start of the stabilization effort requires that the team make, with the end of a Build Track, the transition from a mindset focused on building features to one focused on getting a solution to a known state of readiness. A successful conclusion of the stabilization effort requires that the team make another transition from driving a project to one of supporting operations and support teams in their assuming control and responsibility for a solution, starting with the pilot deployment.

Chapter 11
MSF Deploy Track: Deploying a Solution

Stakeholders and the project team agree: a solution is ready for release. Operations and support teams are poised to assume responsibility for a solution. Resources needed to deploy a solution are ready, including people, equipment, facilities, tools, and scripts. Deployment plans and approaches have been vetted. Solution deployment to the target environment(s) can commence.

A deployment plan, completed in the Plan Track, should have worked out optimal approaches to deploy the various aspects of a solution. For instance, the chosen installation approach is phased; a deployment mechanism is to use a partially scripted installation; and a deployment team consists of on-site staff with remote assistance from a project team.

As with other tracks, you can approach deployment in numerous ways. Accordingly, this chapter discusses common activities and checkpoints associated with deploying the various aspects of a solution.

Goal

The goals for a Deploy Track are to integrate a solution successfully into production within designated environment(s), and to transfer responsibility for the remaining solution delivery from a project team to operations and support teams as smoothly and soon as possible. Ideally, the Operations team is able and willing to deploy a solution at the beginning of a Deploy Track. In this case, the project team plays a supporting role. In the worst case, the Operations team is not able and willing to deploy a solution and, as such, a project team leads the deployment while working with the Operations team to increase their readiness with each successive site deployment.

Team Focus

With all aspects of a solution and its supporting collateral approved for release, the remaining team members work with operations and support teams to deploy their respective solution components. After the deployment plan has been practiced and vetted in the Stabilize Track, a team follows the plan in preparing, installing, and stabilizing various aspects of the solution deployed to their designated environment(s) as well as training users, transitioning solution responsibility to operations, and obtaining sign-off for each deployment.

Although a solution was deemed ready, a team is often trimmed down to only those members needed to handle issues as they arise, which most likely will be related to deployment and integration into the target environment(s). In addition, stabilizing activities might continue during this period as solution components are transferred from a preproduction environment to a production environment. Table 11-1 describes the focus and responsibility areas of each team advocacy group during a Deploy Track. As operations and support teams assume more responsibility, a project team can be reduced even further.

Table 11-1   Team Focal Areas During Deploying

Advocacy Group	Focus
Product Management	Customer feedback, assessment, sign-off for each site deployment
Program Management	Deployment plan and schedule updates, stabilization management
Architecture	Solution/scope comparison
Development	Issue resolution, escalation support
User Experience	Training, user readiness
Test	Issue triage, deployment stabilization
Release/Operations	Site deployment management, change approval

Key Deliverables

The key deliverables for a Deploy Track are the following:

- Operations and support information systems
- Revised processes and procedures
- End-user and administrator training
- Documented configurations (commonly called "as built" documents)
- Repository of all solution collateral, including the final versions of documentation, load sets, knowledge bases, configurations, scripts, and code

Key Checkpoints

The key checkpoints for the Deploy Track listed and described here:

Major Checkpoint

The major checkpoint concluding a Deploy Track is *deployment completed*.

Deployment Completed

Lead Advocacy Group: Release/Operations

A *deployment completed* checkpoint concludes a solution delivery effort for this version or release of a solution (i.e., delivery of subsequent versions or releases might still be in the works). It signifies that all deployments have been completed, stabilized, and verified to be operationally stable. The appropriate operations and support systems, processes, and procedures are in place and functional. By this time, the deployed solution should be providing the expected business value to the customer(s). With this checkpoint ending solution delivery activities, all that potentially remains is project closure, which is discussed in the next chapter.

Interim Checkpoints

The interim checkpoints for a Deploy Track are *core solution components deployed*, *site deployments completed*, and *deployment stabilized*, as depicted in Figure 11-1.

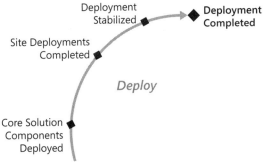

Figure 11-1   Deploy Track checkpoints

Core Solution Components Deployed

Lead Advocacy Group: Release/Operations

Often, solutions are built around a core set of components that provide key services and are the nucleus or backbone for the entire solution. These are typically major components that are deployed to centralized operations centers. This checkpoint signifies that these core solution components have been deployed to their designated environments and have been verified to be operationally stable.

These components do not typically represent an operational solution from a user's perspective. Instead, solution components that are considered core typically satisfy one or more of these criteria:

- Is an enabling component (e.g., domain controllers, mail routers, remote access servers, database servers)
- Site deployments depend on these components
- Is too significant or costly for site deployment (e.g., mainframe)
- Is a legacy component
- Enables a performance or cost benefit to be realized by centrally locating the component
- Services the whole organization

To avoid delays, core components can be reviewed, approved, and deployed in advance of other solution components that are still being stabilized. All of this should be detailed in a deployment plan with the proper acceptance checkpoints.

Site Deployments Completed

Lead Advocacy Group: Release/Operations

Some solutions are deployed to distributed locations and, as such, involve site deployments. This checkpoint signifies that all site deployments have been completed, including being integrated with the core components and possibly with other sites. At this checkpoint, all users should have access to a solution.

Because deployments are complete but not yet fully stabilized (that is the next checkpoint), it is expected that some issues will arise with the various site deployments. However, from an overall perspective, the whole solution should be operationally stable; enough for each site owner to sign off on the deployment. One measure of achieving site-owner satisfaction is site owners' willingness to sign off on their site deployment. Signing off provides validation of customer acceptance at the specific site.

After achieving this checkpoint, the team makes a concentrated effort to resolve the remaining issues, finish deployment stabilization activities, and close out a project. Depending on a deployment plan, achieving this checkpoint is typically when the bulk of the remaining team starts to roll off a project. Only those needed to finish stabilization and project closure typically remain.

It is essential that operations and support teams assume responsibility prior to this checkpoint. Because site deployments tend to be similar, it is a great learning opportunity for them to increase their readiness to a sufficient level. If they are not ready to assume responsibility by this checkpoint, it is highly likely operations acceptance of a solution will delay a project.

Deployment Stabilized

Lead Advocacy Group: Release/Operations

As with other stabilization efforts, this checkpoint signifies that all issues deemed necessary to resolve have been resolved and that the customer and team agree that solution operations, including the sites, satisfy predefined customer acceptance criteria.

As an added indicator of stability, typically operational feedback is solicited from users and stakeholders. Based on this feedback, some final adjustments might be deemed important enough to address.

Deploying to a Production Environment

Although deploying solution components can involve different approaches, the process of how to go about them is the same. As depicted in Figure 11-2, each deployment needs preparation, components installed and integrated into their designated environments, end-user training on what was deployed, and stabilization of what was deployed. Each of these is discussed in the sections that follow.

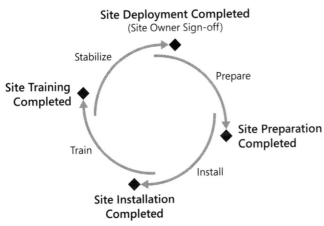

Figure 11-2   Site deployment life cycle

Preparing for Deployment

Lead Advocacy Group: Release/Operations

As often happens, the best-laid plans often go awry. Therefore, preparing for the various deployments should involve either validating information collected during planning or conducting new site surveys. This is especially true when working with sites fraught with logistical challenges and long lead times. The updated information is used to refine and finalize deployment plans and schedules; add more specifics and needed logistics (e.g., server names); ensure predeployment activities are complete (e.g., purchasing and installing equipment; and preparing facilities to receive a solution); and potentially redefine which components are considered core and which are deployed to the various sites.

Because deployments potentially involve many sites each with many users and can be somewhat disruptive, it is essential to work closely with site personnel to share the latest information of when their deployment will occur. Ideally, the means of sharing the latest information with site owners and users is outlined in the communications plan (e.g., conducting project events such as training and launch events). The communications plan should map out key information related to the impending site deployment (e.g., telling them what, why, and when).

Performing Deployments

Lead Advocacy Group: Release/Operations

Deployment approaches vary widely. The selected approach(es) should have considered the various drivers and influences such as capability of site staff to perform deployment(s), logistical challenges of deploying at each site, financial considerations, and schedule. All of these come together to provide the optimal approach(es) to deployment. Note that deployment approaches of core components as well as deployment to each site can differ.

Installation Approach

An installation approach can involve one or a combination of serial or parallel deployments to "push" a solution by geographical site or by business unit; or can involve users taking action to "pull" a solution to their desktop. An installation approach might be to install component(s) on new hardware or perform an in-place upgrade of an existing component.

Deployment Mechanisms

Three basic approaches facilitate a deployment. First, it can be fully automated using a centralized tool such as the Microsoft System Center Configuration Manager (formerly known as Microsoft Systems Management Server [SMS]) to push deployments to sites and to users. Second, deployments can be done manually by on-site personnel or remote personnel pushing a solution to sites and users. Last, a deployment can be a combination of the two (i.e., partially scripted installation).

Deployment Resources

Depending on the readiness of site personnel to perform a deployment, it might be necessary to send qualified internal operations staff or bring in contractors local to a site. This decision is mainly financially driven.

Training During Deployment

Lead Advocacy Group: User Experience

Site support and end-user readiness often need to accompany a solution deployment. Site support staff training must be implemented before their site deployment. End-user training is often implemented in parallel with users' respective site deployment.

Ideally, effective training provides tailored instruction to each user. However, with it being likely that users have a wide variety of backgrounds and experiences, delivering training to meet their unique needs is not always possible. Accordingly, a reasonable approach is to make training available through many different formats and media.

As with site deployments, delivering training to site personnel depends on availability of local trainers who have the ability and capability to deliver the necessary training. Here, too, qualified internal personnel or external trainers might need to be brought in to deliver the training.

Stabilizing a Deployment

Lead Advocacy Group: Release/Operations

Issues are expected during each deployment, even with all of the planning and practicing. As such, the team needs to continue to be ready to triage issues and implement contingency plans to ensure business continuity. Ideally, each deployment is stabilized while deployment resources are still on site (given that there was some manual deployment)—starting with the core components deployment. Once the various deployments are stable, the team needs to ensure stability of a solution as a whole.

As part of the stabilization process, a deployment plan can call for soliciting feedback from users and stakeholders. This feedback can be gathered across the enterprise upon achieving a deployment completed checkpoint, by site, by business unit, or by random sampling using surveys. Something not recommended but sometimes done is to infer feedback by the number and content of trouble tickets opened after a site deployment is completed.

Transitioning to Operations and Support

Lead Advocacy Group: Release/Operations

Transitioning a solution and its supporting collateral to operations and support does not happen through osmosis. Ideally, operations and support personnel have been part of a project team. Being on the team enables them to form a much deeper understanding of a solution and its behavioral characteristic than any training is able to provide. However, it is prudent to allocate time and resources in the various plans and schedules to properly transition solution operations and support functions to permanent staff before a project team disengages.

History shows that a solution hand-off with little overlap leads to disastrous results. Ideally, transitioning of processes, procedures, and systems to operations and support should have commenced as part of preparing for the pilot(s). That way, operations and support teams have significant exposure to the deployed solution and its support systems. Otherwise, how will the stakeholders know that they are sufficiently ready?

Transitioning to operations and support does not just mean that these teams finish deployment efforts. It means that corrective actions, maintenance, and trend analysis of the pilot deployment(s) as well as any production deployments have been assimilated into regular operations. Reporting systems have been set up with support calls already going to the support folks. The support knowledge base is up and operational.

> **Lesson Learned**   Some organizations prepare their operations and support teams only by sending them to training. Although this is a good start, training needs to be reinforced with hands-on experience. Too many times organizations make the mistake of assuming training provides the necessary competency and proficiency.

The Quiet Period

Lead Advocacy Group: Release/Operations

The period between a deployment stabilized checkpoint and deployment completed checkpoint is sometimes referred to as a "quiet period." Typically, the duration of the quiet period is proportional to the stabilization period (e.g., typically, 20 percent of the duration but no shorter than 15 to 30 days long). The purpose of the quiet period is to measure how well a solution behaves in normal operations and to establish a baseline for understanding how much maintenance is required to run a solution. Typically, this is derived from information such as the number of incidents, the amount of downtime, and other various performance metrics. This data also helps form the assumptions used by an operations team to define the various Service Level Agreements (SLAs) on expected yearly levels of service and performance.

Although the remaining team members no longer have planned solution delivery activities, they continue with a project to respond to escalated issues while they shift focus to project closeout activities (discussed in the next chapter).

Success Criteria for a Deploy Track

A Deploy Track has been successfully completed when the deployment completed checkpoint is achieved. To achieve this checkpoint successfully, a few efforts, including the following, need to be successfully completed. All site owners have signed off that their deployments were successfully completed and are operationally stable. Holistically, a solution is also completely deployed and operationally stable. Operations and support teams have assumed full responsibility and are fully capable of performing their duties. Operational and support processes and procedures as well as supporting systems are operationally stable.

Chapter 12
MSF Governance Track: Guiding the Solution Delivery

Good project governance provides just enough oversight, process, guidance, and rigor to efficiently and effectively use project resources, deliver a solution, and handle trade-off decisions while optimally balancing adherence to a set of potentially changing project constraints. The MSF Governance Track strives to provide, and continuously improve, good project governance. It consists of discrete and persistent activities throughout a project. Although governance-related activities and checkpoints have been discussed previously within the enactment tracks, this chapter discusses additional governance activities and checkpoints.

A Governance Track likely starts before the enactment tracks because preenvisioning activities are needed to be able to kick off a project. The Governance Track supports and guides the enactment tracks. It ends with customer acceptance of a solution, marking the end of a project.

Goal

The goals for the Governance Track are the following:

- Guide enactment activities to repeatably and reliably deliver a solution

- Optimize and continuously improve team performance and throughput, solution quality, and process improvement

- Secure approval from:

  ❑ Users that a solution meets their needs and is sufficiently usable

❑ Operations that a solution is ready to deploy

❑ Customer that a project is complete

Team Focus

For a Governance Track, a team has persistent focus in some areas and changing focus in others as a project evolves from project initiation through project execution and concludes with project closeout. Table 12-1 reflects discrete activities and responsibility areas for each team advocacy group during the Governance Track. Table 12-2 reflects persistent activities for each team advocacy group throughout the track. In addition, all advocacy groups participate in various reviews and process improvement activities.

Table 12-1   Team Focal Areas During a Governance Track

Advocacy Group	Focus
Product Management	Customer acceptance
Program Management	Ramping up the team, ramping down the team
Architecture	Establishing planning process
Development	Establishing build process
User Experience	User acceptance
Test	Establishing testing process
Release/Operations	Establishing deployment process, operations acceptance

Table 12-2   Persistent Team Activities Throughout a Governance Track

Advocacy Group	Focus
Product Management	Customer feedback, assessment, and sign-off; requirements trade-off and reprioritization
Program Management	Project initiation, execution, and closure
Architecture	Planning process improvement, architectural refinement, and realignment to changing requirements
Development	Build process improvement, task estimate accuracy, timely task completion
User Experience	Usability assessments; user feedback, assessment, and sign-off.
Test	Forecasting quality attainment
Release/Operations	Defining and refining solution-related agreements, such as Service Level Agreements (SLAs) (i.e., agreements between Operations and Business Unit customers); Operational Level Agreements (OLAs) (i.e., agreements between Operations and internal suppliers); and Under-pinning Contracts (UCs) (i.e., agreements between Operations and external suppliers)

Key Deliverables

The key deliverables for a Governance Track are the following:

- Starting a project:
  - ❑ Project charter
  - ❑ Team orientation guide
- Ongoing:
  - ❑ Status reports
  - ❑ Deliverable status
- Ending a project:
  - ❑ Customer and user satisfaction data
  - ❑ Final versions of all project collateral
  - ❑ Project closeout report
  - ❑ Road map of next steps
  - ❑ Lessons learned

Key Checkpoints

The key checkpoints for a Governance Track are described here:

Major Checkpoint

The major checkpoint concluding a Governance Track is *customer acceptance*.

Customer Acceptance

Lead Advocacy Group: Product Management

A customer acceptance checkpoint signifies that the customer(s) is satisfied with what was delivered as per the previously defined *customer acceptance criteria*. To achieve this checkpoint, customers usually require prior acceptance from users, operations, and site owners; delivery of a project closeout report; and sometimes administrative closure of a project.

This checkpoint signifies the conclusion of a project, even though a solution might not be fully deployed yet. This situation occurs when an operations team assumes responsibility for the remainder of a solution deployment and is confident and capable enough to no longer need project team support.

Interim Checkpoints

The interim checkpoints for a Governance Track are project charter completed, project kicked off, user acceptance, operations acceptance, and customer acceptance, as depicted in Figure 12-1.

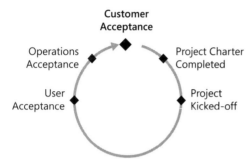

Figure 12-1   Governance Track checkpoints

User Acceptance

Lead Advocacy Group: User Experience

This interim checkpoint signifies that the stakeholders formally acknowledge that a representative population of users, through various feedback mechanisms (e.g., user acceptance testing, surveys), have assessed a solution and concur that it meets their needs and is sufficiently usable. This checkpoint is typically achieved in a Stabilize Track in concert with the achievement of a *user acceptance testing completed* interim checkpoint. However, some organizations choose to tie the achievement of this checkpoint with the affirmative feedback received from surveying a sample user population once a solution is deployed.

Operations Acceptance

Lead Advocacy Group: Release/Operations

This interim checkpoint signifies that an Operations team formally accepts responsibility for a solution. Typically, this checkpoint occurs in a Deploy Track when operations and support teams are ready, willing, and capable of assuming responsibility to finish deploying a solution.

Kicking Off a Project

Lead Advocacy Group: Program Management

An Envision Track contains deliverables, checkpoints, and activities to consider at the beginning of a project. However, it is extremely likely that a whole bunch of pre–Envisioning Track activities and approvals are needed to be able to kick off a project.

The following sections briefly highlight some common activities that enable a project to be kicked off. This assumes that a business case justifying the need for a project has already been assembled for business sponsors to review and approve. Hopefully, operations and support teams have also been involved in project proposal activities to make sure that they are ready, willing, and capable of assuming operations and maintenance of a solution.

Defining a Project Charter (Deliverable)

At its essence, a project charter is a founding agreement between the sponsoring organization(s), solution delivery organization(s), and key stakeholders as to the who, what, when, where, why, and how rationale for undertaking a project. It contains the motivation, authorization, and justification for commissioning a project. It establishes the driving and defining elements of a project. It contains a high-level summary of the intent and purpose of a project. As much as is known, it provides the agreed-to scope, goals, objectives, time frame, approaches, risks, and deliverables of a project. It establishes the foundation of how a project and the team will be structured and managed. It identifies project sponsors and participating organizations, and maps out their roles and responsibilities. Other basic elements of a project charter include these:

- Business needs and drivers
- Desired timelines
- High-level requirements
- Assumptions and constraints
- Success criteria

Once a project is kicked off, a project charter is a useful historical document that provides an overview of the initial project rationale, drivers, and motivators.

Handling Kickoff Logistics

A little-recognized key to a successful project kickoff is to make sure some basic logistics have been taken care of prior to the kickoff, such as the following:

- Suitable and equipped area in which the team can work
- User accounts with appropriate rights on the systems and tools needed for a project
- Unfettered access to all facilities associated with solution delivery
- Orientation guide for on-boarding team members
- Team collaboration site (e.g., Microsoft SharePoint) to store project collateral and governance templates (e.g., status report template)

Kickoff logistics are implicitly assumed to be handled properly, but it is quite obvious and disruptive if they are not—much like the "dissatisfier" category of requirements described in

Chapter 8, "MSF Plan Track: Planning a Solution." A good kickoff enables a team to focus on their work rather than spending time preparing to work.

Establishing a Deliverable Acceptance Procedure

A key to making sure a solution meets the needs and expectations of the stakeholders is to make sure the deliverables do as well. To help instrument this, a team should establish a *deliverable acceptance procedure* that is consistent with the deliverable life cycle discussed in Chapter 6, "Establishing a Solution Delivery Life Cycle." This procedure can be as agile or as rigorous as needed. Regardless, the procedure consists of the following steps:

1. **Submit deliverable** The deliverable is submitted to the appropriate stakeholders for review and, hopefully, approval.

2. **Review deliverable** The review period should be planned into the schedule—allowing sufficient time for the stakeholders to review the deliverable.

3. **Accept or reject deliverable** To have a record of the acceptance, the team should provide a completed *deliverable acceptance form* to the appropriate stakeholder(s) for signature. Should the deliverable be rejected, the form should be returned with the reasons why it was rejected.

4. **Refine deliverable** Most likely, stakeholders will not reject a deliverable but will send it back for further refinement. Given the likelihood that most deliverables will need some refinement upon their first submittal, time to perform this step should also be reasonably planned into the schedule. Unless the deliverable was conditionally accepted (i.e., accepted pending refinements that do not need to be re-reviewed), the deliverable needs to be resubmitted after being refined.

It is expected that the team shares mature versions of the deliverables with appropriate stakeholders to solicit stakeholder feedback along the way. If done correctly, this deliverable acceptance process should be a non-event because the team already has a high degree of confidence that the deliverable meets stakeholder needs and expectations.

It is important to establish which stakeholders need to approve each deliverable and which stakeholders are provided the deliverable for informational purposes only. For technical deliverables, it is good practice to have the appropriate architect sign off on the deliverable before submitting it for business approval.

Ongoing Solution Delivery Guidance

The previous chapters are full of governance activities and checkpoints that apply to enacting solution delivery. Additional governance activities depend on which solution delivery methodology is selected. Typically, additional governance activities include tracking and regularly communicating status, as well as continuously improving and optimizing processes and procedures used by the team.

Tracking and Reporting Status (Deliverable)

As discussed in Chapter 8, "MSF Plan Track: Planning a Solution," the communications plan should detail how much, to whom, and what status information is needed by the team and by the various stakeholders. Ideally, providing status is a two-way, free flow of information. Sharin status does not need to be formal or complex. Table 12-3 provides a simple example of tracking deliverable status.

Table 12-3   Example of a Deliverable Status Matrix

Document	Author/ Lead	Lead Reviewer	Deliver Date	Tech Signed Off	Business Signed Off	Comments
AD Migration Plan	Bassem R.	Brian W.	26-Apr	X	X	
AD Detailed Design	Bassem R.	Brian W.	1-May	X	X	
Exchange Design	Frank G.	Jim S.	2-May	X	X	
AD Test Plan	Bassem R.	Kimm F.	11-May	22-May	3-Jun	
Infrastructure Master Test Plan	Peter R.	John F.	14-May			Very overdue
AD Migration Logistics	Brian W.	Bassem R.	18-May	27-May	TBD	Need to schedule Biz sign-off
Infrastructure Pilot Plan	Scott W.	John F.	1-Jun			May need to slip 2 days
Exchange Test Plan	Frank G.	Kimm F.	3-Jun			
AD Test Logistics	Brian W.	Bassem R.	4-Jun			
Exchange Test Logistics	Jim S.	Frank G.	7-Jun			
Exchange Deployment Plan	Jim S.	Frank G.	7-Jun			
Exchange Migration/Con-solidation Plan	Frank G.	Jim S.	25-Jun			
Exchange Migration/Con-solidation Logistics	Jim S.	Frank G.	7-Jul			

Current as of 6/01/2006

In addition to documenting status, it is a recommended practice to share status interactively with stakeholders on a regular basis (e.g., monthly stakeholder steering committee meetings). It is also recommended to provide status on the team's collaboration site.

Continuously Improving Processes and Procedures

Similar to how Microsoft Solutions Framework (MSF) espouses an incremental and iterative approach to solution construction, MSF espouses an incremental and iterative approach to process and procedure improvement throughout a solution delivery life cycle. Because books and books have been written on continuous improvement (known as *kaizen*, as referenced in Chapter 3, "Foundational Principles, Mindsets, and Proven Practices"), this section provides just a cursory introduction to the topic.

As a team becomes familiar and comfortable with making continuous improvement part of their normal work, they will realize that through small, gradual changes, they are able to evolve and refine all aspects of solution delivery as opposed to disrupt it with larger and/or sudden changes. A process improvement need not be complex. It could be as simple as streamlining a status report template. Other typical areas of improvement include the following:

- Improving estimating and planning accuracy
- Refining matching of team member skills with required tasks competencies
- Simplifying the method and reducing the time needed to share information
- Eliminating (or at least greatly reducing) unnecessary communications
- Minimizing elongated review cycles
- Reducing unproductive governance

Completing a Project

Lead Advocacy Group: Program Management

Even with clear completion criteria, teams and stakeholders sometimes find it challenging to conclude a project. Typically, these challenges to extend a project come from overt external influences and from internal pride in workmanship, including the desire to broaden a solution within the current project scope (e.g., "it works OK, but it would be much better if we just added..."); to stabilize a solution beyond the previously agreed-to acceptance criteria; and to handle the ongoing issues that surface after deployment.

When a team is ready to close down a project, this process involves two activities: *ramping down a team* and *closing out a project*.

Ramping Down a Team

Rarely does a project need all of its team members until the end. Team members should be rolled off a project as they complete their planned work—some might be needed only to build a solution, some are needed to stabilize a solution, and even fewer are needed to deploy a solution. Sometimes members of a project team are transitioned to an operations team for ongoing maintenance and support of a solution. Sometimes team members are transitioned to the project team that handles the next release of a solution. Just as team members are not casually added to the team, so they should not be casually rolled off a project.

Closing Down a Project

Properly closing down a project is key to harvesting lessons learned, making sure all project collateral is properly archived, tying up any loose ends, and setting the stage for follow-on activities. Activities associated with project closeout include these:

- Surveying customer satisfaction
- Conducting project reviews
- Preparing a closeout report
- Administratively closing a project

Surveying Customer Satisfaction

By this point in a project, it is hoped that customers are satisfied. However, this is not always the case. Although customers were involved to help deliver the best solution possible within project constraints, it does not necessarily mean that they are satisfied with the outcome, how a project was conducted, and so forth. Accordingly, it is a best practice to conduct a customer satisfaction survey to root out areas of dissatisfaction. The survey often takes the form of interviews and/or questionnaires. Typically, this feedback is a good source for future process improvements.

Conducting Project Reviews

A project review is a good, informal way at the end of a project for the team to reflect on the processes and outcomes of delivering a solution. As part of that reflection, the team should review what went well (and why it went well), what could of gone better (and how to make it better next time), and what lessons learned or best practices can be gleaned from a project. It goes beyond a normal checkpoint review in that it looks back on the whole project.

Once a team has had a chance to get together, it is a best practice to repeat the session, but this time to invite key stakeholders to elicit their perspectives. It is often productive to start using the information the team came up with during the first session.

Preparing a Closeout Report (Deliverable)

The final deliverable of any project is a *project closeout report*. This report documents final project and solution status. It provides evidence that all customer acceptance criteria have been satisfied, including user and operations acceptance information. Typically, it summarizes and calls out noteworthy feedback from stakeholder and user satisfaction surveys. It often outlines follow-on activities. It might include deferred change requests and deferred scope.

Other elements included in the report are dependent on whether this project is part of a larger program with multiple releases or is a stand-alone project.

Administratively Closing a Project

The last step of closing out a project is *administrative closure*. As the name implies, administrative closure concludes and finalizes any remaining governance activities, including the following:

- Releasing the remaining project team

- Ensuring lessons learned are documented

- Verifying project collateral has been properly archived

- Delivering project closeout report

- Obtaining customer sign-off

- If necessary, achieving financial closure such as concluding all contracts, finalizing cost analysis, and ensuring all outstanding purchase orders and payments have been processed

Success Criteria for a Governance Track

The Governance Track successfully starts with the outlining of a project using a project charter and a productive kickoff of process enactment. The Governance Track has been successfully completed when the customer acceptance checkpoint is achieved, signifying that the team has satisfied the customer acceptance criteria, which is marked by the customer signing off on a project and taking receipt of a solution. It also signifies that a project has ended after delivering a solution that meets the needs and expectations of the stakeholders, users, and operations teams.

A successful Governance Track facilitates solution delivery in the least obtrusive means possible while proactively improving processes and procedures used by the team. It also enables the team and stakeholders to put into action the foundational principles and mindsets in a positive and reaffirming way. This includes capturing and providing project knowledge and lessons learned to those in operations and subsequent project teams.

Although a solution might not be fully deployed, the end of the Governance Track marks the end of a project and the disengagement of a project team. It is a positive sign that operations and support teams are confident and capable enough to finish deployments without project team support.

Appendix
MSFv3 Credits

Previous material on Microsoft Solutions Framework (MSF) version 3 was published in white papers and provided through training courses. Although this is the first book on MSF, it builds heavily on the great work put into those white papers that were written by the following people.

Chapter 3: Foundational Principles, Mindsets, and Proven Practices

This chapter borrows from the "MSF v3 Overview" white paper published in June 2003.

Contributors

Derick Campbell, Product Manager, Microsoft Solutions Framework

Geoffrey Lory, Director, GTD Ltd.

Allison Robin, Director, Microsoft Solutions Framework

Patricia Rytkonen, Technical Editor, Volt Technical Services

Gaile Simmons, Technical Editor, Microsoft

Reviewers

Jeff Carter, MSFmentor, U.S.

Nathan Dolly, Microsoft Consulting Services, U.S.

John S. Dranchak, Logic Control

Holly Dyas, Microsoft

Paul Glen, C2 Consulting, U.S.

Tom Gordon, Framework Deliveries, LLC

Paul Haynes, Microsoft

Hiroshi Koisumi, Microsoft Consulting Services, Japan

Eran Kolber, LIH Ltd, Israel

Shawn LaBelle, Microsoft Premier Support, U.S.

David Millet, Microsoft Consulting Services, U.S.

Ed Musters, Systemgroup Management Services, Canada

Alex Nicol, Microsoft Consulting Services, Canada

David Preedy, Gainsford Associates, UK

Jane Marie Rief, Thomson West

Dolph Santello, Microsoft Consulting Services, U.S.

Chapter 4: Building an MSF Team

This chapter borrows from two white papers: "MSF Team Model v3.1" and "MSF Project Management Discipline v1.1"—both published in June 2002.

"MSF Team Model v3.1" White Paper

Contributors

Scott Getchell, Program Manager, Microsoft Solutions Framework

Patrick Griffin, Managing Consultant, Microsoft Consulting Services, U.S.

Laura Hargrave, Technical Editor, Microsoft Solutions Framework

Paul Haynes, Program Manager, Microsoft Solutions Framework

Nancy Huber, Technical Editor, Microsoft Solutions Framework

Pervez Kazmi, Program Manager, Microsoft Solutions Framework

Paulo Henrique Leocadio, Microsoft Consulting Services, Brazil

Mike Lubrecht, Technical Writer, Microsoft Solutions Framework

Rob Oikawa, Program Manager, Microsoft Solutions Framework

Enzo Paschino, Program Manager, Microsoft Solutions Framework

Allison Robin, Director, Microsoft Solutions Framework

Paulo Rocha, Microsoft Consulting Services, New Zealand

Dolph Santello, Microsoft Consulting Services, U.S.

Ralph Schimpl, Director, Microsoft Austria

Mark Short, Program Manager, Microsoft Solutions Framework

Suzana Vukcevic, Program Manager, Microsoft Belgium

"MSF Project Management Discipline v1.1" White Paper

Contributors

Scott Getchell, Program Manager, Microsoft Solutions Framework

Paul Haynes, Program Manager, Microsoft Solutions Framework

Nancy Huber, Technical Editor, Microsoft Solutions Framework

Rob Oikawa, Principal Consultant, Microsoft Solutions Framework

Enzo Paschino, Program Manager, Microsoft Solutions Framework

Allison Robin, Director, Microsoft Solutions Framework

Mark Short, Program Manager, Microsoft Solutions Framework

Reviewers

Brian Willson, Senior Consultant, Microsoft Consulting Services, U.S.

Elizabeth Carson, Managing Consultant, Microsoft Consulting Services, Canada

Joseph Lopesilvero, Principal Project Manager, Microsoft Services

Francis Delgado Millan, Practice Manager, Microsoft Consulting Services, Germany

Guy Morris, Director, Project Management Office, Microsoft Services

David Preedy, Practice Manager, Microsoft Consulting Services, UK

David Roberts, Principal Consultant, Microsoft Consulting Services, U.S.

Dolph Santello, Principal Consultant, Microsoft Consulting Services, U.S.

Suzana Vukcevic, Senior Consultant, Advanced Technical Services, Belgium

Chapter 5: Managing Project Risks

This chapter borrows from the "MSF Risk Management Discipline v1.1" white paper published in June 2002.

Contributors

Marijke Born, Release Manager, Microsoft Frameworks

Derick Campbell, Product Manager, Microsoft Solutions Framework

Scott Getchell, Program Manager, Microsoft Solutions Framework

Laura Hargrave, Technical Editor, Microsoft Frameworks

Paul Haynes, Program Manager, Microsoft Solutions Framework

Nancy Huber, Technical Editor, Microsoft Frameworks

Pervez Kazmi, Program Manager, Microsoft Solutions Framework

Rob Oikawa, Program Manager, Microsoft Solutions Framework

Enzo Paschino, Program Manager, Microsoft Solutions Framework

David Preedy, Program Manager, Microsoft Solutions Framework

Allison Robin, Director, Microsoft Solutions Framework

Reviewers

Brian Carter, Consultant, MCS National Practices

Paulo Henrique Leocadio, Senior Principal Consultant, MCS Brazil

Joseph Lopesilvero, Principal Project Manager, Microsoft Project Management Office

Francis Delgado Millan, Practice Manager, Microsoft Enterprise Services

David Millett, Principal Consultant, MCS NorCal

Paulo Rocha, Principal Consultant, MCS New Zealand

Dolph Santello, Principal Consultant, MCS Northeast

Anthony Saxby, Microsoft Consulting Services, UK

Ralph Schimpl, Microsoft Consulting Services, Austria

Ron Stutz, Managing Consultant, MCS Rocky Mountain

Rick Varvel, Principal Consultant, MCS PacWest

Andres Vinet, Microsoft Consulting Services, Chile

Brian Willson, Automotive Industry Strategy Consultant, MCS Great Lakes

Chapter 6: Establishing a Solution Delivery Life Cycle

This chapter borrows from "MSF Process Model v3.1" white paper published in June 2002.

Contributors

Scott Getchell, Program Manager, U.S. Frameworks

Laura Hargrave, Technical Editor, U.S. Frameworks

Paul Haynes, Program Manager, U.S. Frameworks

Pervez Kazmi, Program Manager, U.S. Frameworks

Mike Lubrecht, Technical Writer, U.S. Frameworks

Rob Oikawa, Principal Consultant, Microsoft Consulting Services, U.S.

Enzo Paschino, Program Manager, U.S. Frameworks

Allison Robin, Director, U.S. Frameworks

Mark Short, Program Manager, U.S. Frameworks

Reviewers

Andrew Delin, Microsoft Consulting Services, Australia

Paulo Henrique Leocadio, Microsoft Consulting Services, LATAM

Joe Lopesilvero, Microsoft Consulting Services, U.S.

David Millet, Microsoft Consulting Services, U.S.

Thierry Paquay, Microsoft Premier Support, U.S.

Paulo Rocha, Microsoft Consulting Services, New Zealand

Anthony Saxby, Microsoft Consulting Services, UK

Ralph Schimpl, Microsoft Consulting Services, Austria

Ron Stutz, Microsoft Consulting Services, U.S.

Andres Vinet, Microsoft Consulting Services, Chile

Brian Willson, Microsoft Consulting Services, U.S.

Chapter 7: MSF Envision Track: Defining a Solution

This chapter borrows from "MSF Readiness Management Discipline v1.1" white paper published in June 2002.

Contributors

Scott Getchell, Program Manager, Microsoft Solutions Framework

Paul Haynes, Program Manager, Microsoft Solutions Framework

Jeff Hickey, Technical Writer, Microsoft Solutions Framework

Nancy Huber, Technical Editor, Microsoft Solutions Framework

Pervez Kazmi, Program Manager, Microsoft Solutions Framework

Mike Lubrecht, Technical Writer, Microsoft Solutions Framework

Rob Oikawa, Principal Consultant, Microsoft Consulting Services, U.S.

Enzo Paschino, Program Manager, Microsoft Solutions Framework

Allison Robin, Director, Microsoft Solutions Framework

Mark Short, Program Manager, Microsoft Solutions Framework

Suzana Vukcevic, Program Manager, Microsoft Belgium

Reviewers

Eric Halsey, Microsoft Corporation

Geof Lory, GTD Consulting, LLC

David Millet, Microsoft Consulting Services, U.S.

John Mulder, Microsoft Netherlands

Bill Reed, Microsoft Consulting Services, U.S.

Paulo Rocha, Microsoft Consulting Services, New Zealand

Dolph Santello, Microsoft Consulting Services, U.S.

Anthony Saxby, Microsoft Consulting Services, UK

Fitz Stewart, Microsoft Consulting Services, U.S.

Ron Stutz, Microsoft Consulting Services, U.S.

Brian Willson, Microsoft Consulting Services, U.S.

Andres Vinet, Microsoft Consulting Services, Chile

Index

A

abstract vs. specific solutions, 44–46
Accessibility functional area, 80
accountability
  overview, 28
  readiness, 175
  risk management, 106
  solution delivery life cycles, 145
  team building, 53
adapting to change
  overview, 31–32
  readiness, 176
  risk management, 106
  solution delivery life cycles, 145
  team building, 54
administratively closing projects, 280
advocacy groups. *See also* team of advocates
  Architecture Advocacy Group. *See* Architecture Advocacy Group
  Development Advocacy Group. *See* Development Advocacy Group
  overview, xix, 48–49
  Product Management. *See* Product Management Advocacy Group
  Program Management. *See* Program Management Advocacy Group
  quality goals. *See* quality goals
  Release/Operations Advocacy Group. *See* Release/Operations Advocacy Group
  roles, 55–56
  Test Advocacy Group. *See* Test Advocacy Group
  User Experience Advocacy Group. *See* User Experience Advocacy Group
advocates
  Architecture Advocacy Group, 70
  Product Management Advocacy Group, 60
  Program Management Advocacy Group, 65
  Release/Operations Advocacy Group, 83
  Test Advocacy Group, 76
  User Experience Advocacy Group, 79
agility
  overview, 31–32
  readiness, 176
  risk management, 106
  solution delivery life cycles, 145
  team building, 54
analyzing and prioritizing risks
  additional analysis methods, 127
  deactivating risks, 125–126
  goals, 120
  inputs, 121

multiattribute impact scoring, 124
multiattribute prioritization approach, 125
outputs, 126
overview, 119–120
prioritized master risk list, 126
risk analysis activities, 121
risk-driven scheduling, 162
risk exposure simple prioritization approach, 124–125
risk impact, 122–124
risk prioritization activities, 124
risk probability, 121–122
single-attribute impact scoring, 123–124
top risks list, 126
applying information from this book, xxii
Architecture Advocacy Group
  advocates, 70
  constituents, 70–71
  focus, 71
  functional areas overview, 71
  overview, xix, 70
  quality goals, 71
  Solution Architecture functional area, 71–72
  Technical Architecture functional area, 73
assessing challenges
  business environments, 10
  corporate culture, 10–11
  internal governance, 11–12
  organizational structure, 12–13
  overview, 9–10
  people, 12–13
  process and procedure, 11–12
  skills, 12
  team chemistry, 12
  technology, 13
assessing readiness
  creating learning plans, 184–185
  identifying readiness gaps, 184
  measuring knowledge, skills, and abilities, 184
  overview, 183
  revisiting readiness needs, 184
assessing solution stability
  deployment testing, 259
  functional testing, 258
  overview, 258
  regression testing, 258
  release testing, 259
  system testing overview, 259
  usability testing, 258–259
audience for this book, xxii

About the Author

Michael S. V. Turner, DSc, PMP, is a versatile and seasoned software executive with more than 18 years of senior engineering experience in both startup companies and mature enterprises. He is a senior manager with Microsoft Services HQ where he helps define, develop, and deploy tools, processes, and methodologies for solutions delivery for Microsoft Services. Prior to working with Microsoft Services HQ, Mike was a senior program manager with Microsoft Consulting Services where he managed a diverse portfolio of high-profile application development and infrastructure engagements for various clients in entrepreneurial and regulated environments. Prior to joining Microsoft, Mike held Vice President of Engineering and Development positions and provided technical leadership for all aspects of software development and service delivery for in-house, offshore, and outsourced engineering teams in fast-paced dynamic environments.

Mike is also the founder of North Star Analytics, a side venture that builds artificial intelligence-based software based on his doctoral research. He likes architecting and putting in place development methodologies, processes and procedures, systems, and schedules that ensure delivery of a consistent stream of predictable, right-quality, innovative, commercially viable products and services to market on time and within budget.

To contact Mike, e-mail him at the following addresses: *msturner@microsoft.com* or *mike.turner@NorthStarAnalytics.com.*

What do you think of this book?
We want to hear from you!

Do you have a few minutes to participate in a brief online survey? Microsoft is interested in hearing your feedback about this publication so that we can continually improve our books and learning resources for you.

To participate in our survey, please visit:

www.microsoft.com/learning/booksurvey

And enter this book's ISBN, 0-7356-2353-8. As a thank-you to survey participants in the United States and Canada, each month we'll randomly select five respondents to win one of five $100 gift certificates from a leading online merchant.* At the conclusion of the survey, you can enter the drawing by providing your e-mail address, which will be used for prize notification *only*.

Thanks in advance for your input. Your opinion counts!

Sincerely,

Microsoft Learning

Learn More. Go Further.